SHANE
WARNE

CRICKET STATISTICS

SHANE WARNE

CRICKET STATISTICS

MATTHEW PINKNEY & CHARLIE WAT

The Five Mile Press

The Five Mile Press

Published by
The Five Mile Press Pty Ltd
950 Stud Road, Rowville
Victoria 3178 Australia
Website: www.fivemile.com.au
Email: publishing@fivemile.com.au

Published in 2007

Introduction © Matthew Pinkney, 2007
Career statistics © Charlie Wat, 2007

Cover photograph: Shane Warne, India 2004. AP/AAP Aman Sharma
Formatting: SBR Productions Olinda Victoria
            Charlie Wat
Printed in Australia by Griffin Press

National Library of Australia Cataloguing-in-Publication data
Pinkney, Matthew.
Shane Warne: cricket statistics.
1st ed.

ISBN 9781741785593 (pbk.).

1. Warne, Shane. 2. Cricket players - Australia - Statistics.
3. Cricket - Australia - Records. 4. Cricket -Australia - Statistics.
I. Wat, Charlie. II. Title.

796.3580994

Contents

Introduction   *7*

Statistical Introduction   *30*

First Class Record   *38*

First Class Wickets   *53*

Test Record   *106*

Test Record Match by Match   *128*

Limited Over Internationals Record   *168*

Limited Over Internationals Record
Match by Match   *179*

Limited Over Match Record   *195*

First XI Record for St Kilda in Victorian District
Premier Cricket   *205*

When Shane Warne approached the wicket to bowl his first delivery of Australia's 1993 Ashes campaign at Old Trafford in England, he was just another promising Aussie.

Warne had made his Test debut in January of the previous year, and many experienced observers still had their doubts. Here was a young man with obvious talent. But a love of junk food, the odd smoke and several beers raised questions about his discipline in a game requiring total dedication.

That he became possibly the greatest bowler cricket has known is even more amazing, as Shane Warne never discarded the habits that many thought would doom his career.

From his first match to his last, he was a one-off, a technical genius but the most ordinary of blokes.

It's easy to believe that Shane Warne showed signs of greatness from the very beginning. But what we saw in England at the start of the 1993 Ashes series was a highpoint of a somewhat difficult early career.

Warne had made his first class debut in early 1991, representing Victoria against Western Australia. He produced the modest figures of 0/61 and 1/41, but showed enough to earn selection in the Australia B side in September.

A lot of batsmen in world cricket will be delighted to learn he's leaving the game, but I think the game will be poorer without him. He has been a matchwinner, flamboyant and just incredible to watch.

New Zealand great Sir Richard Hadlee

He bowled well in the B team's tour of Zimbabwe and was promoted to the Australia A side in December where he took wickets against the touring West Indies.

With ageing spinner Peter Taylor struggling to make an impression in the Test team, Warne capped a stunning rise by earning his Baggy Green for the third Test against India.

His elevation from the comparatively humble ranks of grade cricket to the Test arena was meteoric and Warne himself seemed surprised to be striding onto the Sydney Cricket Ground to take on the Indians in the summer of 1991-2.

Surprise turned to horror however, as the young Victorian watched the classy subcontinental batsmen lashing him to all points of the ground.

By the time the Indians had finished with him, he was nursing both an aching spinning wrist and battered pride. His single victim had been bought for the punishing price of 150 runs.

He was picked for the next Test and while nobody had expected him to dominate, a return of 0/18 and 0/60 gave him an overall analysis of 1/228 from his first two Tests – the first on what is traditionally a spinner's wicket.

Little did he know, but India's Ravi Shastri – Warne's only scalp from these early trials – would eventually be joined by another 707 befuddled and bemused batsmen.

Despite doubts in the minds of some Australian selectors – he was dropped from the national side after the Indian Test debacles – 22-year-old Warne was picked for the short tour of Sri Lanka in late 1992.

Again, the selection was based on a feeling – rather than any direct proof – that Australia might just have unearthed something special.

Despite this, Warne had played two very ordinary Tests, and he was beginning to wonder whether some of his critics had a point – that he was a decent player, but not good enough to wear the baggy green for any length of time.

He remembers leaving the team hotel on the final day of

the first Test at the Sinhalese Sports Club ground believing that perhaps this was to be the final chapter in the briefest of international careers.

This anxiety was heightened by the fact that in the first innings, he'd returned a disappointing and demoralising 0/107.

So, despite the banter and encouragement of team-mates, Warne travelled the chaotic streets to the stadium burdened by the knowledge that he was a Test bowler with an average of 335.

Play resumed that morning with Australia in a perilous position – 102 runs ahead in its second innings with just three wickets in hand. Sri Lanka were still relative Test newcomers, but with a passionate crowd behind them they seemed to be striding toward a major upset.

I'm absolutely gobsmacked by this. I've lost a lot of money because I backed him to take 1000 Test wickets and it's not going to happen now.

Former Australia fast bowler Geoff Lawson

With every run precious, the Aussie tail wagged with Warne, Greg Matthews and Mike Whitney managing to drag the lead out to 181. And while his 35 was a crucial contribution, it seemed it would be in vain: Sri Lanka needed to score 182 from 58 overs, a very achievable task.

With typical dash and flair, Sri Lanka carved 76 from the target without losing a wicket. But then off-spinner Matthews and fast bowler Craig McDermott made a series of crucial breakthroughs and suddenly, from a position of real comfort, the hosts were staggering.

Warne had watched the transformation from the sidelines, fielding the occasional ball and encouraging his team-mates.

But then, when he probably thought he'd remain a spectator, skipper Allan Border tossed him the ball.

For me, he was the reason you played cricket. To be in a Test against him, you knew you were in a battle with Warne, verbally, physically, mentally and technically.

Former England captain Nasser Hussain

It was a remarkable show of faith, but also a big risk – not only for the immediate fate of the team, but for the brittle confidence of the young leg-spinner.

Warne's first over of the crucial spell was a maiden. Then, over the course of 13 mesmerising deliveries, he managed to bamboozle the Sri Lankan tail – picking up the wickets of Pramodya Wickramasinghe, Don Anurasiri and Ranjith Madurasinghe without conceding a run.

It was the first – and tantalising – glimpse of Warne's potential. In a remarkable victory, Australia snatched the Test by just 16 runs, Shane Warne returning the figures of 5.1 overs, three maidens, three wickets for 11 runs.

Australia had always struggled on the subcontinent and the victory was the basis for an all-too-rare series victory. But it was far more important than that: it was – Warne later recounted – the moment he first truly believed that he might have something to offer to Australian cricket.

'(Team-mate and off-spinner) Greg Matthews was on fire. He took five-for and was absolutely outstanding,' Warne said several years later.

'Then Allan Border told me to warm up when they needed 30-odd runs to win. I thought, "Oh no, we're in trouble here".

'I came on and bowled a maiden and thought, "It's not over yet". And as the next couple of overs went on, I took 3–0 and I actually felt like I might have contributed … I hadn't felt like I belonged up to that stage. But then I felt like I was part of the team, and that was important.

'Everyone that plays sport has a moment when you think, "I can do this at this level".'

It's very hard to judge across eras but Warne would sit pretty comfortably as the second best player ever. He has been responsible for winning more Test matches than anyone else I have seen or played with.

Warne's former captain and team-mate, Steve Waugh

'Once you get the confidence and you know you are going to play the next game, that you're not going out to play for your spot and you've got nothing to prove, that's when you can actually go out there and achieve things.'

It must have come as a deflating surprise then, to be dropped for the first Test of the next series – a five-rubber home clash against the Windies.

He was back, however, for the second Test in Melbourne and gave his home crowd only a little to cheer about with his first innings return of 1/65.

Despite the promise of that dramatic afternoon in Sri Lanka, the modest performance meant Warne was again under pressure to prove he could play at the elite level.

'It was the last day, and there was a lot of talk that it was about time for Shane Warne to deliver,' he recalled. 'I'd played (four) Tests at that stage and been smashed all over the park against everyone.'

But where some players would respond to such pressure with nerves and an unwillingness to take a risk, Warne seemed to channel the adrenaline and expectation.

By the time the Windies had crashed to defeat, he had collected seven scalps for 52 runs – a magnificent, match-winning performance. Crucially, he had taken the wickets of elite batsmen in a side that was only just coming down from its position as the world's best.

I don't think I've ever seen a competitor as determined and focused as Warne. Test cricket and cricket in general will miss him, and a lot of batsmen around the world will be saying, 'Thank God it's over'.

Retired South Africa paceman Allan Donald

'To come out and get 7/52 and help us win that Test match made me feel I belonged in that side," he said later. 'And if I could bowl like that I knew I could take wickets at this level no matter who we were playing.'

The performance was also notable for the fact that despite the hype that surrounded his first Ashes delivery, Warne's seven-wicket bag included perhaps his favourite all-time delivery – a perfect flipper that skittled a totally duped Richie Richardson.

Warne later described it as 'a delivery that might well have saved my Test career.'

Finally, Shane Keith Warne was on his way, and while he only took two more wickets in the series, his immediate future was secure; he and the selectors now understood what he could bring to cricket.

A three-match away series against New Zealand was a further step forward, with Warne at last adding consistency to his performances. He took wickets in all six innings of the series and bags of 4/63, 3/23 and 4/8 contributed to an impressive 17-wicket haul.

The scene was set, then, for his appearance in one of the greatest and longest-running rivalries of international sport: an Ashes series against England.

And it was here, on a typically overcast Manchester day, he was tossed the ball to begin his first-ever bowling spell in an Ashes match. At the other end was England's former skipper and renowned player of spin – Mike Gatting.

England was 1–80 and travelling comfortably. But as Australian skipper Allan Border had discovered in Sri Lanka and against the West Indies in Melbourne, 23-year-old Warne was the sort of bloke who relished a tough situation.

With wicketkeeper Ian Healy providing his customary encouraging chatter, Warne began his short, relaxed approach. Choosing to bowl his stock delivery – the big turning leg-break – Warne produced a ball that fizzed as it curved from off to leg through the air.

I think he's had the greatest influence on the game of cricket outside of Sir Donald Bradman.

Australia selector and former team-mate, David Boon

Dipping suddenly as it approached Gatting, it pitched outside leg stump before ripping past the outside edge of the Englishman's bat to take the top of off stump.

Gatting thought he'd had everything covered, but when he looked back, he saw the timber disturbed. As Healy leapt in triumph and Warne produced a fist-pumping victory roar, Gatting simply stood – looking totally and hopelessly befuddled.

He then turned to the square leg umpire to confirm his dawning realisation that something extraordinary had happened.

Umpire Ken Parker gave the smallest of nods, and with eyebrows raised and head shaking, Gatting trudged off the park.

Even some of the experts struggled to describe what had just happened, with veteran radio commentator Jonathan Agnew forced to admit he didn't really have a clue.

'Shane Warne off only two or three paces,' Agnew told listeners. 'He bowls and Gatting is taken on the pad. He's bowled? ... (pause) .... Well, Gatting's still standing there, he can't believe it. That must have turned a very long way, we haven't got a view of this, we'll have to wait for a replay to tell you exactly what happened.'

He is one of the great bowlers. From what I have seen, his leg spinner is as good as ever ... he should always be respected, because he is a great bowler.

Sri Lanka spinner Muttiah Muralidaran

Fittingly, it was former Australian skipper and leg-spinning all-rounder Richie Benaud who best described the action for Australian TV audiences.

'He's done it!' Benaud said. 'He's started off with the most beautiful delivery. Gatting has absolutely no idea what has happened to it. He still doesn't know.'

Several hours later, he *still* didn't know, and coming across his vanquisher he asked, 'Bloody hell, Warnie, what happened?'

The delivery was immediately dubbed 'The Gatting Ball' and then re-named by Benaud 'The Ball of the Century.' It's one of the only deliveries – amongst the hundreds of thousands that have been bowled since Test cricket began – to have its own title.

Geniuses don't come along too often. He stands head and shoulders above all the other past spinners. We've been fortunate to have had two geniuses – one's Don Bradman and the other's Shane Warne.

Former Australia skipper Kim Hughes

And how does Warne describe this career-defining ball? Sheer fluke.

'To be honest I would have been happy with one that hit the right spot and didn't go for runs,' he said.

'I knew it might be more than that by the way it curved into the batsman in flight; this is usually a sign it will turn. Even then it was a fluke to spin as much as it did.

'I might even have apologised to Gatting as he walked off.'

He should really have apologised to the entire English team, both current and future, as 'The Gatting Ball' was the beginning of a long and painful stranglehold that Warne would exert on the old enemy.

In his first Ashes series he took 34 wickets in six Tests. When England attempted to regain the Ashes in 1994–5, he spun them to ignominious defeat with 3/39 and a career-best 8/71 in the first Test of the series.

Shane Warne is without doubt the finest leg-spinner the world has ever seen. You would certainly have Warne right up there as one of the greatest Australians to ever step on the field.

Former Australian captain and leg-spinner, Richie Benaud

He then backed up with 6/64 and 3/16 (including a hat trick) in the second Test to get their campaign off to a disastrous start.

In the 2001 Ashes series in England, he again spun a suffocating web, taking bags of 5/71, 6/33 and 7/165 in another 30-plus wicket series.

But even when England turned the cricket world on its head with their epic performances in the 2005 Ashes series, they still couldn't handle Warne – his return of 40 wickets in a losing side one of the greatest Ashes performances ever.

And of course, when England returned to defend the urn in 2006–7, Warne was their tormentor-in-chief. With 23 wickets and having scored more runs than most in the English side, he was a key to England's humiliation – a 5–0 whitewash, the first in 86 years of Ashes cricket.

He just has that capacity, unlike any other wrist spinner we've seen, to put the ball in the danger area ball after ball after ball. His special talent has been to spin the ball and at the same time be accurate.

Mentor, coach and former Test bowler, Terry Jenner

Between the Ashes contests, he dominated batsmen from every Test-playing nation (with the frustrating exception of India), on every type of wicket in all conditions. From the dusty tracks and infernal temperatures of Pakistan to the bouncy pitches of South Africa and Australia, he tailored his game plan to maximum efficiency and effect.

More than that, he took a scholar's interest in the batsmen he was going to bowl to, watching them intensely, learning what shots they liked, whether they got frustrated by being tied down, even their response to the odd sledge from the bowler's end.

Warne's most recent Ashes performance was easily good enough to suggest he had at least another two years of highly-effective Test cricket in him – after all, he would still be amongst the first picked in any current international side.

But as he revealed during his shock retirement announcement, he'd been thinking about leaving the game as early as 2005, and it was only the burning urge to regain the Ashes from England that kept him from quitting.

Warne's decision to stay on heaped more misery on the batsmen of the West Indies, South Africa and Bangladesh, all of whom had to suffer the determination of a man desperate to be in the best possible form and condition for England's Ashes defence.

In the 12 Test matches between Australia's 2005 humbling in England and the beginning of the 2006–7 Ashes series, Warne took 62 wickets, confirming the suspicion that his 2003 12-month suspension for taking two diuretic pills was a hidden blessing.

If there is one thing he has that I would love to have, it is the ability to spin the ball the way he does. Warney has been very open about what he thinks and how he bowls. I am very happy to have played with him and competed with him. I have learnt a lot from him, not just by talking to him but by watching the way he bowls.

Champion Indian spinner, Anil Kumble

While he missed Australia's triumphant 2003 World Cup campaign, the suspension from all first-class cricket allowed his increasingly creaky body to recover – particularly his bowling shoulder and troublesome spinning finger.

But despite the reinvigorating effect of the enforced break and his superb form following it, Warne's body was beginning to struggle with the demands of touring, training and playing.

I think he'd be just about the best player that's ever played cricket.

Former team-mate and Test fast bowler, Jason Gillespie

He had given up one-day cricket to extend his Test career, but with his 40th birthday on the horizon, recovery was taking longer and training seemed that much tougher.

As he'd revealed, he had been psychologically prepared to go if Australia retained the Ashes in 2005. So when the Aussies clinched the Perth Test to take an unassailable 3–0 lead in the 2006–7 Ashes battle, the decision to retire was relatively easy.

It wasn't quite as easy for his team-mates:

'I knew as soon as I saw Shane Warne walking towards me during our post-match celebrations in the dressing rooms that something was up,' skipper Ricky Ponting wrote after that key Perth Test.

He literally is a legend. It's probably an overused term but in cricketing terms he is the ultimate legend, probably the best bowler that has been on this planet.

England Test and one-day batsman, Paul Collingwood

'He had said he wanted a chat, but as he got closer I thought "This doesn't look right". He just came out with it, and said to me; "It's my time".

'I sat back and tried to process the news. I hadn't heard any whispers at all, I had no inkling. My initial reaction wasn't so much disappointment that he was finishing, but more sadness than anything else. Shane was a guy that I played cricket with for so long, and had learned so much about the game from him.

'Then we probably sat there in the rooms for an hour, and talked about a lot of things. I made no attempt to try to talk him out of it.

'I would love to keep playing with him. Don't get me wrong; everyone would love to see him continue playing Test cricket for Australia. But I said to him, "Mate, I'm not even going to try to talk you out of it. You've obviously thought long and hard about it, you're not going to make a decision like this without doing that."'

Warne's former skipper and the man who had shown so much faith during his difficult early period, could scarcely believe it. 'I just got the inkling that he was even considering one more tilt at England in England (the 2009 Ashes series) and that would see him out,' Allan Border said. 'What he's brought to the game is immeasurable.'

Whatever you say about Shane Warne it isn't enough. His performances have not only shaped cricket in Australia but worldwide. Most people go through a purple patch and Shane Warne has had a purple patch for 15 or 16 years.

Former Victorian and Australian team-mate, Merv Hughes

After fifteen years of amazing highs, serious injuries, unprecedented on-field success and off-field drama, Shane Warne was about to draw the curtains on a game-changing career – but not before he staged one great finale.

From the earliest days of playing grade cricket for St Kilda, Warne had relished the role of entertainer. He loved the spotlight and the drama of turning a seemingly hopeless position into a platform for unlikely triumph.

His crucial role in the nerve-shredding 1999 World Cup semifinal tie against South Africa, his MCG Test hat-trick, even the drama of falling one short of his maiden Test century against New Zealand in 2001–2 – it was what he played for.

I thank him for the massive contribution he's made to Australian cricket. He's made a huge contribution to both maintaining and further stimulating interest in cricket in this and many other countries and I wish him well.

Long-serving Prime Minister, John Howard

So while his retirement shocked many, its timing and nature embodied the true performer's motto: always leave them wanting more. And for a man so attuned to the theatre of sport, the timing of his farewell Test at the MCG could scarcely have been better.

Warne arrived at Australia's greatest sports stadium one wicket shy of becoming the first man to take 700 Test wickets. With the newly redeveloped 'G packed with an emotional home crowd, he began his spell to a subdued hush.

As always, he was immediately on a length – probing and testing the English bats. And it wasn't long before he produced the spiritual successor to 'The Gatting Ball' – a magnificent delivery that uprooted one of England's best batsmen, Andrew Strauss.

It was a typically controlled, superbly-placed and sharply-spinning ball that drifted away from the left-handed Strauss before biting and angling back into his middle-stump. It was 3:18pm on Boxing Day, and for the 89,155 spectators who rose for one of the great standing ovations, a moment to lock in the memory vault.

Warne immediately sprinted away for what appeared would be a victory lap, but later admitted he stopped when he realised how much running was involved. And not only did he break the previously unthinkable 700 wicket mark, he took 5/39, setting England well on the way toward yet another Test loss.

'There's some special things that happen in your life and there's some special days in your life, and that's definitely one of them,' he said later that day.

'The birth of your children, getting married, playing your first Test – they're pretty special – but that one today, from an individual point of view, that's got to be one of the best days I ever had.'

Warne finally closed the circle on his career by playing his last Test where he played his first – the Sydney Cricket Ground. When he trapped Monty Panesar LBW to end England's first innings, Warne had taken his 1000th wicket in Tests and One Day Internationals.

He then scored an ebullient 71 off 65 balls to give Australia a crucial first-innings lead. Day three saw him take the final wicket of his Test career – the crucial scalp of England skipper Andrew Flintoff, stumped by Warne's great collaborator, Adam Gilchrist.

Not only is he a great bowler but he's also a great thinker. He got a lot of people out with wonderful deliveries but also out-thought a lot.

Former Australian captain, Mark Taylor

It was over, and Warne – who left the SCG with his great mate and co-retiree Glenn McGrath – brought to a close one of cricket's golden eras. Amazingly, the pair ended their careers ranked third and fourth respectively on the International Cricket Council's bowler rankings.

In the thousands of words that have been written about Shane Warne since his retirement, there's one common theme: he's a one-off.

He's been described as the Don Bradman of bowling, the Michael Jordan of cricket and poetically compared by author Gideon Haigh to the Roman emperor Augustus. 'It was said of Augustus that he found Rome brick and left it marble: the same is true of Warne and spin bowling,' Haigh wrote.

But why was he so great? What was it that allowed him to surprise and confuse elite batsmen who'd spent hours studying the nuances of Warne's various deliveries on video and DVD?

How did he manage to dominate the English for so long – even after they'd designed a special bowling robot to simulate his leg-breaks, flippers, wrong'uns and zooters?

According to those who were closest to the action, Warne was a freak because he combined several elite-level skills into an unstoppable package.

Technically, he was a genius; able to drop the ball almost exactly where he wanted over long periods and in all sorts of conditions. Although the technology that allowed pitch-mapping arrived relatively late in his career, the computerised analyses of where he was pitching his deliveries showed an incredible accuracy.

Not only that, he was able to maintain that accuracy while bowling a range of deliveries that demanded subtle changes to his grip, arm speed and delivery height. And of course, these variations had to be well enough disguised to fool the batsman into thinking he was bowling something else.

Second, Warne had an uncanny knack of analysing the strategic aspects of the game – the match situation, the changing nature of the pitch and the general morale of Australia's opponents. If containment was needed, he could bowl tight with relatively few variations.

I suppose I can say that 'I was there' at the moment he first indicated his potential to the wider world. There or thereabouts, anyway. Thanks to him, there are many more legspinners in the game. We may not see his like again.

Former England skipper and victim of 'The Ball of the Century', Mike Gatting

---

But if Australia needed wickets and had runs to play with, he'd unlock his box of tricks, using the crease to alter his angle, varying his pace and trajectory, tossing in the odd flipper (a delivery he joyfully re-mastered late in his career) and very occasionally, a fiery bouncer.

Third, he was an acutely tactical thinker who prepared himself with a military discipline for each opponent. Although he gave the impression of the easy-going joker, Warne's intensely competitive nature meant he'd plan the downfall of each of his opponents meticulously.

And he was patient – almost serenely so. Warne came into Test cricket at a time when fast bowling was king. For close to a decade, the West Indies had steamrolled sides through the intimidatory power of super-fast, hyper-aggressive bowlers. The typical response of the Windies' opponents was to try to intimidate them back.

But when Warne began to get into his stride, the game changed. Nobody was going to get hurt facing him, and there was even time to change your mind about a shot while the ball was in the air. He'd even offer a batsman a complimentary ball to smash to the boundary in order to get their confidence up.

He'd then hit them with the second element of his two-part plan; a wrong'un or a flipper that looked exactly the same as the previous delivery but went straight and low or jagged in the opposite direction.

'Occasionally I'll do that on purpose to set the batsman up for the flipper,' Warne said. 'Their confidence usually grows after a good shot. Sometimes they can forget that you have a dangerous delivery up your sleeve.'

Warne never blasted anyone out, he thought them out – an amazing 708 times.

Shortly after his retirement, Ricky Ponting was asked what Warne had offered the team.

'He's such an unbelievable competitor. It didn't matter if he was feeling a million dollars or rubbish, he would perform for you,' Ponting said.

'A lot of people don't understand how hard it is to bowl leg-spin. To be able to bowl one good leg-spinner is a great skill, but to be able to do it as regularly as he does for as long as he has says everything about the bloke.

'Everyone realises how talented he is and the contribution he has made. But the way he thinks about the game and sets batsmen up continues to amaze me.

'He told me how an entire over against England's Kevin Pietersen was going to unfold at The Oval last year (2005).

During the tea break, he said to me "I'm going to start around the wicket for the first three balls, bowl them way outside leg stump and he'll pad up to every one of them."

'Then he said, "I'll go back over the wicket fourth or fifth ball, bowl him a slow, loopy leg-spinner that pitches outside off stump that he'll try to slog sweep over mid-wicket, and he'll miss it". And that's what happened.

'It's one thing to be able to bowl all those balls in exactly the right spot. But to know what the batter's going to do because of the pressure he had created during the over was remarkable.'

Adam Gilchrist – who, along with former keeper Ian Healy – has seen more of Warne's Test match deliveries than anyone on the planet, says standing behind the stumps to the master leggie is the clear highlight of his career.

And he sheepishly admits that having studied Warne from the best possible vantage point through long training sessions and searing Test match afternoons, he can still get fooled by his good mate's trickery.

'He totally bamboozled me,' Gilchrist said of a delivery in the most recent Ashes-clinching Test in Perth.

There are a generation of Australians who were privileged enough to see Bradman. We are the generation that will always say we were privileged to see Warne.

Cricket Australia's chief executive, James Sutherland

Bowling to the left-handed English opener Alastair Cook, Warne tossed up what appeared to be a standard leggie – a ball which if it behaved as it should, was about to spear down the leg side.

Gilchrist moved quickly to cut off any possible byes, but to his amazement, the ball spun in the opposite direction and finished in the hands of first slip.

'I walked down to Warnie at the end of the over and, with a wry smile on his face he said "Did I do you then, Gilly?".

'I must admit I felt pretty foolish because I always felt I had a pretty good understanding of what he was bowling. I've always lived by the theory that I can pick everything. I think I made up an excuse that Cook's bat got in the way. He had me guessing after all those years.'

Plenty of former team-mates have been asked to describe their Warne highlight, but it's Gilchrist who remembers a blue-collar all-round performance that summarised Warne's hunger, work ethic and immense value to the team.

It was Warne's 100th Test – playing a strong South African side in Cape Town, early 2002. 'All the attention was on him, and rightly so,' Gilchrist said. 'He's enjoyed the limelight. He's always stepped up under that glare.'

In South Africa's first innings, Warne took 2/70 on a very unresponsive pitch. Then during Australia's first knock, he formed a crucial 132-run partnership – Warne scoring 63, Gilchrist 138 not-out.

Warne then produced a marathon performance of 70 overs in South Africa's second innings, taking 6/61 when the Proteas were attempting to kill the game. All under an injury cloud.

'His bowling on a very unresponsive wicket was a testament to his courage and physical strength, even though people claimed he wasn't fit,' Gilchrist said.

'That was a really taxing, exhausting effort which proved that he wasn't just the showman, front page, tabloid glitzy Warnie.

'It was a tradesman's effort, and he had the ability to do both and be both. It was a very special Test for all of us because we won it to win the series.'

After more than 40,000 Test deliveries, more than 120 catches, thousands of one-day deliveries, the most Test runs of any batsman not to have scored a century, and all those wickets, Shane Warne's career was finally brought to a close in early 2007.

He could undoubtedly have continued playing for some time, but when it comes to the game and choosing the right path, the man named one of Wisden's top five cricketers of the 20th century, has rarely put a foot wrong.

As he said during his retirement announcement, 'My time is now and I couldn't have asked for things to go any better.'

I think it's perfect timing for a champion player ... if you make a mistake it's best to get out a little early than a little late.

Former Australia captain and Warne mentor, Ian Chappell

Clearly, the Australian team and the Australian public will miss him desperately. But while he won't be playing, his presence will be felt throughout the coming decades.

On summery Saturday mornings, across thousands of dewy ovals, the kids that grew up watching Shane Warne will be attempting a zooter, trying out a flipper or just attempting to bowl their version of 'The Gatting Ball'.

Shane Warne revived the spinner's art, and while he may have suffered from some calamitous off-field misjudgements, even these may have contributed to the package that so many found compelling.

In a period when pace was everything, Shane Warne made it cool to be a spinner – and by doing this, he opened up the game for thousands of kids who just weren't built to bowl fast.

Not just in Australia, either. He rejuvenated spin bowling across the globe. Some of the kids who were inspired by Warne will become Test cricketers, and for that, we thank him.

Matthew Pinkney
Melbourne 2007

By the years:
Warne's highs and lows

1992:   Debut v India at the SCG. Dismisses Ravi Shastri as he
        takes 1/150.
        Takes 3/11 against Sri Lanka.

1993:   Seventeen wickets in three Tests against New Zealand.
        Gets engaged to blonde model Simone Callahan.
        Old Trafford, Manchester. First ball of his Ashes debut
        delivers 'The Gatting Ball', later renamed 'The Ball of the
        Century'.

1993–4: 100th Test wicket. Brian McMillan, South Africa.

1994:   Australian Cricket Board fines Warne $4000 for sledging
        South African Andrew Hudson while on tour.
        Career-best 8/71 against England in Brisbane.
        Hat-trick at the MCG in the Boxing Day Test.
        Named Wisden Cricketer of the Year

1995:   200th wicket – Sri Lanka's Chaminda Vaas – in his 42nd
        Test.

1996:   Undergoes surgery on his main spinning finger.

1997:   Key role as Australia retains the Ashes. Takes 250th
        wicket – England's Alec Stewart, the batsman doomed to
        be dismissed most often by Warne.

1998:   Major shoulder surgery to repair wear and tear.
        Was paid $5000 for providing pitch conditions to 'John' an
        Indian bookmaker. He denied any involvement in match-
        fixing but was fined $8000 by cricket authorities.

1998–9: South Africa's Jacques Kallis becomes his 300th
        wicket.

1999:   Dropped for the final Test against West Indies.
        Bounces back with a key role in Australia's thrilling semi-
        final tie against South Africa in the World Cup. Australia
        goes on to lift the trophy, with Warne named Man of the
        Match in the final.

2000:   Becomes Australia's highest Test wicket-taker,
        surpassing great fast bowler Dennis Lillee.
        Is stripped of the vice-captain's position after a text
        message scandal with a British nurse.
        Named One-Day International Player of the Year.
        Named as one of Wisden's five cricketers of the 20th
        century.

2001:   Takes his 400th wicket. The wicket of his prize victim
        Alec Stewart gets him to the milestone.
        Makes his highest Test score – 99 – against New Zealand.
        It's later revealed the delivery that got him out was a no-
        ball.

2002:   Dislocates his shoulder during a one-day match.
        Questions are raised about his long-term future.

2003:   Takes two diuretic pills given to him by his mother. Is
        suspended by cricket authorities for a year and is sent
        home from the World Cup in South Africa in disgrace.
        Announces he is retiring from one-day internationals to
        extend his Test career.

2003–4: Takes his 500th Test wicket. Sri Lanka's Hashan
        Tillakaratne is his victim.

2005:   Separates from wife Simone.
        Takes his 600th Test wicket by dismissing England's
        Marcus Trescothick during the Ashes series.
        Takes 40 wickets in five Tests against the English and
        finishes the 2005 calendar year with an amazing 96
        wickets – the most by any bowler in a year.

2006:   Announces his retirement between the third and fourth
        Ashes Tests.
        Hometown farewell at the MCG in the Boxing Day Test.
        Helps bowl Australia to victory with 5/59 – including his
        700th wicket – 40 not out, and 2/46. Andrew Strauss is
        his 700th scalp.

2007:   Plays his final Test at the Sydney Cricket Ground, taking
        1/69 and 1/23 and scoring 71 with the bat. Helps
        Australia to a 5–0 clean sweep.

Shane Warne
Career Statistics

WARNE, Shane Keith

(RHB, LBG) b Ferntree Gully, 13 September 1969.

Key: HS – highest score; HSA – highest score in Australia; HSV highest score for Victoria; BB Best Bowling; BBV – best bowling for Victoria; Int Test – International Tests (between two countries); Multi Test – Multinational Tests (against multinational teams e.g. the ICC World XI); DLO – Domestic Limited over matches; LOI – Limited over International matches.

MAJOR FIRST CLASS TEAMS

Played for Victoria 1990-91 to 2006-07; Australia 1991-92 to 2006-07; Hampshire 2000, 2004 to 2006 (captain from 2004).

MAJOR TOURS

Zimbabwe 1991-92 (Australia B); Sri Lanka 1992-93; New Zealand 1992-93; England 1993; South Africa 1993-94; Sharjah 1993-94; Sri Lanka/Pakistan 1994-95; West Indies 1994-95; India/Pakistan (World Cup) 1995-96; South Africa 1996-97; England 1997; India 1997-98; West Indies 1998-99; England (World Cup) 1999; Sri Lanka and Zimbabwe 1999-2000; New Zealand 1999-2000; India 2000-01; England 2001; South Africa 2001-02; Sri Lanka 2003-04; India 2004-05; New Zealand 2004-05; England 2005; South Africa 2005-06 & Bangladesh 2005-06. He was selected for the 2002-03 World Cup in South Africa, but had to withdraw after testing positive to a banned substance.

FIRST CLASS RECORD

Debut 1990-91 Victoria v Western Australia (St Kilda) (20; 0/61 + 1/41). HS 107* Hampshire v Kent (Canterbury) 2005; HSA 99 Australia v New Zealand (Perth) 2001-02; HSV 75 Victoria v South Australia (Melbourne) 2004-05. BB 8/71 Australia v England (Brisbane) 1994-95 including 3 wickets in 4 balls and 11/110 in the match; BBV 7/100 (10/164 in the match) Victoria v Queensland (St Kilda) 2005-06.

TEST RECORD

Debut 1991-92 Australia v India (Sydney) (20 + 1*; 1/150). HS 99 as above. BB 8/71 as above.

DLO RECORD

Debut 1992-93 Victoria v Tasmania (Devonport) (26; 3/31). HS 32 Victoria v South Australia (Adelaide) 1994-95. BB 5/35 Victoria v Tasmania (Carlton) 1996-97.

LOI RECORD

Debut 1992-93 Australia v New Zealand (Wellington) (3; 2/40). HS 55 Australia v South Africa (Port Elizabeth) 1993-94. BB 5/33 Australia v West Indies (Sydney) 1996-97.

BEST SEASONS

2005 in England took 87 wickets @ 22.50; 1994-95 in Pakistan, Australia & West Indies took 86 wickets @ 22.84; 2004-05 in Australia, India & Sri Lanka took 77 wickets @ 22.88; 1993 in England took 75 wickets @ 22.64 (including 34 wickets @ 25.79 in Tests - record for a leg-spinner in England); 2000 in England took 70 wickets @ 23.14; 1993-94 in Australia took 63 wickets @ 19.92 (87 wickets @ 20.77 in Australia & South Africa); 1999-2000 in Sri Lanka, Zimbabwe, Australia & New Zealand took 62 wickets @ 27.96; 2004-05 in Australia & India took 60 wickets @ 29.36; 1997-98 in Australia & India took 59 wickets @ 35.93; 2006 in England took 58 wickets @ 27.08; 1997 in England took 57 wickets @ 20.24; 2005-06 in Australia took 52 wickets @ 24.90; 2001-02 in Australia & South Africa took 51 wickets @ 32.49; 2004 in England took 51 wickets @ 24.17.

OTHER MISCELLANEOUS ACHIEVEMENTS & FACTS

Took 3 wickets in 4 balls for Australia v England (Brisbane) 1994-95. Took a hat trick for Australia v England (Melbourne) 1994-95. He is the leading wicket-taker in Test cricket. He has scored more runs in Test cricket than any other player without recording a century. He has had more sixes hit off his bowling than any other player in Test history. He scored his maiden first class century in his 238th match & 321st innings - both are records for an Australian. He announced his retirement from Test cricket & Australian first class cricket in December 2006.

Batting record by competition

Competition	Debut	M	I	NO	Runs	HS	Avge	100	50	C
First Class	1990-91	286	385	48	6555	107*	19.45	2	25	248
Sheffield Shield	1990-91	46	58	7	872	75	17.09	0	4	38
For State	1990-91	46	58	7	872	75	17.09	0	4	38
Int Test	1991-92	144	197	17	3142	99	17.45	0	12	125
Multi Test	2005-06	1	2	0	12	7	6.00	0	0	0
DLO	1992-93	30	22	1	210	32	10.00	0	0	12
LOI	1992-93	193	106	28	1016	55	13.02	0	1	80

Bowling record by competition

Competition	Debut	M	Balls	Mdns	Runs	Wkts	Avge	5w	10w	Best
First Class	1990-91	286	72200	2977	32972	1269	25.98	64	11	8/71
Sheffield Shield	1990-91	46	11854	446	5591	161	34.72	8	1	7/100
For State	1990-91	46	11854	446	5591	161	34.72	8	1	7/100
Int Test	1991-92	144	40518	1754	17924	702	25.53	37	10	8/71
Multi Test	2005-06	1	186	7	71	6	11.83	0	0	3/23
DLO	1992-93	30	1609	18	1201	43	27.93	1		5/35
LOI	1992-93	193	10600	110	7514	291	25.82	1		5/33

SHANE WARNE'S HUNDREDS

107*	Hampshire	v	Kent	Canterbury	2005
101	Hampshire	v	Middlesex	Southgate	2005

SHANE WARNE'S FIVE WICKETS IN AN INNINGS

Southampton[1] – County Ground
Southampton[2] – Rose Bowl

7/49	Australians	v	Zimbabwe	Harare	1991-92
5/49	Victoria	v	Western Australia	St Kilda	1992-93
7/52	AUSTRALIA	v	WEST INDIES	Melbourne	1992-93
5/61	Australians	v	Gloucestershire	Bristol	1993
5/82	AUSTRALIA	v	ENGLAND	Birmingham	1993
6/42	Victoria	v	Western Australia	Melbourne	1993-94
6/31	AUSTRALIA	v	NEW ZEALAND	Hobart	1993-94
5/77	Victoria	v	New South Wales	Sydney	1993-94
7/56	AUSTRALIA	v	SOUTH AFRICA	Sydney	1993-94
5/72	AUSTRALIA	v	SOUTH AFRICA	Sydney	1993-94

5/89	AUSTRALIA	v	PAKISTAN	Karachi	1994-95
6/136	AUSTRALIA	v	PAKISTAN	Lahore	1994-95
5/104	Victoria	v	Tasmania	Melbourne	1994-95
8/71	AUSTRALIA	v	ENGLAND	Brisbane	1994-95
6/64	AUSTRALIA	v	ENGLAND	Melbourne	1994-95
5/122	Victoria	v	New South Wales	Melbourne	1995-96
7/23	AUSTRALIA	v	PAKISTAN	Brisbane	1995-96
7/103	Australians	v	Derbyshire	Derby	1997
5/42	Australians	v	Leicestershire	Leicester	1997
6/48	AUSTRALIA	v	ENGLAND	Manchester	1997
5/57	Australians	v	Somerset	Taunton	1997
5/88	AUSTRALIA	v	NEW ZEALAND	Hobart	1997-98
5/75	AUSTRALIA	v	NEW ZEALAND	Sydney	1997-98
6/34	AUSTRALIA	v	NEW ZEALAND	Sydney	1997-98
5/52	AUSTRALIA	v	SRI LANKA	Kandy	1999-2000
5/110	AUSTRALIA	v	PAKISTAN	Hobart	1999-2000
5/86	Hampshire	v	Leicestershire	Leicester	2000
5/31	Hampshire	v	Surrey	The Oval	2000
5/90	Hampshire	v	Surrey	Southampton[1]	2000
6/36	Hampshire	v	Kent	Canterbury	2000
5/92	Hampshire	v	Yorkshire	Southampton[1]	2000
5/49	Victoria	v	Western Australia	Perth	2000-01
7/56	Australians	v	Mumbai	Mumbai (Brabourne)	2000-01
5/71	AUSTRALIA	v	ENGLAND	Birmingham	2001
6/33	AUSTRALIA	v	ENGLAND	Nottingham	2001
7/165	AUSTRALIA	v	ENGLAND	The Oval	2001
5/113	AUSTRALIA	v	SOUTH AFRICA	Adelaide	2001-02
6/161	AUSTRALIA	v	SOUTH AFRICA	Cape Town	2001-02
7/94	AUSTRALIA	v	PAKISTAN	Colombo,PSS	2002-03
5/74	AUSTRALIA	v	PAKISTAN	Sharjah	2002-03
5/116	AUSTRALIA	v	SRI LANKA	Galle	2003-04
5/43	AUSTRALIA	v	SRI LANKA	Galle	2003-04
5/65	AUSTRALIA	v	SRI LANKA	Kandy	2003-04
5/90	AUSTRALIA	v	SRI LANKA	Kandy	2003-04
5/68	Hampshire	v	Durham	Southampton[2]	2004
6/65	Hampshire	v	Glamorgan	Cardiff	2004
6/127	Hampshire	v	Somerset	Taunton	2004
6/125	AUSTRALIA	v	INDIA	Chennai	2004-05
5/39	AUSTRALIA	v	N.ZEALAND	Christchurch	2004-05
6/88	Hampshire	v	Warwickshire	Stratford	2005
6/46	AUSTRALIA	v	England	Birmingham	2005

6/122	AUSTRALIA	v	England	The Oval	2005
6/124	AUSTRALIA	v	England	The Oval	2005
5/48	AUSTRALIA	v	WEST INDIES	Brisbane	2005-06
6/80	AUSTRALIA	v	WEST INDIES	Adelaide	2005-06
7/100	Victoria	v	Queensland	St Kilda	2005-06
6/86	AUSTRALIA	v	SOUTH AFRICA	Durban	2005-06
5/113	AUSTRALIA	v	BANGLADESH	Chittagong	2005-06
7/99	Hampshire	v	Middlesex	Southampton[2]	2006
5/52	Hampshire	v	Warwickshire	Birmingham	2006
6/136	Hampshire	v	Sussex	Hove	2006
5/135	Hampshire	v	Durham	Chester-le-Street	2006
5/103	Victoria	v	South Australia	Adelaide	2006-07
5/39	AUSTRALIA	v	ENGLAND	Melbourne	2006-07

SHANE WARNE'S TEN WICKETS IN A MATCH

12/128(7/56 + 5/72)	Australia	v	South Africa	Sydney	1993-94
11/110(3/39 + 8/71)	Australia	v	England	Brisbane	1994-95
11/77(7/23 + 4/54)	Australia	v	Pakistan	Brisbane	1995-96
11/109(5/75 + 6/34)	Australia	v	South Africa	Sydney	1997-98
11/188(7/94 + 4/94)	Australia	v	Pakistan	Colombo (PSS)	2002-03
11/229(7/165 + 4/64)	Australia	v	England	Brisbane	2002-03
10/159(5/116 + 5/43)	Australia	v	Sri Lanka	Galle	2003-04
10/155(5/65 + 5/90)	Australia	v	Sri Lanka	Kandy	2003-04
10/162(4/116 + 6/46)	Australia	v	England	Birmingham	2005
12/246(6/122 + 6/124)	Australia	v	England	The Oval	2005
10/164(7/100 + 3/64)	Victoria	v	Queensland	St Kilda	2005-06

Sheffield Shield batting & fielding record against each State

Opponent	M	I	NO	Runs	HS	Avge	100	50	C
New South Wales	10	12	1	186	52	16.90	0	1	8
Queensland	8	11	4	140	31*	20.00	0	0	9
South Australia	9	9	1	146	75	18.25	0	1	8
Tasmania	9	11	1	160	62	16.00	0	1	5
Western Australia	10	15	0	240	69	16.00	0	1	8
TOTAL	46	58	7	872	75	17.09	0	4	38

Sheffield Shield batting & fielding record on each ground

Ground	M	I	NO	Runs	HS	Avge	100	50	C
Adelaide	5	6	0	39	18	6.50	0	0	4
Bellerive	2	3	0	18	10	6.00	0	0	1
Brisbane	1	1	0	9	9	9.00	0	0	0
MCG	18	20	4	331	75	20.68	0	1	16
North Sydney	1	1	1	5	5*	-	0	0	1
Perth	7	12	0	150	38	12.50	0	0	7
Richmond	2	1	1	4	4*	-	0	0	3
St Kilda	5	8	1	195	69	27.85	0	2	1
Sydney	5	6	0	111	52	18.50	0	1	5
TOTAL	46	58	7	872	75	17.09	0	4	38

Sheffield Shield bowling record against each State

Opponent	M	Balls	Mdns	Runs	Wkts	Avge	5w	10w	Best
New South Wales	10	2650	94	1324	30	44.13	2	0	5/77
Queensland	8	2226	67	1072	28	38.28	1	1	7/100
South Australia	9	2549	104	1129	31	36.41	1	0	5/103
Tasmania	9	2245	90	1038	36	28.83	1	0	5/104
Western Australia	10	2184	91	1028	36	28.55	3	0	6/42
TOTAL	46	11854	446	5591	161	34.72	8	1	7/100

Sheffield Shield bowling record on each ground

Ground	M	Balls	Mdns	Runs	Wkts	Avge	5w	10w	Best
Adelaide	5	1462	55	662	17	38.94	1	0	5/103
Bellerive	2	390	20	209	4	52.25	0	0	2/26
Brisbane	1	366	9	173	4	43.25	0	0	3/111
MCG	18	5041	206	2242	73	30.71	3	0	6/42
North Sydney	1	348	9	195	3	65.00	0	0	2/78
Perth	7	1301	49	669	19	35.21	1	0	5/49
Richmond	2	276	4	156	4	39.00	0	0	4/118
St Kilda	5	1269	38	616	22	28.00	2	1	7/100
Sydney	5	1401	56	669	15	44.60	1	0	5/77
TOTAL	46	11854	446	5591	161	34.72	8	1	7/100

DLO batting & fielding record against each State

Opponent	M	I	NO	Runs	HS	Avge	100	50	C
ACT	1	1	0	9	9	9.00	0	0	0
New South Wales	6	6	0	69	25	11.50	0	0	1
Queensland	6	2	0	22	22	11.00	0	0	3
South Australia	6	4	1	49	32	16.33	0	0	3
Tasmania	4	3	0	42	26	14.00	0	0	3
Western Australia	7	6	0	19	15	3.16	0	0	2
TOTAL	30	22	1	210	32	10.00	0	0	12

DLO batting & fielding record on each ground

Ground	M	I	NO	Runs	HS	Avge	100	50	C
Adelaide	4	3	1	49	32	24.50	0	0	3
Ballarat	1						0	0	1
Bankstown	1	1	0	25	25	25.00	0	0	1
Bellerive	1	1	0	9	9	9.00	0	0	0
Carlton	1						0	0	3
Devonport	1	1	0	26	26	26.00	0	0	0
MCG	8	6	0	53	24	8.83	0	0	1
North Sydney	2	2	0	15	14	7.50	0	0	0
Perth	3	3	0	2	2	0.66	0	0	1
Richmond	3	3	0	9	9	3.00	0	0	1
St Kilda	2						0	0	0
Sydney	1	1	0	0	0	0.00	0	0	0
Woolloongabba	2	1	0	22	22	22.00	0	0	1
TOTAL	30	22	1	210	32	10.00	0	0	12

DLO bowling record against each State

Opponent	M	Balls	Mdns	Runs	Wkts	Avge	5w	Best
ACT	1	60	0	31	2	15.50	0	2/31
New South Wales	6	270	3	223	6	38.83	0	3/43
Queensland	6	320	2	238	7	34.00	0	2/20
South Australia	6	342	7	228	9	25.33	0	4/45
Tasmania	4	215	2	155	11	14.09	1	5/35
Western Australia	7	402	4	316	8	39.50	0	3/48
TOTAL	30	1609	18	1201	43	27.93	1	5/35

DLO bowling record on each ground

Ground	M	Balls	Mdns	Runs	Wkts	Avge	5w	Best
Adelaide	4	222	5	128	4	32.00	0	2/34
Ballarat	1	50	0	20	2	10.00	0	2/20
Bankstown	1	60	1	49	1	49.00	0	1/49
Bellerive	1	60	0	41	2	20.50	0	2/41
Carlton	1	60	1	35	5	7.00	1	5/35
Devonport	1	35	0	31	3	10.33	0	3/31
MCG	8	414	3	340	8	42.50	0	4/45
North Sydney	2	84	1	90	3	30.00	0	3/43
Perth	3	174	4	116	6	19.33	0	3/48
Richmond	3	180	1	126	5	25.20	0	2/31
St Kilda	2	120	1	92	1	92.00	0	1/39
Sydney	1	60	0	54	1	54.00	0	1/54
Woolloongabba	2	90	1	79	2	39.50	0	1/36
TOTAL	30	1609	18	1201	43	27.93	1	5/35

SHANE WARNE'S FIRST CLASS RECORD

First class batting and fielding in each season

Season (Country)	M	I	NO	Runs	HS	Avge	100s	50s	C
1990-91 (Australia)	1	1	0	20	20	20.00	0	0	0
1991-92 (Zimbabwe)	2	3	2	53	35*	53.00	0	0	1
1991-92 (Australia)	9	11	4	120	30*	17.14	0	0	2
1992-93 (Sri Lanka)	3	4	0	67	35	16.75	0	0	1
1992-93 (Australia)	9	13	1	172	69	14.33	0	2	5
1992-93 (New Zealand)	4	5	2	51	22*	17.00	0	0	1
1993 (England)	16	15	4	246	47	22.36	0	0	8
1993-94 (Australia)	10	12	2	151	74*	15.10	0	1	10
1993-94 (South Africa)	5	8	1	84	34	12.00	0	0	1
1994-95 (Pakistan)	4	5	0	73	33	14.60	0	0	2
1994-95 (Australia)	7	14	1	101	36*	7.76	0	0	5
1994-95 (West Indies)	6	6	0	51	23	8.50	0	0	5
1995-96 (Australia)	9	9	2	132	36	18.85	0	0	9
1996-97 (Australia)	7	10	0	159	30	15.90	0	0	8
1996-97 (South Africa)	5	7	0	101	44	14.42	0	0	4
1997 (England)	12	17	1	293	53	18.31	0	1	5
1997-98 (Australia)	9	12	2	138	36	13.80	0	0	7
1997-98 (India)	5	8	1	129	35	18.42	0	0	3
1998-99 (Australia)	5	7	2	98	38	19.60	0	0	8
1998-99 (West Indies)	6	10	0	190	33	19.00	0	0	6
1999-00 (Sri Lanka)	5	7	1	55	27	9.16	0	0	5
1999-00 (Zimbabwe)	2	3	1	8	6	4.00	0	0	0
1999-00 (Australia)	6	7	1	187	86	31.16	0	2	7
1999-00 (New Zealand)	4	5	0	60	24	12.00	0	0	6

2000 (England)	15	22	2	431	69	21.55	0	3	14
2000-01 (Australia)	2	2	0	39	27	19.50	0	0	2
2000-01 (India)	4	7	0	59	39	8.42	0	0	2
2001 (England)	8	10	2	237	69	29.62	0	2	13
2001-02 (Australia)	8	11	1	296	99	29.60	0	2	8
2001-02 (South Africa)	4	6	1	129	63	25.80	0	1	5
2002-03 (Sri Lanka)	1	2	0	0	0	0.00	0	0	0
2002-03 (United Arab Emirates)	2	2	0	30	19	15.00	0	0	2
2002-03 (Australia)	5	6	0	143	57	23.83	0	1	1
2003-04 (Australia)	1	1	0	18	18	18.00	0	0	1
2003-04 (Sri Lanka)	4	8	0	118	32	14.75	0	0	4
2004 (England)	12	16	2	381	57	27.21	0	1	9
2004-05 (Australia)	11	14	1	223	75	17.15	0	2	19
2004-05 (India)	3	5	0	38	31	7.60	0	0	4
2004-05 (New Zealand)	3	3	1	53	50*	26.50	0	1	1
2005 (England)	16	27	3	742	107*	30.91	2	2	18
2005-06 (Australia)	10	15	1	202	62	14.42	0	1	9
2005-06 (South Africa)	3	4	0	82	36	20.50	0	0	1
2005-06 (Bangladesh)	2	2	0	11	6	5.50	0	0	1
2006 (England)	13	17	5	371	61*	30.91	0	2	16
2006-07 (Australia)	8	6	1	213	71	42.60	0	1	8
Total	286	385	48	6555	107*	19.45	2	25	247

First class bowling in each season

Season (Country)	M	Balls	Mdns	Runs	Wkts	Avge	5wi	10wm	Best
1990-91 (Australia)	1	222	13	102	1	102.00	0	0	1/41
1991-92 (Zimbabwe)	2	586	28	207	11	18.81	1	0	7/49
1991-92 (Australia)	9	1872	81	853	20	42.65	0	0	4/42
1992-93 (Sri Lanka)	3	229	8	158	3	52.66	0	0	3/11
1992-93 (Australia)	9	1859	56	983	27	36.40	2	0	7/52
1992-93 (New Zealand)	4	1127	81	337	19	17.73	0	0	4/8
1993 (England)	16	4595	281	1698	75	22.64	2	0	5/61
1993-94 (Australia)	10	3446	176	1255	63	19.92	5	1	7/56
1993-94 (South Africa)	5	1668	96	552	24	23.00	0	0	4/86
1994-95 (Pakistan)	4	1264	59	598	23	26.00	2	0	6/136
1994-95 (Australia)	7	2240	123	814	40	20.35	3	1	8/71
1994-95 (West Indies)	6	1068	46	553	23	24.04	0	0	4/70
1995-96 (Australia)	9	2699	131	1057	42	25.16	2	1	7/23
1996-97 (Australia)	7	1885	87	795	27	29.44	0	0	4/95
1996-97 (South Africa)	5	1014	60	397	16	24.81	0	0	4/43
1997 (England)	12	2602	111	1154	57	20.24	4	0	7/103
1997-98 (Australia)	9	2993	115	1381	47	29.38	3	1	6/34
1997-98 (India)	5	1254	43	739	12	61.58	0	0	4/85
1998-99 (Australia)	5	1069	33	631	10	63.10	0	0	2/80
1998-99 (West Indies)	6	977	37	509	11	46.27	0	0	3/26
1999-00 (Sri Lanka)	5	617	30	272	15	18.13	1	0	5/52
1999-00 (Zimbabwe)	2	553	27	238	10	23.80	0	0	3/50
1999-00 (Australia)	6	1541	72	705	20	35.25	1	0	5/110
1999-00 (New Zealand)	4	950	38	519	17	30.52	0	0	4/68
2000 (England)	15	3838	183	1620	70	23.14	5	0	6/34
2000-01 (Australia)	2	287	8	140	9	15.55	1	0	5/49

2000-01 (India)	4	1156	40	642	18	35.66	1	0	7/56
2001 (England)	8	1578	56	784	42	18.66	3	1	7/165
2001-02 (Australia)	8	2238	63	1156	29	39.86	1	0	5/113
2001-02 (South Africa)	4	1068	40	501	22	22.77	1	0	6/161
2002-03 (Sri Lanka)	1	330	10	188	11	17.09	1	1	7/94
2002-03 (United Arab Emirates)	2	414	19	154	16	9.62	1	0	5/74
2002-03 (Australia)	5	1189	43	528	20	26.40	0	0	4/93
2003-04 (Australia)	1	216	11	100	6	16.66	0	0	4/51
2003-04 (Sri Lanka)	4	1184	43	621	29	21.41	4	2	5/43
2004 (England)	12	2471	88	1231	51	24.13	3	0	6/65
2004-05 (Australia)	11	2857	95	1341	46	29.15	0	0	4/15
2004-05 (India)	3	840	27	421	14	30.07	1	0	6/125
2004-05 (New Zealand)	3	789	25	374	17	22.00	1	0	5/39
2005 (England)	16	3903	98	1958	87	22.50	4	2	6/46
2005-06 (Australia)	10	2813	96	1295	52	24.90	3	1	7/100
2005-06 (South Africa)	3	766	19	423	15	28.20	1	0	6/86
2005-06 (Bangladesh)	2	524	12	300	11	27.27	1	0	5/113
2006 (England)	13	3142	91	1571	58	27.08	4	0	7/99
2006-07 (Australia)	8	2267	74	1115	33	33.78	2	0	5/39
Total	286	72200	2973	32970	1269	25.98	64	11	8/71

First class batting and fielding for each team

Team	M	I	NO	Runs	HS	Avge	100s	50s	C
Australia in International Tests	144	197	17	3142	99	17.45	0	12	125
Australia v ICC World XI	1	2	0	12	7	6.00	0	0	0
Australia B	2	3	2	53	35*	53.00	0	0	1
Australian XI	2	2	1	7	6	7.00	0	0	0
Australians	40	50	9	793	69	19.34	0	2	31
Hampshire	51	73	12	1676	107*	27.47	2	7	52
Victoria	46	58	7	872	75	17.09	0	4	38
Total	286	385	48	6555	107*	19.45	2	25	247

First-class bowling for each team

Team	M	Balls	Mdns	Runs	Wkts	Avge	5wi	10wm	Best
Australia in International Tests	144	40518	1754	17924	702	25.53	37	10	8/71
Australia v ICC World XI	1	186	7	71	6	11.83	0	0	3/23
Australia B	2	586	28	207	11	18.81	1	0	7/49
Australian XI	2	423	16	240	12	20.00	0	0	4/42
Australians	40	6796	299	3354	151	22.21	5	0	7/56
Hampshire	51	11837	423	5583	226	24.70	13	0	7/99
Victoria	46	11854	446	5591	161	34.72	8	1	7/100
Total	286	72200	2973	32970	1269	25.98	64	11	8/71

First class batting and fielding against each opponent

Opponent	M	I	NO	Runs	HS	Avge	100s	50s	C
Bangladesh	2	2	0	11	6	5.50	0	0	1
Boland	1	1	0	9	9	9.00	0	0	1
Border	1	1	0	15	15	15.00	0	0	0
Combined Universities	1	2	0	52	47	26.00	0	0	0
Derbyshire	5	5	2	62	34	20.66	0	0	0
Durham	6	7	1	100	41	16.66	0	0	6
England	36	48	5	946	90	22.00	0	4	30
Essex	2	4	0	55	34	13.75	0	0	2
Glamorgan	5	6	1	141	42	28.20	0	0	5
Gloucestershire	3	5	0	106	62	21.20	0	1	1
Guyana	1	1	0	23	23	23.00	0	0	1
Hampshire	2	3	0	54	38	18.00	0	0	2
ICC World XI	1	2	0	12	7	6.00	0	0	0
India	14	22	1	309	86	14.71	0	1	10
Indian Board President's XI	1	1	0	2	2	2.00	0	0	2
Kent	6	10	4	328	107*	54.66	1	1	11
Lancashire	4	4	2	62	30*	31.00	0	1	3
Leicestershire	5	7	2	181	57	36.20	0	0	1
Marylebone Cricket Club	1	2	1	99	69	99.00	1	1	2
Middlesex	5	8	2	255	101	42.50	0	1	6
Mumbai	2	4	1	31	11*	10.33	0	0	1
Natal	1	1	0	44	44	44.00	0	0	1
New South Wales	10	12	1	186	52	16.90	0	1	8
New Zealand	20	22	5	558	99	32.82	0	5	18
New Zealand Board XI	1	1	0	2	2	2.00	0	0	0
Northern Districts	1	1	0	24	24	24.00	0	0	2
Nottinghamshire	6	5	0	98	46	19.60	0	0	3

First class batting and fielding against each opponent (continued)

Opponent	M	I	NO	Runs	HS	Avge	100s	50s	C
Orange Free State	1	2	1	34	34	34.00	0	0	0
Pakistan	15	19	2	275	86	16.17	0	1	13
President's XI	1	1	0	4	4	4.00	0	0	0
Queensland	8	11	4	140	31*	20.00	0	0	9
Somerset	5	6	0	88	47	14.66	0	0	0
South Africa	24	37	4	460	63	13.93	0	1	19
South Africa A	1	1	0	0	0	0.00	0	0	0
South Australia	9	9	1	146	75	18.25	0	1	8
Southern Districts XI	1	1	0	1	1	1.00	0	0	0
Sri Lanka	13	18	0	193	35	10.72	0	0	15
Sri Lanka Board President's XI	1	2	0	39	31	19.50	0	0	1
Sri Lanka Board XI	2	3	1	49	27	24.50	0	0	3
Surrey	4	7	1	132	50	22.00	0	1	4
Sussex	2	3	0	93	53	31.00	0	1	3
Tasmania	9	11	1	160	62	16.00	0	1	5
Warwickshire	2	3	0	21	17	7.00	0	0	0
West Indians	2	2	1	7	6	7.00	0	0	0
West Indies	19	28	0	384	47	13.71	0	0	19
West Indies A	1	2	0	46	33	23.00	0	0	2
West Indies Board President's XI	2	1	0	4	4	4.00	0	0	2
West Indies Board XI	1	1	0	2	2	2.00	0	0	1
Western Australia	10	15	0	240	69	16.00	0	1	8
Worcestershire	2	3	1	112	68	56.00	0	1	4
Yorkshire	4	6	0	99	65	16.50	0	1	3
Zimbabwe	1	1	0	6	6	6.00	0	0	0
Zimbabwe B	2	3	2	53	35*	53.00	0	0	1
Zimbabwe.C.U President's XI	1	2	1	2	1*	2.00	0	0	0
Total	286	385	48	6555	107*	19.45	2	25	247

First class bowling against each opponent

Opponent	M	Balls	Mdns	Runs	Wkts	Avge	5wi	10wm	Best
Bangladesh	2	524	12	300	11	27.27	1	0	5/113
Boland	1	215	16	73	4	18.25	0	0	3/49
Border	1	18	2	1	3	0.33	0	0	3/1
Combined Universities	1	204	13	66	5	13.20	0	0	3/45
Derbyshire	5	1268	68	505	19	26.57	1	0	7/103
Durham	6	1092	41	561	29	19.34	2	0	5/68
England	36	10757	488	4535	195	23.25	11	4	8/71
Essex	2	402	9	231	7	33.00	0	0	4/118
Glamorgan	5	1218	42	544	26	20.92	1	0	6/65
Gloucestershire	3	650	24	264	15	17.60	1	0	5/61
Guyana	1	156	11	63	6	10.50	0	0	3/21
Hampshire	2	312	9	130	9	14.44	0	0	4/31
ICC World XI	1	186	7	71	6	11.83	0	0	3/23
India	14	3925	139	2029	43	47.18	1	0	6/125
Indian Board President's XI	1	156	5	88	2	44.00	0	0	2/88
Kent	6	1658	81	620	29	21.37	1	0	6/34
Lancashire	4	866	36	382	11	34.72	0	0	4/61
Leicestershire	5	856	41	342	25	13.68	2	0	5/42
Marylebone Cricket Club	1	114	3	58	3	19.33	0	0	2/10
Middlesex	5	1389	32	657	26	25.26	1	0	7/99
Mumbai	2	339	10	248	8	31.00	1	0	7/56
Natal	1	198	11	114	2	57.00	0	0	2/25
New South Wales	10	2650	94	1324	30	44.13	2	0	5/77
New Zealand	20	5770	252	2511	103	24.37	3	0	6/31
New Zealand Board XI	1	173	8	81	2	40.50	0	0	2/21
Northern Districts	1	174	5	105	2	52.50	0	0	2/53
Nottinghamshire	6	1037	26	629	14	44.92	0	0	3/53
Orange Free State	1	308	11	143	5	28.60	0	0	3/73

First class bowling against each opponent (continued)

Pakistan	15	4050	192	1816	90	20.17	6	2	7/23
President's XI	1	174	9	94	5	18.80	0	0	3/42
Queensland	8	2226	67	1072	28	38.28	1	1	7/100
Somerset	5	991	41	466	22	21.18	2	0	6/127
South Africa	24	7928	367	3142	130	24.16	7	2	7/56
South Africa A	1	96	2	59	2	29.50	0	0	2/59
South Australia	9	2549	104	1129	31	36.41	1	0	5/103
Southern Districts XI	1	did not bowl							
Sri Lanka	13	3167	132	1507	59	25.54	5	2	5/43
Sri Lanka Board President's XI	1	176	6	100	3	33.33	0	0	2/79
Sri Lanka Board XI	2	280	10	157	7	22.42	0	0	3/74
Surrey	4	1053	45	487	23	21.17	2	0	5/31
Sussex	2	519	14	289	12	24.08	1	0	6/136
Tasmania	9	2245	90	1038	36	28.83	1	0	5/104
Warwickshire	2	508	23	198	13	15.23	2	0	6/88
West Indians	2	423	16	240	12	20.00	0	0	4/42
West Indies	19	4078	159	1947	65	29.95	3	0	7/52
West Indies A	1	186	10	89	4	22.25	0	0	3/26
West Indies Board President's XI	2	300	6	216	6	36.00	0	0	3/82
West Indies Board XI	1	72	3	20	1	20.00	0	0	1/20
Western Australia	10	2184	91	1028	36	28.55	3	0	6/42
Worcestershire	2	322	16	194	4	48.50	0	0	2/38
Yorkshire	4	919	19	562	19	29.57	1	0	5/92
Zimbabwe	1	319	13	137	6	22.83	0	0	3/68
Zimbabwe B	2	586	27	207	13	15.92	1	0	7/49
Zimbabwe.C.U President's XI	1	234	14	101	4	25.25	0	0	3/50
Total	286	72200	2973	32970	1269	25.98	64	11	8/71

First class batting and fielding on each ground

Ground	M	I	NO	Runs	HS	Ave	100	50	C
Adelaide Oval	18	25	3	368	86	16.72	0	2	18
Aigburth, Liverpool	1	2	1	29	18*	29.00	0	0	0
Antigua Recreation Ground, St John's	3	4	0	59	33	14.75	0	0	3
Arundel Castle Cricket Club Ground	1	2	1	99	69	99.00	0	1	2
Asgiriya Stadium, Kandy	2	4	0	30	18	7.50	0	0	1
Basin Reserve, Wellington	3	3	1	79	50*	39.50	0	1	3
Bellerive Oval, Hobart	10	11	3	137	70	17.12	0	1	7
Bir Shrestha Shahid Ruhul Amin Stadium, Chittagong	1					-	0	0	1
Bourda, Georgetown	1	1	0	23	23	23.00	0	0	1
Brabourne Stadium, Mumbai	2	4	1	31	11*	10.33	0	0	1
Brisbane Cricket Ground, Woolloongabba	12	13	1	374	86	31.16	0	3	15
Buffalo Park, East London	1	1	0	15	15	15.00	0	0	0
Bulawayo Athletic Club	1	1	0	0	0	0.00	0	0	0
Cazaly's Stadium, Cairns	1	2	0	6	4	3.00	0	0	3
Centurion Park	1	2	0	12	12	6.00	0	0	0
Colombo Cricket Club Ground	2	3	0	66	31	22.00	0	0	1
County Ground, Bristol	2	3	0	22	17	7.33	0	0	0
County Ground, Chelmsford	1	2	0	34	34	17.00	0	0	1
County Ground, Derby	3	2	1	14	12	14.00	0	0	2
County Ground, Hove	2	3	0	93	53	31.00	0	1	3
County Ground, New Road, Worcester	2	3	1	112	68	56.00	0	1	4
County Ground, Southampton	6	8	0	181	65	22.62	0	1	5
County Ground, Taunton	4	4	0	88	47	22.00	0	0	0
Eden Gardens, Kolkata	2	4	0	20	11	5.00	0	0	0
Eden Park, Auckland	3	5	1	25	12	6.25	0	0	2
Edgbaston, Birmingham	5	7	0	164	47	23.42	0	0	3

First class batting and fielding on each ground (continued)

Ground	M	I	NO	Runs	HS	Ave	100	50	C
Fatullah Khan Saheb Osmani Stadium, Fatullah	1	2	0	11	6	5.50	0	0	0
Gaddafi Stadium, Lahore	1	1	0	33	33	33.00	0	0	0
Galle International Stadium	2	3	0	23	23	7.66	0	0	2
Goodyear Park, Bloemfontein	1	2	1	34	34	34.00	0	0	0
Grace Road, Leicester	4	6	1	152	57	30.40	0	1	1
Guaracara Park, Pointe-a-Pierre	1	1	0	4	4	4.00	0	0	0
Harare Sports Club	2	3	2	59	35*	59.00	0	0	1
Headingley, Leeds	5	5	0	0	0	0.00	0	0	3
Indira Priyadarshini Stadium, Visakhapatnam	1	1	0	2	2	2.00	0	0	2
John Walker's Ground, Southgate	1	2	0	105	101	52.50	1	0	3
Junction Oval, St Kilda	5	8	1	195	69	27.85	0	2	1
Kennington Oval, London	6	8	1	161	50	23.00	0	1	10
Kensington Oval, Bridgetown	2	3	0	51	32	17.00	0	0	2
Kingsmead, Durban	4	6	0	133	44	22.16	0	0	4
Lancaster Park, Christchurch	2	2	1	24	22*	24.00	0	0	0
Lord's Cricket Ground, St John's Wood, London	6	7	2	151	61*	30.20	0	1	6
M.A.Chidambaram Stadium, Chepauk, Chennai	3	6	0	67	35	11.16	0	0	2
M.Chinnaswamy Stadium, Bangalore	2	3	0	65	33	21.66	0	0	0
Marrara Cricket Ground, Darwin	1	2	0	3	2	1.50	0	0	1
May's Bounty, Basingstoke	1	1	0	0	0	0.00	0	0	1
Melbourne Cricket Ground	29	35	6	454	75	15.65	0	1	23
Mindoo Phillip Park, Castries	1					–	0	0	2
National Stadium, Karachi	1	2	0	22	22	11.00	0	0	1
New Wanderers Stadium, Johannesburg	4	6	0	76	36	12.66	0	0	2
Newlands, Cape Town	3	4	1	96	63	32.00	0	1	1
North Sydney Oval	1	1	1	5	5*	–	0	0	1
North West Cricket Stadium, Potchefstroom	1	1	0	0	0	0.00	0	0	0
Old Trafford, Manchester	4	6	1	198	90	39.60	0	2	2

Ground									
P.Saravanamuttu Stadium, Colombo	2	4	1	22	18	7.33	0	0	3
Pukekura Park, New Plymouth	1	1	0	2	2	2.00	0	0	0
Queen's Park Oval, Port of Spain	2	4	0	57	25	14.25	0	0	2
Queens Sports Club, Bulawayo	1	2	1	2	1*	2.00	0	0	0
Rawalpindi Cricket Stadium	2	2	0	18	14	9.00	0	0	1
Richmond Cricket Ground, Melbourne	2	1	1	4	4*	-	0	0	3
Riverside Ground, Chester-le-Street	3	3	1	60	41	30.00	0	0	3
Sabina Park, Kingston	2	3	0	47	24	15.66	0	0	1
Seddon Park, Hamilton	2	2	0	34	24	17.00	0	0	3
Sharjah Cricket Association Stadium	2	2	0	30	19	15.00	0	0	2
Sinhalese Sports Club Ground, Colombo	3	5	0	91	35	18.20	0	0	3
Sophia Gardens, Cardiff	2	3	0	68	29	22.66	0	0	3
St George's Park, Port Elizabeth	1	2	0	21	18	10.50	0	0	3
St Lawrence Ground, Canterbury	4	6	4	243	107*	121.50	1	0	6
Stellenbosch University Ground	1	1	0	9	9	9.00	0	0	1
Stratford-upon-Avon Cricket Club Ground	1	2	0	4	4	2.00	0	0	0
Sydney Cricket Ground	19	25	3	387	71	17.59	0	2	15
The Gnoll, Neath	1	1	0	18	18	18.00	0	0	0
The Rose Bowl, Southampton	18	26	4	423	62	19.22	0	1	20
The University Parks, Oxford	1	2	0	52	47	26.00	0	0	0
Trent Bridge, Nottingham	7	8	1	157	46	22.42	0	0	1
Tyronne Fernando Stadium, Moratuwa	1	1	0	7	7	7.00	0	0	0
United Services Recreation Ground, Portsmouth	1	2	0	73	69	36.50	0	1	4
Uyanwatte Stadium, Matara	1	1	0	1	1	1.00	0	0	0
Vidarbha Cricket Association Ground, Nagpur	1	1	0	2	2	2.00	0	0	0
Wankhede Stadium, Mumbai	1	1	0	39	39	39.00	0	0	3
Western Australia Cricket Association Ground, Perth	19	28	0	479	99	17.10	0	1	22
Total	286	385	48	6555	107*	19.45	2	25	247

First class bowling on each ground

Ground	M	Balls	Mdns	Runs	Wkts	Ave	5wi	10wm	Best
Adelaide Oval	18	5527	232	2367	73	32.42	3	0	6/80
Aigburth, Liverpool	1	100	4	61	4	15.25	0	0	4/61
Antigua Recreation Ground, St John's	3	468	22	210	8	26.25	0	0	3/26
Arundel Castle Cricket Club Ground	1	114	3	58	3	19.33	0	0	2/10
Asgiriya Stadium, Kandy	2	385	12	225	15	15.00	3	1	5/52
Basin Reserve, Wellington	3	854	49	351	14	25.07	0	0	4/68
Bellerive Oval, Hobart	10	2186	86	1070	44	24.31	3	0	6/31
Bir Shrestha Shahid Ruhul Amin Stadium, Chittagong	1	326	7	160	8	20.00	1	0	5/113
Bourda, Georgetown	1	156	11	63	6	10.50	0	0	3/21
Brabourne Stadium, Mumbai	2	339	10	248	8	31.00	1	0	7/56
Brisbane Cricket Ground, Woolloongabba	12	3686	171	1554	72	21.58	3	2	8/71
Buffalo Park, East London	1	18	2	1	3	0.33	0	0	3/1
Bulawayo Athletic Club	1	268	13	118	3	39.33	0	0	3/76
Cazaly's Stadium, Cairns	1	450	21	199	7	28.42	0	0	4/70
Centurion Park	1	216	11	89	0	-	0	0	0/89
Colombo Cricket Club Ground	2	245	8	146	5	29.20	0	0	2/79
County Ground, Bristol	2	380	19	158	9	17.55	1	0	5/61
County Ground, Chelmsford	1	108	6	60	2	30.00	0	0	2/40
County Ground, Derby	3	636	26	273	11	24.81	1	0	7/103
County Ground, Hove	2	519	14	289	12	24.08	1	0	6/136
County Ground, New Road, Worcester	2	322	16	194	4	48.50	0	0	2/38
County Ground, Southampton	6	1569	69	717	27	26.55	2	0	5/90
County Ground, Taunton	4	793	31	383	21	18.23	2	0	6/127
Eden Gardens, Kolkata	2	577	10	364	3	121.33	0		2/65
Eden Park, Auckland	3	783	38	350	18	19.44	0	0	4/8
Edgbaston, Birmingham	5	1503	78	654	32	20.43	4	1	6/46
Fatullah Khan Saheb Osmani Stadium, Fatullah	1	198	5	140	3	46.66	0	0	3/28

Gaddafi Stadium, Lahore	1	431	14	240	9	26.66	1	0	6/136
Galle International Stadium	2	516	26	193	13	14.84	2	1	5/43
Goodyear Park, Bloemfontein	1	308	11	143	5	28.60	0	0	3/73
Grace Road, Leicester	4	718	31	299	21	14.23	2	0	5/42
Guaracara Park, Pointe-á-Pierre	1	216	6	132	4	33.00	0	0	3/82
Harare Sports Club	2	637	28	226	14	16.14	1	0	7/49
Headingley, Leeds	5	1194	48	500	12	41.66	0	0	4/68
Indira Priyadarshini Stadium, Visakhapatnam	1	156	5	88	2	44.00	0	0	2/88
John Walker's Ground, Southgate	1	316	8	165	4	41.25	0	0	2/57
Junction Oval, St Kilda	5	1269	38	616	22	28.00	2	1	7/100
Kennington Oval, London	6	2074	90	930	46	20.21	4	2	7/165
Kensington Oval, Bridgetown	2	470	13	260	6	43.33	0	0	3/64
Kingsmead, Durban	4	1151	52	513	20	25.65	1	0	6/86
Lancaster Park, Christchurch	2	612	28	237	14	16.92	1	0	5/39
Lord's Cricket Ground, St John's Wood, London	6	1452	51	634	27	23.48	0	0	4/57
M.A.Chidambaram Stadium, Chepauk, Chennai	3	933	30	513	13	39.46	1	0	6/125
M.Chinnaswamy Stadium, Bangalore	2	720	27	379	9	42.11	0	0	3/106
Marrara Cricket Ground, Darwin	1	155	3	81	3	27.00	0	0	3/20
May's Bounty, Basingstoke	1	178	9	56	8	7.00	0	0	4/22
Melbourne Cricket Ground	29	8179	335	3526	129	27.33	6	0	7/52
Mindoo Phillip Park, Castries	1	84	0	84	2	42.00	0	0	2/84
National Stadium, Karachi	1	379	22	150	8	18.75	1	0	5/89
New Wanderers Stadium, Johannesburg	4	1047	52	448	21	21.33	0	0	4/43
Newlands, Cape Town	3	1217	57	465	17	27.35	1	0	6/161
North Sydney Oval	1	348	9	195	3	65.00	0	0	2/78
North West Cricket Stadium, Potchefstroom	1	96	2	59	2	29.50	0	0	2/59
Old Trafford, Manchester	4	1492	85	536	25	21.44	1	0	6/48
P.Saravanamuttu Stadium, Colombo	2	541	18	299	16	18.68	1	1	7/94
Pukekura Park, New Plymouth	1	173	8	81	2	40.50	0	0	2/21

First class bowling on each ground (continued)

Ground	M	Balls	Mdns	Runs	Wkts	Ave	5wi	10wm	Best
Queen's Park Oval, Port of Spain	2	179	9	77	1	77.00	0	0	1/16
Queens Sports Club, Bulawayo	1	234	14	101	4	25.25	0	0	3/50
Rawalpindi Cricket Stadium	2	454	23	208	6	34.66	0	0	3/42
Richmond Cricket Ground, Melbourne	2	276	4	156	4	39.00	1	0	4/118
Riverside Ground, Chester-le-Street	3	521	21	308	13	23.69	1	0	5/135
Sabina Park, Kingston	2	472	22	236	7	33.71	0	0	4/70
Seddon Park, Hamilton	2	444	21	211	5	42.20	0	0	2/53
Sharjah Cricket Association Stadium	2	414	19	154	16	9.62	1	0	5/74
Sinhalese Sports Club Ground, Colombo	3	607	24	336	9	37.33	0	0	4/92
Sophia Gardens, Cardiff	2	515	16	223	14	15.92	1	0	6/65
St George's Park, Port Elizabeth	1	248	12	82	5	16.40	0	0	3/62
St Lawrence Ground, Canterbury	4	1086	51	416	20	20.80	1	0	6/34
Stellenbosch University Ground	1	215	16	73	4	18.25	0	0	3/49
Stratford-upon-Avon Cricket Club Ground	1	146	2	88	6	14.66	1	0	6/88
Sydney Cricket Ground	19	5461	220	2469	79	31.25	5	2	7/56
The Gnoll, Neath	1	260	9	111	6	18.50	0	0	4/67
The Rose Bowl, Southampton	18	3517	103	1757	67	26.22	2	0	7/99
The University Parks, Oxford	1	204	13	66	5	13.20	0	0	3/45
Trent Bridge, Nottingham	7	2000	81	930	37	25.13	1	0	6/33
Tyronne Fernando Stadium, Moratuwa	1	66	3	40	0	-	0	0	0/40
United Services Recreation Ground, Portsmouth	1	412	24	150	4	37.50	0	0	4/81
Uyanwatte Stadium, Matara	1			did not bowl					
Vidarbha Cricket Association Ground, Nagpur	1	225	10	103	4	25.75	0	0	2/47
Wankhede Stadium, Mumbai	1	300	18	107	5	21.40	0	0	4/47
Western Australia Cricket Association Ground, Perth	19	4156	158	2018	56	36.03	1	0	5/49
Total	286	72200	2973	32970	1269	25.98	64	11	8/71

SHANE WARNE'S FIRST CLASS WICKETS IN CHRONOLOGICAL ORDER:

No	Batsman	How Out	Inns

Victoria v Western Australia, Junction Oval, Melbourne, 15, 16, 17, 18, February 1991

No	Batsman	How Out	Inns
1	T.M.Moody	c D.W.Fleming	2

Australia B v Zimbabwe, Bulawayo Athletic Club, 16, 17, 18, 19, September 1991

No	Batsman	How Out	Inns
2	A.J.Pycroft	lbw	2
3	D.L.Houghton	b	2
4	M.P.Jarvis	c P.R.Reiffel	2

Australia B v Zimbabwe, Harare Sports Club, 21, 23, 24, 25, September 1991

No	Batsman	How Out	Inns
5	A.G.Huckle	lbw	1
6	G.W.Flower	lbw	2
7	A.D.R.Campbell	c T.M.Moody	2
8	A.Flower	b	2
9	K.J.Arnott	b	2
10	N.P.Hough	c T.M.Moody	2
11	M.G.Burmester	c M.A.Taylor	2
12	A.G.Huckle	lbw	2

Victoria v Tasmania, Melbourne Cricket Ground, 1, 2, 3, 4, November 1991

No	Batsman	How Out	Inns
13	B.A.Cruse	b	1
14	R.J.Tucker	cw D.S.Berry	1
15	J.Cox	cw D.S.Berry	1
16	D.R.Gilbert	c S.P.O'Donnell	1

Victoria v South Australia, Melbourne Cricket Ground, 15, 16, 17, 18, November 1991

No	Batsman	How Out	Inns
17	J.A.Brayshaw	b	1
18	J.D.Siddons	st D.S.Berry	1
19	D.J.Hickey	lbw	1

Australian XI v West Indians, Bellerive Oval, Hobart, 20, 21, 22, 23, December 1991

No	Batsman	How Out	Inns
20	B.C.Lara	c W.N.Phillips	1
21	A.C.Cummins	b	1
22	B.P.Patterson	c P.R.Reiffel	1

23	C.L.Hooper	c M.G.Bevan	2
24	R.C.Haynes	c C.D.Matthews	2
25	H.A.G.Anthony	c sub	2
26	B.P.Patterson	st I.A.Healy	2

**Australia v India, Sydney Cricket Ground,
2, 3, 4, 5, 6, January 1992**

| 27 | R.J.Shastri | c D.M.Jones | 1 |

**Victoria v Tasmania, Bellerive Oval, Hobart,
17, 18, 19, 20, January 1992**

28	C.D.Matthews	cw D.S.Berry	1
29	D.R.Gilbert	c D.S.Lehmann	1
30	G.A.Hughes	c S.P.O'Donnell	2

**Victoria v New South Wales, Melbourne Cricket Ground,
13, 14, 15, 16, February 1992**

| 31 | T.H.Bayliss | c W.N.Phillips | 2 |

**Victoria v South Australia, Adelaide Oval,
21, 22, 23, 24, February 1992**

| 32 | J.D.Siddons | c A.I.C.Dodemaide | 1 |

**Australia v Sri Lanka, Sinhalese Sports Club Ground, Colombo,
17, 18, 19, 21, 22, August 1992**

33	G.P.Wickramasinghe	c M.E.Waugh	2
34	S.D.Anurasiri	c M.E.Waugh	2
35	M.A.W.R.Madurasinghe	c G.R.J.Matthews	2

**Victoria v New South Wales, Sydney Cricket Ground,
6, 7, 8, 9, November 1992**

36	M.G.Bevan	c W.N.Phillips	1
37	M.A.Taylor	cw D.S.Berry	2
38	M.E.Waugh	st D.S.Berry	2

**Australian XI v West Indians, Bellerive Oval, Hobart,
14, 15, 16, 17, November 1992**

39	P.V.Simmons	c D.C.Boon	1
40	C.L.Hooper	c C.D.Matthews	1
41	A.L.Logie	c sub	1
42	J.C.Adams	lbw	1
43	R.B.Richardson	c D.A.Freedman	2

**Victoria v Queensland, Junction Oval, Melbourne,
20, 21, 22, 23, November 1992**

| 44 | T.J.Barsby | c W.G.Ayres | 1 |
| 45 | M.L.Hayden | c D.S.Lehmann | 2 |

Victoria v Western Australia, Junction Oval, Melbourne, 4, 5, 6, 7, December 1992

46	G.R.Marsh	b	1
47	J.L.Langer	cw D.S.Berry	1
48	T.J.Zoehrer	c D.S.Lehmann	1
49	J.Angel	c A.I.C.Dodemaide	1
50	B.A.Reid	c G.J.Allardice	1
51	M.R.J.Veletta	b	2
52	J.L.Langer	b	2

Australia v West Indies, Melbourne Cricket Ground, 26, 27, 28, 29, 30, December 1992

53	C.E.L.Ambrose	c C.J.McDermott	1
54	R.B.Richardson	b	2
55	K.L.T.Arthurton	st I.A.Healy	2
56	C.L.Hooper	c M.R.Whitney	2
57	P.V.Simmons	c D.C.Boon	2
58	D.Williams	c M.E.Waugh	2
59	I.R.Bishop	c M.A.Taylor	2
60	C.A.Walsh	c M.G.Hughes	2

Australia v West Indies, Sydney Cricket Ground, 2, 3, 4, 5, 6, January 1993

| 61 | C.L.Hooper | b | 1 |

Australia v West Indies, Adelaide Oval, 23, 24, 25, 26, January 1993

| 62 | R.B.Richardson | cw I.A.Healy | 2 |

Australians v New Zealand Board XI, Pukekura Park, New Plymouth, 16, 17, 18, February 1993

| 63 | C.Z.Harris | c J.L.Langer | 2 |
| 64 | M.B.Owens | c M.E.Waugh | 2 |

Australia v New Zealand, Lancaster Park, Christchurch, 25, 26, 27, 28, February 1993

65	K.R.Rutherford	b	1
66	J.G.Wright	lbw	1
67	M.B.Owens	lbw	1
68	C.L.Cairns	c M.A.Taylor	2
69	A.C.Parore	c D.C.Boon	2

| 70 | D.N.Patel | b | 2 |
| 71 | K.R.Rutherford | cw I.A.Healy | 2 |

Australia v New Zealand, Basin Reserve, Wellington, 4, 5, 6, 7, 8, March 1993

72	W.Watson	c M.A.Taylor	1
73	M.B.Owens	b	1
74	A.H.Jones	lbw	2
75	T.E.Blain	cw I.A.Healy	2

Australia v New Zealand, Eden Park, Auckland, 12, 13, 14, 15, 16, March 1993

76	K.R.Rutherford	st I.A.Healy	1
77	D.N.Patel	cw I.A.Healy	1
78	C.Z.Harris	c M.A.Taylor	1
79	M.L.Su'a	c S.R.Waugh	1
80	M.D.Crowe	c J.L.Langer	2
81	A.H.Jones	b	2

Australians v Worcestershire, County Ground, New Road, Worcester, 5, 6, 7, May 1993

| 82 | D.B.D'Oliveira | b | 2 |

Australians v Somerset, County Ground, Taunton, 8, 9, 10, May 1993

83	N.A.Folland	lbw	1
84	C.J.Tavaré	c M.A.Taylor	2
85	A.N.Hayhurst	b	2
86	N.A.Folland	st T.J.Zoehrer	2
87	A.P.van Troost	c S.R.Waugh	2

Australians v Surrey, The Oval, Kennington, 25, 26, 27, May 1993

88	M.A.Lynch	b	1
89	M.A.Butcher	lbw	1
90	G.J.Kersey	lbw	1
91	G.P.Thorpe	cw T.J.Zoehrer	2
92	M.A.Butcher	st T.J.Zoehrer	2
93	J.E.Benjamin	st T.J.Zoehrer	2
94	A.J.Murphy	c W.J.Holdsworth	2

Australians v Leicestershire, Grace Road, Leicester, 29, 30, 31, May 1993

| 95 | P.E.Robinson | cw I.A.Healy | 1 |

96	B.F.Smith	b	1
97	P.A.Nixon	c M.L.Hayden	1
98	P.E.Robinson	b	2
99	V.J.Wells	b	2
100	B.F.Smith	lbw	2

Australia v England, Old Trafford, Manchester, 3, 4, 5, 6, 7, June 1993

101	M.W.Gatting	b	1
102	R.A.Smith	c M.A.Taylor	1
103	G.A.Gooch	c B.P.Julian	1
104	A.R.Caddick	cw I.A.Healy	1
105	M.A.Atherton	c M.A.Taylor	2
106	R.A.Smith	b	2
107	A.J.Stewart	cw I.A.Healy	2
108	C.C.Lewis	c M.A.Taylor	2

Australians v Gloucestershire, County Ground, Bristol, 12, 13, 14, June 1993

109	T.H.C.Hancock	c M.L.Hayden	1
110	B.C.Broad	c M.L.Hayden	1
111	A.J.Wright	c M.A.Taylor	1
112	R.I.Dawson	b	1
113	R.C.Russell	c D.R.Martyn	1

Australia v England, Lord's Cricket Ground, St John's Wood, 17, 18, 19, 20, 21, June 1993

114	C.C.Lewis	lbw	1
115	N.A.Foster	c A.R.Border	1
116	M.A.Atherton	b	1
117	P.M.Such	c M.A.Taylor	1
118	G.A.Gooch	cw I.A.Healy	2
119	M.W.Gatting	lbw	2
120	P.M.Such	b	2
121	P.C.R.Tufnell	b	2

Australians v Combined Universities, The University Parks, Oxford, 23, 24, 25, June 1993

122	R.R.Montgomerie	st D.R.Martyn	1
123	G.B.T.Lovell	st T.J.Zoehrer	1
124	R.Q.Cake	c B.P.Julian	1
125	S.F.Shephard	lbw	2
126	J.R.Wileman	c M.A.Taylor	2

Australia v England, Trent Bridge, Nottingham,
1, 2, 3, 5, 6, July 1993

127	M.A.Atherton	c D.C.Boon	1
128	A.J.Stewart	c M.E.Waugh	1
129	N.Hussain	c D.C.Boon	1
130	R.A.Smith	cw I.A.Healy	2
131	M.N.Lathwell	lbw	2
132	G.A.Gooch	c M.A.Taylor	2

Australia v England, Headingley, Leeds,
22, 23, 24, 25, 26, July 1993

133	M.J.McCague	c M.A.Taylor	1

Australians v Lancashire, Old Trafford, Manchester,
28, 29, 30, July 1993

134	G.D.Mendis	b	1
135	N.J.Speak	c & b	1
136	P.A.J.DeFreitas	c W.J.Holdsworth	1
137	G.D.Mendis	c M.A.Taylor	2

Australians v Glamorgan, The Gnoll, Neath,
31, July, 1, 2, August 1993

138	P.A.Cottey	b	1
139	R.D.B.Croft	lbw	1
140	D.L.Hemp	b	1
141	S.D.Thomas	st I.A.Healy	1
142	A.Dale	cw I.A.Healy	2
143	D.L.Hemp	b	2

Australia v England, Edgbaston, Birmingham,
5, 6, 7, 8, 9, August 1993

144	A.J.Stewart	c & b	1
145	M.A.Atherton	c A.R.Border	2
146	R.A.Smith	lbw	2
147	G.A.Gooch	b	2
148	A.J.Stewart	lbw	2
149	G.P.Thorpe	st I.A.Healy	2

Australians v Kent, St Lawrence Ground, Canterbury,
11, 12, 13, August 1993

150	G.R.Cowdrey	lbw	1
151	T.R.Ward	c M.A.Taylor	2

Australia v England, The Foster's Oval, Kennington, 19, 20, 21, 22, 23, August 1993

152	M.P.Maynard	b	1
153	N.Hussain	c M.A.Taylor	1
154	G.A.Gooch	cw I.A.Healy	2
155	S.L.Watkin	lbw	2
156	P.M.Such	lbw	2

Victoria v South Australia, Adelaide Oval, 27, 28, 29, 30, October 1993

157	P.C.Nobes	cw D.S.Berry	1
158	J.D.Siddons	c A.I.C.Dodemaide	1
159	D.S.Lehmann	c D.J.Ramshaw	1
160	J.A.Brayshaw	c & b	1

Victoria v Western Australia, Melbourne Cricket Ground, 4, 5, 6, 7, November 1993

161	M.R.J.Veletta	c D.J.Ramshaw	1
162	B.P.Julian	b	1
163	J.Angel	c D.M.Jones	1
164	T.M.Moody	st D.S.Berry	2
165	T.J.Zoehrer	c M.T.G.Elliott	2
166	B.P.Julian	c D.J.Ramshaw	2
167	D.J.Spencer	lbw	2
168	J.Angel	c B.J.Hodge	2
169	W.K.Wishart	c D.J.Ramshaw	2

Australia v New Zealand, W.A.C.A. Ground, Perth, 12, 13, 14, 15, 16, November 1993

170	C.L.Cairns	b	1

Victoria v New South Wales, Melbourne Cricket Ground, 19, 20, 21, 22, November 1993

171	S.R.Waugh	c P.R.Reiffel	1
172	M.G.Bevan	c D.J.Ramshaw	1
173	M.J.Slater	b	1
174	W.J.Holdsworth	c D.J.Ramshaw	1
175	M.E.Waugh	b	2
176	M.G.Bevan	b	2

Australia v New Zealand, Bellerive Oval, Hobart, 26, 27, 28, 29, November 1993

177	D.N.Patel	c M.A.Taylor	1
178	M.L.Su'a	c M.A.Taylor	1

179	S.B.Doull	lbw	1
180	B.A.Pocock	st I.A.Healy	2
181	K.R.Rutherford	b	2
182	M.L.Su'a	b	2
183	D.K.Morrison	b	2
184	T.E.Blain	c & b	2
185	S.B.Doull	c T.B.A.May	2

Australia v New Zealand, Brisbane Cricket Ground, Woolloongabba, 3, 4, 5, 6, 7, December 1993

186	A.H.Jones	b	1
187	C.L.Cairns	c & b	1
188	D.K.Morrison	cw I.A.Healy	1
189	R.P.de Groen	c A.R.Border	1
190	A.H.Jones	c A.R.Border	2
191	B.A.Young	b	2
192	D.N.Patel	b	2
193	S.B.Doull	c M.A.Taylor	2

Victoria v New South Wales, Sydney Cricket Ground, 18, 19, 20, 21, December 1993

194	M.A.Taylor	b	1
195	P.A.Emery	lbw	1
196	M.G.Bevan	c D.M.Jones	1
197	R.Chee Quee	c C.Howard	1
198	W.J.Holdsworth	b	1
199	M.A.Taylor	st D.S.Berry	2
200	M.E.Waugh	c D.W.Fleming	2
201	W.J.Holdsworth	c P.R.Reiffel	2

Australia v South Africa, Melbourne Cricket Ground, 26, 27, 28, 29, 30, December 1993

202	W.J.Cronje	c D.C.Boon	1

Australia v South Africa, Sydney Cricket Ground, 2, 3, 4, 5, 6, January 1994

203	D.J.Cullinan	b	1
204	J.N.Rhodes	lbw	1
205	G.Kirsten	st I.A.Healy	1
206	D.J.Richardson	c M.A.Taylor	1
207	K.C.Wessels	c & b	1
208	C.R.Matthews	c M.A.Taylor	1
209	P.L.Symcox	b	1

210	K.C.Wessels	b	2
211	D.J.Cullinan	lbw	2
212	C.R.Matthews	c M.E.Waugh	2
213	P.S.de Villiers	lbw	2
214	A.A.Donald	cw I.A.Healy	2

Australia v South Africa, Adelaide Oval, 28, 29, 30, 31, January, 1, February 1994

215	P.N.Kirsten	c M.E.Waugh	1
216	W.J.Cronje	lbw	2
217	G.Kirsten	b	2
218	B.M.McMillan	lbw	2
219	R.P.Snell	c & b	2

Australians v Orange Free State, Goodyear Park, Bloemfontein, 26, 27, 28, February, 1, March 1994

220	J.M.Arthur	b	1
221	B.T.Player	lbw	1
222	N.Boje	st I.A.Healy	1
223	N.Boje	b	2
224	P.J.L.Radley	lbw	2

Australia v South Africa, Wanderers Stadium, Johannesburg, 4, 5, 6, 7, 8, March 1994

225	D.J.Richardson	lbw	1
226	A.C.Hudson	b	2
227	K.C.Wessels	c A.R.Border	2
228	D.J.Richardson	c A.R.Border	2
229	B.M.McMillan	b	2

Australians v Boland, Stellenbosch University Ground, 12, 13, 14, March 1994

230	K.C.Jackson	b	1
231	B.J.Drew	c S.R.Waugh	1
232	D.Smith	lbw	1
233	J.S.Roos	c P.R.Reiffel	2

Australia v South Africa, Newlands, Cape Town, 17, 18, 19, 20, 21, March 1994

234	P.N.Kirsten	lbw	1
235	B.M.McMillan	b	1
236	P.S.de Villiers	c M.A.Taylor	1
237	G.Kirsten	lbw	2
238	P.N.Kirsten	c M.A.Taylor	2

239	P.S.de Villiers	lbw	2

**Australia v South Africa, Kingsmead, Durban,
25, 26, 27, 28, 29, March 1994**

240	W.J.Cronje	c S.R.Waugh	1
241	J.N.Rhodes	lbw	1
242	D.J.Richardson	c P.R.Reiffel	1
243	C.R.Matthews	lbw	1

**Australians v President's XI, Rawalpindi Cricket Stadium,
23, 24, 25, September 1994**

244	Ijaz Ahmed	c D.C.Boon	1
245	Mohsin Kamal	cw I.A.Healy	1
246	Ata-ur-Rehman	st I.A.Healy	1
247	Ijaz Ahmed	c S.R.Waugh	2
248	Manzoor Akhtar	lbw	2

**Australia v Pakistan, National Stadium, Karachi,
28, 29, 30, September, 1, 2, October 1994**

249	Aamer Sohail	c M.G.Bevan	1
250	Inzamamul Haq	c M.A.Taylor	1
251	Rashid Latif	c M.A.Taylor	1
252	Zahid Fazal	c D.C.Boon	2
253	Akram Raza	lbw	2
254	Wasim Akram	c & b	2
255	Basit Ali	lbw	2
256	Waqar Younis	cw I.A.Healy	2

**Australia v Pakistan, Rawalpindi Cricket Stadium,
5, 6, 7, 8, 9, October 1994**

257	Inzamamul Haq	lbw	1

**Australia v Pakistan, Gaddafi Stadium, Lahore,
1, 2, 3, 4, 5, November 1994**

258	Saeed Anwar	b	1
259	Basit Ali	c M.E.Waugh	1
260	Ijaz Ahmed	c D.C.Boon	1
261	Akram Raza	b	1
262	Aaqib Javed	c M.E.Waugh	1
263	Mohsin Kamal	lbw	1
264	Aamer Sohail	st P.A.Emery	2
265	Akram Raza	lbw	2
266	Aaqib Javed	b	2

Victoria v Tasmania, Melbourne Cricket Ground, 17, 18, 19, 20, November 1994

267	D.F.Hills	c G.J.Clarke	1
268	J.Cox	c S.H.Cook	1
269	M.J.di Venuto	c G.J.Clarke	1
270	D.C.Boon	c G.J.Clarke	1
271	R.J.Tucker	c S.H.Cook	1
272	M.J.di Venuto	c I.A.Wrigglesworth	2
273	S.Young	c D.M.Jones	2

Australia v England, Brisbane Cricket Ground, Woolloongabba, 25, 26, 27, 28, 29, November 1994

274	G.P.Thorpe	c & b	1
275	P.A.J.DeFreitas	cw I.A.Healy	1
276	P.C.R.Tufnell	c M.A.Taylor	1
277	A.J.Stewart	b	2
278	M.A.Atherton	lbw	2
279	G.P.Thorpe	b	2
280	G.A.Hick	cw I.A.Healy	2
281	G.A.Gooch	cw I.A.Healy	2
282	P.A.J.DeFreitas	b	2
283	M.J.McCague	lbw	2
284	D.Gough	c M.E.Waugh	2

Victoria v Western Australia, W.A.C.A. Ground, Perth, 16, 17, 18, 19, December 1994

285	D.R.Martyn	c P.R.Reiffel	1
286	T.M.Moody	st D.S.Berry	1
287	J.Angel	c B.J.Hodge	2
288	M.P.Lavender	b	2
289	M.W.Goodwin	c sub	2
290	A.C.Gilchrist	b	2

Australia v England, Melbourne Cricket Ground, 24, 26, 27, 28, 29, December 1994

291	M.A.Atherton	lbw	1
292	G.P.Thorpe	c M.E.Waugh	1
293	M.W.Gatting	c S.R.Waugh	1
294	S.J.Rhodes	c M.E.Waugh	1
295	A.J.Stewart	c & b	1
296	P.A.J.DeFreitas	st I.A.Healy	1
297	P.A.J.DeFreitas	lbw	2

| 298 | D.Gough | cw I.A.Healy | 2 |
| 299 | D.E.Malcolm | c D.C.Boon | 2 |

Australia v England, Sydney Cricket Ground,
1, 2, 3, 4, 5, January 1995

| 300 | D.E.Malcolm | b | 1 |

Australia v England, Adelaide Oval,
26, 27, 28, 29, 30, January 1995

301	G.P.Thorpe	c M.A.Taylor	1
302	J.P.Crawley	b	1
303	S.J.Rhodes	c D.W.Fleming	2
304	P.C.R.Tufnell	lbw	2

Australia v England, W.A.C.A. Ground, Perth,
3, 4, 5, 6, 7, February 1995

| 305 | G.P.Thorpe | st I.A.Healy | 1 |
| 306 | M.R.Ramprakash | b | 1 |

Australians v Guyana, Bourda, Georgetown, Guyana,
20, 21, 22, March 1995

307	K.F.Semple	cw I.A.Healy	1
308	S.Chanderpaul	cw I.A.Healy	1
309	R.A.Harper	c & b	1
310	S.Chanderpaul	b	2
311	L.A.Joseph	b	2
312	K.A.Wong	lbw	2

Australians v West Indies Board President's XI, Mindoo Phillip Park,
Castries, St Lucia,
25, 26, 27, 28, March 1995

| 313 | R.I.C.Holder | c & b | 1 |
| 314 | S.Chanderpaul | c & b | 1 |

Australia v West Indies, Kensington Oval, Bridgetown, Barbados,
31, March, 1, 2, April 1995

315	W.K.M.Benjamin	c M.A.Taylor	1
316	C.A.Walsh	c S.R.Waugh	1
317	S.L.Campbell	c S.R.Waugh	2
318	J.R.Murray	c S.R.Waugh	2
319	K.C.G.Benjamin	b	2

Australia v West Indies, Antigua Recreation Ground, St John's,
Antigua, 8, 9, 10, 12, 13, April 1995

| 320 | S.C.Williams | c D.C.Boon | 1 |

| 321 | J.C.Adams | lbw | 1 |
| 322 | K.L.T.Arthurton | c M.A.Taylor | 1 |

Australia v West Indies, Queen's Park Oval, Port of Spain, Trinidad, 21, 22, 23, April 1995

| 323 | W.K.M.Benjamin | c M.J.Slater | 1 |

Australia v West Indies, Sabina Park, Kingston, Jamaica, 29, 30, April, 1, 3, May 1995

324	B.C.Lara	cw I.A.Healy	1
325	C.O.Browne	c D.C.Boon	1
326	K.L.T.Arthurton	lbw	2
327	C.E.L.Ambrose	st I.A.Healy	2
328	C.A.Walsh	c G.S.Blewett	2
329	K.C.G.Benjamin	c M.A.Taylor	2

Victoria v Queensland, Brisbane Cricket Ground, Woolloongabba, 19, 20, 21, 22, October 1995

330	M.L.Hayden	st D.S.Berry	1
331	J.P.Maher	cw D.S.Berry	1
332	M.S.Kasprowicz	lbw	1
333	W.A.Seccombe	lbw	2

Victoria v New South Wales, Melbourne Cricket Ground, 1, 2, 3, November 1995

334	M.J.Slater	st D.S.Berry	1
335	P.A.Emery	c P.A.Broster	1
336	G.R.J.Matthews	lbw	1
337	S.Lee	lbw	1
338	G.D.McGrath	c J.R.Bakker	1

Australia v Pakistan, Brisbane Cricket Ground, Woolloongabba, 9, 10, 11, 13, November 1995

339	Rameez Raja	c M.A.Taylor	1
340	Aamer Sohail	st I.A.Healy	1
341	Inzamamul Haq	c S.R.Waugh	1
342	Moin Khan	c C.J.McDermott	1
343	Basit Ali	c M.A.Taylor	1
344	Wasim Akram	c D.C.Boon	1
345	Mohammad Akram	c G.S.Blewett	1
346	Wasim Akram	c M.J.Slater	2
347	Saleem Malik	c C.J.McDermott	2
348	Waqar Younis	lbw	2
349	Mohammad Akram	lbw	2

Australia v Pakistan, Sydney Cricket Ground, 30, November, 1, 2, 3, 4, December 1995

350	Rameez Raja	c M.J.Slater	1
351	Inzamamul Haq	cw I.A.Healy	1
352	Ijaz Ahmed	c G.D.McGrath	1
353	Mushtaq Ahmed	c C.J.McDermott	1
354	Ijaz Ahmed	lbw	2
355	Rameez Raja	c M.E.Waugh	2
356	Basit Ali	b	2
357	Rashid Latif	lbw	2

Australia v Sri Lanka, W.A.C.A. Ground, Perth, 8, 9, 10, 11, December 1995

358	P.A.de Silva	c & b	1
359	R.S.Kaluwitharana	c M.A.Taylor	1
360	W.P.U.J.C.Vaas	cw I.A.Healy	1
361	P.A.de Silva	c R.T.Ponting	2
362	W.P.U.J.C.Vaas	cw I.A.Healy	2
363	H.P.Tillakaratne	c R.T.Ponting	2

Australia v Sri Lanka, Melbourne Cricket Ground, 26, 27, 28, 29, 30, December 1995

364	H.P.Tillakaratne	c M.A.Taylor	1
365	U.C.Hathurusingha	lbw	2
366	R.S.Kaluwitharana	st I.A.Healy	2
367	G.P.Wickramasinghe	st I.A.Healy	2
368	M.Muralidaran	c M.A.Taylor	2

Australia v Sri Lanka, Adelaide Oval, 25, 26, 27, 28, 29, January 1996

369	G.P.Wickramasinghe	b	2

Victoria v Queensland, Melbourne Cricket Ground, 23, 24, 25, 26, March 1996

370	J.P.Maher	c M.T.G.Elliott	1
371	A.R.Border	c D.M.Jones	1

Victoria v New South Wales, Sydney Cricket Ground, 8, 9, 10, 11, November 1996

372	A.M.Stuart	st D.S.Berry	1
373	S.C.G.MacGill	lbw	1

Victoria v South Australia, Melbourne Cricket Ground, 15, 16, 17, 18, November 1996

374	J.C.Scuderi	c B.A.Williams	1

| 375 | P.E.McIntyre | st D.S.Berry | 1 |
| 376 | S.P.George | c D.M.Jones | 1 |

Australia v West Indies, Brisbane Cricket Ground, Woolloongabba, 22, 23, 24, 25, 26, November 1996

377	I.R.Bishop	lbw	1
378	K.C.G.Benjamin	lbw	1
379	R.G.Samuels	c M.A.Taylor	2
380	J.C.Adams	lbw	2

Australia v West Indies, Sydney Cricket Ground, 29, 30, November, 1, 2, 3, December 1996

381	C.L.Hooper	lbw	1
382	S.Chanderpaul	c & b	1
383	I.R.Bishop	c M.T.G.Elliott	1
384	R.G.Samuels	b	2
385	S.Chanderpaul	b	2
386	K.C.G.Benjamin	c M.A.Taylor	2
387	C.A.Walsh	c G.D.McGrath	2

Australia v West Indies, Melbourne Cricket Ground, 26, 27, 28, December 1996

388	R.G.Samuels	c M.A.Taylor	1
389	C.E.L.Ambrose	b	1
390	C.A.Walsh	c M.E.Waugh	1

Australia v West Indies, Adelaide Oval, 25, 26, 27, 28, January 1997

391	B.C.Lara	c G.S.Blewett	1
392	S.Chanderpaul	c M.A.Taylor	1
393	J.C.Adams	c & b	1
394	C.L.Hooper	lbw	2
395	I.R.Bishop	c M.G.Bevan	2
396	B.C.Lara	cw I.A.Healy	2

Australia v West Indies, W.A.C.A. Ground, Perth, 1, 2, 3, February 1997

| 397 | B.C.Lara | cw I.A.Healy | 1 |
| 398 | R.G.Samuels | c M.E.Waugh | 1 |

Australians v Natal, Kingsmead, Durban, 20, 21, 22, February 1997

| 399 | M.L.Bruyns | cw I.A.Healy | 2 |
| 400 | D.J.Watson | st I.A.Healy | 2 |

Australia v South Africa, Wanderers Stadium, Johannesburg, 28, February, 1, 2, 3, 4, March 1997

401	W.J.Cronje	c M.E.Waugh	1
402	P.R.Adams	lbw	1
403	G.Kirsten	b	2
404	D.J.Cullinan	cw I.A.Healy	2
405	J.N.Rhodes	lbw	2
406	J.H.Kallis	b	2

Australians v Border, Buffalo Park, East London, 7, 8, March 1997

407	S.C.Pope	lbw	2
408	D.Taljard	lbw	2
409	M.Ntini	b	2

Australia v South Africa, St George's Park, Port Elizabeth, 14, 15, 16, 17, March 1997

410	D.J.Richardson	c G.D.McGrath	1
411	B.M.McMillan	c S.R.Waugh	1
412	A.A.Donald	c & b	1
413	S.M.Pollock	lbw	2
414	P.R.Adams	c M.A.Taylor	2

Australians v Gloucestershire, County Ground, Bristol, 27, 28, 29, May 1997

415	R.P.Davis	lbw	1
416	R.J.Cunliffe	c M.S.Kasprowicz	1
417	R.C.Russell	c M.G.Bevan	1
418	A.M.Smith	c J.N.Gillespie	1

Australians v Derbyshire, County Ground, Derby, 31, May, 1, 2, June 1997

419	C.J.Adams	lbw	1
420	D.M.Jones	b	1
421	C.J.Adams	c sub	2
422	A.S.Rollins	lbw	2
423	I.D.Blackwell	c & b	2
424	V.P.Clarke	c B.P.Julian	2
425	K.M.Krikken	c M.G.Bevan	2
426	P.A.J.DeFreitas	c sub	2
427	A.J.Harris	lbw	2

Australia v England, Edgbaston, Birmingham, 5, 6, 7, 8, June 1997

| 428 | N.Hussain | cw I.A.Healy | 1 |

Australians v Leicestershire, Grace Road, Leicester, 14, 15, 16, June 1997

429	G.I.Macmillan	c M.G.Bevan	1
430	J.J.Whitaker	lbw	2
431	A.Habib	c R.T.Ponting	2
432	P.A.Nixon	st I.A.Healy	2
433	J.Ormond	b	2
434	A.R.K.Pierson	c J.L.Langer	2

Australia v England, Lord's Cricket Ground, St John's Wood, 19, 20, 21, 22, 23, June 1997

| 435 | N.Hussain | c & b | 2 |
| 436 | M.A.Butcher | b | 2 |

Australians v Hampshire, County Ground, Southampton, 28, 29, 30, June 1997

437	R.A.Smith	cw I.A.Healy	1
438	S.D.Udal	cw I.A.Healy	1
439	S.J.Renshaw	lbw	1
440	S.D.Udal	b	2

Australia v England, Old Trafford, Manchester, 3, 4, 5, 6, 7, July 1997

441	A.J.Stewart	c M.A.Taylor	1
442	G.P.Thorpe	c M.A.Taylor	1
443	N.Hussain	cw I.A.Healy	1
444	J.P.Crawley	cw I.A.Healy	1
445	D.Gough	lbw	1
446	A.R.Caddick	c M.E.Waugh	1
447	A.J.Stewart	b	2
448	G.P.Thorpe	cw I.A.Healy	2
449	A.R.Caddick	c J.N.Gillespie	2

Australians v Middlesex, Lord's Cricket Ground, St John's Wood, 19, 20, 21, July 1997

450	O.A.Shah	c M.E.Waugh	1
451	P.N.Weekes	c & b	2
452	J.C.Pooley	b	2
453	M.R.Ramprakash	cw I.A.Healy	2

Australia v England, Headingley, Leeds,
24, 25, 26, 27, 28, July 1997

454	N.Hussain	c J.N.Gillespie	2

Australians v Somerset, County Ground, Taunton,
1, 2, 3, 4, August 1997

455	S.C.Ecclestone	lbw	1
456	M.E.Trescothick	b	1
457	M.N.Lathwell	c M.E.Waugh	1
458	A.R.Caddick	c G.D.McGrath	1
459	P.S.Jones	lbw	1
460	M.N.Lathwell	st I.A.Healy	2

Australia v England, Trent Bridge, Nottingham,
7, 8, 9, 10, August 1997

461	M.A.Atherton	cw I.A.Healy	1
462	A.J.Stewart	cw I.A.Healy	1
463	N.Hussain	b	1
464	G.P.Thorpe	c G.S.Blewett	1
465	B.C.Hollioake	lbw	2
466	R.D.B.Croft	c G.D.McGrath	2
467	A.R.Caddick	lbw	2

Australia v England, The Oval, Kennington,
21, 22, 23, August 1997

468	A.J.Hollioake	b	1
469	P.C.R.Tufnell	c G.S.Blewett	1
470	N.Hussain	c M.T.G.Elliott	2
471	M.R.Ramprakash	st I.A.Healy	2

Victoria v New South Wales, North Sydney Oval, Sydney,
22, 23, 24, 25, October 1997

472	M.G.Bevan	c I.J.Harvey	1
473	M.A.Taylor	c D.J.Saker	2
474	M.E.Waugh	b	2

Victoria v Queensland, Melbourne Cricket Ground,
31, October, 1, 2, 3, November 1997

475	A.Symonds	st D.S.Berry	1
476	G.I.Foley	c & b	1
477	I.A.Healy	c D.J.Saker	1
478	M.P.Mott	st D.S.Berry	2

Australia v New Zealand, Brisbane Cricket Ground, Woolloongabba,
7, 8, 9, 10, 11, November 1997

479	B.A.Pocock	c M.A.Taylor	1
480	C.D.McMillan	lbw	1
481	A.C.Parore	c M.A.Taylor	1
482	C.Z.Harris	b	1
483	C.Z.Harris	b	2
484	D.L.Vettori	c M.A.Taylor	2
485	G.I.Allott	lbw	2

Australia v New Zealand, W.A.C.A. Ground, Perth,
20, 21, 22, 23, November 1997

486	S.P.Fleming	c G.S.Blewett	1
487	C.L.Cairns	c M.E.Waugh	1
488	S.B.Doull	c M.A.Taylor	1
489	G.I.Allott	b	1
490	D.L.Vettori	c M.A.Taylor	2
491	S.P.Fleming	c G.S.Blewett	2

Australia v New Zealand, Bellerive Oval, Hobart,
27, 28, 29, 30, November, 1, December 1997

492	R.G.Twose	lbw	1
493	C.L.Cairns	st I.A.Healy	2
494	S.P.Fleming	st I.A.Healy	2
495	B.A.Young	c R.T.Ponting	2
496	C.D.McMillan	c M.A.Taylor	2
497	A.C.Parore	c M.T.G.Elliott	2

Victoria v Tasmania, Bellerive Oval, Hobart,
19, 20, 21, 22, December 1997

498	S.Young	cw D.S.Berry	1

Australia v South Africa, Melbourne Cricket Ground,
26, 27, 28, 29, 30, December 1997

499	W.J.Cronje	c G.S.Blewett	1
500	S.M.Pollock	lbw	1
501	L.Klusener	lbw	1
502	A.M.Bacher	c M.A.Taylor	2
503	D.J.Cullinan	b	2
504	B.M.McMillan	c M.A.Taylor	2

Australia v South Africa, Sydney Cricket Ground,
2, 3, 4, 5, January 1998

505	S.M.Pollock	c M.A.Taylor	1

506	D.J.Richardson	b	1
507	W.J.Cronje	c M.A.Taylor	1
508	P.L.Symcox	cw I.A.Healy	1
509	P.R.Adams	c S.R.Waugh	1
510	W.J.Cronje	c R.T.Ponting	2
511	H.H.Gibbs	c G.S.Blewett	2
512	B.M.McMillan	b	2
513	S.M.Pollock	c M.A.Taylor	2
514	D.J.Richardson	c & b	2
515	J.H.Kallis	b	2

Australia v South Africa, Adelaide Oval,
30, 31, January, 1, 2, 3, February 1998

516	W.J.Cronje	b	1
517	D.J.Richardson	c M.A.Taylor	1
518	A.M.Bacher	c S.C.G.MacGill	2

Australians v Indian Board President's XI, Indira Priyadarshini
Stadium, Visakhapatnam,
1, 2, 3, March 1998

519	R.S.Dravid	c & b	1
520	V.V.S.Laxman	c R.T.Ponting	1

Australia v India, MA Chidambaram Stadium, Chepauk, Chennai,
6, 7, 8, 9, 10, March 1998

521	S.R.Tendulkar	c M.A.Taylor	1
522	M.Azharuddin	c P.R.Reiffel	1
523	J.Srinath	c M.A.Taylor	1
524	R.S.Dravid	c G.R.Robertson	1
525	R.S.Dravid	cw I.A.Healy	2

Australia v India, M Chinnaswamy Stadium, Bangalore,
25, 26, 27, 28, March 1998

526	N.S.Sidhu	b	1
527	R.S.Dravid	b	1
528	N.R.Mongia	c R.T.Ponting	1
529	V.V.S.Laxman	c R.T.Ponting	2
530	N.S.Sidhu	c D.S.Lehmann	2

Victoria v Western Australia, W.A.C.A. Ground, Perth,
13, 14, 15, 16, November 1998

531	A.C.Gilchrist	c G.R.Vimpani	2

Victoria v South Australia, Melbourne Cricket Ground, 26, 27, 28, 29, November 1998

532	D.A.Fitzgerald	c & b	1
533	B.N.Wigney	c D.J.Saker	1
534	D.A.Fitzgerald	c P.R.Reiffel	2
535	G.S.Blewett	c D.J.Saker	2

Victoria v Queensland, Melbourne Cricket Ground, 11, 12, 13, 14, December 1998

| 536 | W.A.Seccombe | c J.R.Bakker | 1 |

Victoria v New South Wales, Sydney Cricket Ground, 19, 20, 21, 22, December 1998

| 537 | P.A.Emery | c M.H.W.Inness | 1 |
| 538 | S.H.Cook | c M.P.Mott | 1 |

Australia v England, Sydney Cricket Ground, 2, 3, 4, 5, January 1999

| 539 | M.A.Butcher | lbw | 1 |
| 540 | M.A.Butcher | st I.A.Healy | 2 |

Australians v West Indies Board XI, Antigua Recreation Ground, St John's, Antigua, 22, 23, 24, February 1999

| 541 | R.J.J.McLean | c A.C.Dale | 2 |

Australians v West Indies Board President's XI, Guaracara Park, Pointe-a-Pierre, Trinidad, 27, 28, February, 1, March 1999

542	R.N.Lewis	c G.D.McGrath	1
543	D.C.Rampersad	c G.S.Blewett	2
544	W.Phillip	lbw	2
545	N.A.M.McLean	c M.J.Slater	2

Australia v West Indies, Sabina Park, Kingston, Jamaica, 13, 14, 15, 16, March 1999

| 546 | R.D.Jacobs | c J.N.Gillespie | 1 |

Australians v West Indies A, Antigua Recreation Ground, St John's, Antigua, 20, 21, 22, 23, March 1999

547	S.C.Williams	lbw	1
548	M.G.Sinclair	c J.L.Langer	1
549	N.C.McGarrell	cw I.A.Healy	1
550	R.J.J.McLean	lbw	2

Australia v West Indies, Kensington Oval, Bridgetown, Barbados, 26, 27, 28, 29, 30, March 1999

| 551 | C.A.Walsh | c M.J.Slater | 1 |

Australians v Sri Lanka Board XI, P Saravanamuttu Stadium, Colombo, 3, 4, 5, 6, September 1999

552	R.P.Hewage	st I.A.Healy	1
553	I.S.Gallage	lbw	1
554	T.M.Dilshan	c M.J.Slater	2
555	S.I.de Saram	cw I.A.Healy	2
556	L.P.C.Silva	c M.J.Slater	2

Australia v Sri Lanka, Asgiriya Stadium, Kandy, 9, 10, 11, September 1999

557	D.P.M.D.Jayawardene	c R.T.Ponting	1
558	A.Ranatunga	cw I.A.Healy	1
559	U.D.U.Chandana	c sub	1
560	P.A.de Silva	c R.T.Ponting	1
561	D.N.T.Zoysa	c C.R.Miller	1

Australians v Sri Lanka Board XI, Colombo Cricket Club Ground, 17, 18, 19, September 1999

| 562 | M.M.D.N.R.G.Perera | c C.R.Miller | 1 |
| 563 | H.A.P.W.Jayawardene | b | 2 |

Australia v Sri Lanka, Galle International Stadium, 22, 23, 24, 25, 26, September 1999

564	M.S.Atapattu	cw I.A.Healy	1
565	D.P.M.D.Jayawardene	c G.S.Blewett	1
566	A.Ranatunga	c C.R.Miller	1

Australians v Zimbabwe Cricket Union President's XI, Queens Sports Club, Bulawayo, 9, 10, 11, October 1999

567	E.A.Brandes	c D.W.Fleming	1
568	B.D.Moore-Gordon	b	2
569	E.A.Brandes	c M.E.Waugh	2
570	G.A.Lamb	c G.S.Blewett	2

Australia v Zimbabwe, Harare Sports Club, 14, 15, 16, 17, October 1999

571	T.R.Gripper	lbw	1
572	H.H.Streak	c M.E.Waugh	1
573	G.J.Whittall	cw I.A.Healy	1

574	G.J.Whittall	c M.E.Waugh	2
575	H.H.Streak	lbw	2
576	M.W.Goodwin	c S.R.Waugh	2

Australia v Pakistan, Brisbane Cricket Ground, Woolloongabba, 5, 6, 7, 8, 9, November 1999

577	Saeed Anwar	c M.E.Waugh	1
578	Abdur Razzaq	c R.T.Ponting	2
579	Azhar Mahmood	st A.C.Gilchrist	2

Australia v Pakistan, Bellerive Oval, Hobart, 18, 19, 20, 21, 22, November 1999

580	Azhar Mahmood	b	1
581	Saqlain Mushtaq	lbw	1
582	Wasim Akram	cw A.C.Gilchrist	1
583	Saqlain Mushtaq	lbw	2
584	Saeed Anwar	b	2
585	Azhar Mahmood	lbw	2
586	Wasim Akram	c G.S.Blewett	2
587	Inzamamul Haq	c M.E.Waugh	2

Australia v Pakistan, W.A.C.A. Ground, Perth, 26, 27, 28, November 1999

| 588 | Azhar Mahmood | b | 2 |

Australia v India, Adelaide Oval, 10, 11, 12, 13, 14, December 1999

589	R.S.Dravid	c J.L.Langer	1
590	S.R.Tendulkar	c J.L.Langer	1
591	S.C.Ganguly	st A.C.Gilchrist	1
592	M.S.K.Prasad	b	1
593	R.S.Dravid	cw A.C.Gilchrist	2
594	S.Ramesh	lbw	2

Australia v India, Melbourne Cricket Ground, 26, 27, 28, 29, 30, December 1999

| 595 | H.H.Kanitkar | lbw | 1 |
| 596 | S.R.Tendulkar | lbw | 2 |

Australians v Northern Districts, WestpacTrust Park, Hamilton, 5, 6, 7, 8, March 2000

| 597 | J.A.H.Marshall | c D.W.Fleming | 1 |
| 598 | M.D.Bailey | c G.D.McGrath | 1 |

Australia v New Zealand, Eden Park, Auckland, 11, 12, 13, 14, 15, March 2000

599	M.S.Sinclair	lbw	1
600	N.J.Astle	c M.E.Waugh	1
601	C.D.McMillan	lbw	1
602	N.J.Astle	b	2
603	P.J.Wiseman	cw A.C.Gilchrist	2

Australia v New Zealand, Basin Reserve, Wellington, 24, 25, 26, 27, March 2000

604	S.P.Fleming	c C.R.Miller	1
605	N.J.Astle	c M.E.Waugh	1
606	D.L.Vettori	c J.L.Langer	1
607	S.B.Doull	c M.J.Slater	1
608	N.J.Astle	b	2
609	C.D.McMillan	c M.E.Waugh	2
610	S.B.Doull	c S.R.Waugh	2

Australia v New Zealand, WestpacTrust Park, Hamilton, 31, March, 1, 2, 3, April 2000

611	P.J.Wiseman	b	1
612	N.J.Astle	cw A.C.Gilchrist	2
613	C.D.McMillan	c M.E.Waugh	2

Hampshire v Somerset, County Ground, Southampton, 3, 4, 5, May 2000

614	P.C.L.Holloway	c D.A.Kenway	1

Hampshire v Yorkshire, Headingley, Leeds, 12, 13, 14, May 2000

615	J.D.Middlebrook	c J.P.Stephenson	1
616	G.M.Hamilton	b	1

Hampshire v Leicestershire, Grace Road, Leicester, 17, 18, 19, 20, May 2000

617	T.R.Ward	st A.N.Aymes	1
618	D.I.Stevens	lbw	1
619	J.M.Dakin	lbw	1
620	A.Habib	st A.N.Aymes	1
621	P.A.J.DeFreitas	b	1

Hampshire v Lancashire, County Ground, Southampton, 23, 24, 25, 26, May 2000

622	J.C.Scuderi	cw A.N.Aymes	1
623	G.Chapple	b	1

Hampshire v Surrey, The Oval, Kennington, 1, 2, 3, 4, June 2000

624	J.D.Ratcliffe	b	1
625	Saqlain Mushtaq	lbw	1
626	A.J.Hollioake	b	2
627	J.N.Batty	c J.P.Stephenson	2
628	J.D.Ratcliffe	b	2
629	A.J.Tudor	c J.S.Laney	2
630	Saqlain Mushtaq	cw A.N.Aymes	2

Hampshire v Lancashire, Aigburth, Liverpool, 6, 7, 8, June 2000

631	G.D.Lloyd	lbw	1
632	J.C.Scuderi	lbw	1
633	I.D.Austin	b	1
634	M.P.Smethurst	b	1

Hampshire v Durham, May's Bounty, Basingstoke, 14, 15, 16, June 2000

635	N.J.Speak	c A.J.Sexton	1
636	J.Wood	cw A.N.Aymes	1
637	M.M.Betts	b	1
638	S.J.E.Brown	c A.D.Mascarenhas	1
639	N.J.Speak	cw A.N.Aymes	2
640	S.M.Katich	c W.S.Kendall	2
641	M.P.Speight	b	2
642	N.C.Phillips	c W.S.Kendall	2

Hampshire v Surrey, County Ground, Southampton, 29, 30, June, 1, 2, July 2000

643	J.N.Batty	b	1
644	A.J.Tudor	b	1
645	I.J.Ward	cw A.N.Aymes	2
646	Saqlain Mushtaq	lbw	2
647	A.J.Hollioake	st D.A.Kenway	2
648	A.D.Brown	c G.W.White	2
649	B.C.Hollioake	lbw	2

Hampshire v Somerset, County Ground, Taunton, 7, 8, 9, 10, July 2000

650	K.A.Parsons	c S.R.G.Francis	1
651	P.D.Trego	lbw	1
652	P.C.L.Holloway	cw A.N.Aymes	1

| 653 | R.J.Turner | lbw | 1 |

Hampshire v Kent, United Services Recreation Ground, Portsmouth, 19, 20, 21, 22, July 2000

654	R.W.T.Key	c G.W.White	1
655	D.D.Masters	lbw	1
656	A.P.Wells	b	1
657	M.V.Fleming	lbw	1

Hampshire v Derbyshire, County Ground, Derby, 2, 3, 4, 5, August 2000

| 658 | S.J.Lacey | c D.A.Kenway | 2 |
| 659 | P.Aldred | b | 2 |

Hampshire v Kent, St Lawrence Ground, Canterbury, 22, 23, 24, 25, August 2000

660	E.T.Smith	lbw	1
661	M.J.Walker	c & b	1
662	M.J.McCague	b	1
663	M.J.Walker	cw A.N.Aymes	2
664	D.P.Fulton	lbw	2
665	P.A.Nixon	b	2
666	A.P.Wells	c L.R.Prittipaul	2
667	M.J.McCague	c S.D.Udal	2
668	D.D.Masters	st A.N.Aymes	2

Hampshire v Durham, Riverside Ground, Chester-le-Street, 31, August, 1, 2, 3, September 2000

| 669 | J.J.B.Lewis | b | 1 |
| 670 | J.A.Daley | lbw | 1 |

Hampshire v Derbyshire, County Ground, Southampton, 6, 7, 8, 9, September 2000

671	S.D.Stubbings	b	1
672	M.E.Cassar	cw A.N.Aymes	1
673	T.A.Munton	cw A.N.Aymes	1
674	K.J.Dean	b	1
675	T.A.Munton	c A.C.Morris	2
676	L.J.Wharton	c G.W.White	2

Hampshire v Yorkshire, County Ground, Southampton, 13, 14, 15, 16, September 2000

| 677 | M.P.Vaughan | c W.S.Kendall | 1 |

678	A.McGrath	lbw	1
679	D.Byas	lbw	1
680	G.M.Fellows	lbw	1
681	I.D.Fisher	c G.W.White	1
682	G.M.Fellows	c W.S.Kendall	2
683	D.Byas	c S.D.Udal	2

Victoria v Western Australia, W.A.C.A. Ground, Perth,
4, 5, 6, January 2001

684	M.E.K.Hussey	lbw	1
685	M.J.Walsh	b	1
686	S.M.Katich	cw D.S.Berry	1
687	M.J.North	c I.J.Harvey	1
688	D.R.Martyn	lbw	2
689	M.J.North	c J.L.Arnberger	2
690	S.M.Katich	c C.J.Peake	2
691	J.Angel	c M.H.W.Inness	2
692	S.J.Karppinen	lbw	2

Australians v Mumbai, Brabourne Stadium, Mumbai,
22, 23, 24, February 2001

693	J.V.Paranjpe	c D.W.Fleming	1
694	Wasim Jaffer	c R.T.Ponting	2
695	V.G.Kambli	c M.L.Hayden	2
696	R.F.Morris	st A.C.Gilchrist	2
697	J.V.Paranjpe	c R.T.Ponting	2
698	R.R.Powar	c D.W.Fleming	2
699	S.S.Dighe	c sub	2
700	A.A.Muzumdar	c sub	2

Australia v India, Wankhede Stadium, Mumbai,
27, 28, February, 1, March 2001

701	S.C.Ganguly	c M.L.Hayden	1
702	A.B.Agarkar	c & b	1
703	J.Srinath	c M.E.Waugh	1
704	Harbhajan Singh	c S.R.Waugh	1
705	R.S.Dravid	b	2

Australia v India, Eden Gardens, Kolkata,
11, 12, 13, 14, 15, March 2001

706	R.S.Dravid	b	1
707	V.V.S.Laxman	c M.L.Hayden	1
708	S.Ramesh	c M.E.Waugh	2

Australia v India, MA Chidambaram Stadium, Chepauk, Chennai, 18, 19, 20, 21, 22, March 2001

709	S.Ramesh	c R.T.Ponting	1
710	S.S.Dighe	lbw	1

Australians v Worcestershire, County Ground, New Road, Worcester, 1, 2, 3, June 2001

711	D.J.Pipe	b	1
712	A.Sheriyar	st A.C.Gilchrist	1
713	D.J.Pipe	c N.W.Bracken	2

Australians v Marylebone Cricket Club, Arundel Castle Cricket Club Ground,
25, 26, 27, June 2001

714	Azhar Mahmood	lbw	1
715	G.J.Kruis	lbw	1
716	D.M.Ward	c S.R.Waugh	2

Australia v England, Edgbaston, Birmingham,
5, 6, 7, 8, July 2001

717	M.A.Butcher	c R.T.Ponting	1
718	U.Afzaal	b	1
719	C.White	lbw	1
720	A.F.Giles	cw A.C.Gilchrist	1
721	D.Gough	c J.N.Gillespie	1
722	M.E.Trescothick	c M.E.Waugh	2
723	D.Gough	lbw	2
724	A.F.Giles	c M.E.Waugh	2

Australia v England, Lord's Cricket Ground, St John's Wood,
19, 20, 21, 22, July 2001

725	A.R.Caddick	b	1
726	D.Gough	b	1
727	M.A.Atherton	b	2

Australians v Hampshire, The Rose Bowl, Southampton,
28, 29, 30, July 2001

728	D.A.Kenway	c S.R.Waugh	1
729	W.S.Kendall	b	2
730	N.C.Johnson	lbw	2
731	A.D.Mascarenhas	b	2
732	S.D.Udal	b	2

Australia v England, Trent Bridge, Nottingham,
2, 3, 4, August 2001

733	A.J.Tudor	lbw	1
734	R.D.B.Croft	c R.T.Ponting	1
735	M.E.Trescothick	cw A.C.Gilchrist	2
736	M.A.Atherton	cw A.C.Gilchrist	2
737	A.J.Stewart	b	2
738	M.R.Ramprakash	st A.C.Gilchrist	2
739	C.White	c S.R.Waugh	2
740	A.J.Tudor	c R.T.Ponting	2

Australia v England, Headingley, Leeds,
16, 17, 18, 19, 20, August 2001

741	M.R.Ramprakash	c M.E.Waugh	2

Australia v England, The Oval, Kennington,
23, 24, 25, 26, 27, August 2001

742	M.A.Atherton	b	1
743	M.E.Trescothick	b	1
744	M.A.Butcher	c J.L.Langer	1
745	A.J.Stewart	cw A.C.Gilchrist	1
746	A.R.Caddick	lbw	1
747	J.Ormond	b	1
748	D.Gough	st A.C.Gilchrist	1
749	M.A.Butcher	c S.R.Waugh	2
750	N.Hussain	lbw	2
751	M.R.Ramprakash	c M.L.Hayden	2
752	A.J.Stewart	b	2

Victoria v South Australia, Adelaide Oval,
17, 18, 19, 20, October 2001

753	D.A.Fitzgerald	cw D.S.Berry	1
754	D.M.Dempsey	lbw	2

Victoria v Queensland, Richmond Cricket Ground, Melbourne,
24, 25, 26, 27, October 2001

755	A.Symonds	lbw	1
756	S.G.Law	lbw	1
757	W.A.Seccombe	c J.L.Arnberger	1
758	A.A.Noffke	c M.T.G.Elliott	1

Australia v New Zealand, Brisbane Cricket Ground, Woolloongabba,
8, 9, 10, 11, 12, November 2001

759	M.H.Richardson	lbw	2

| 760 | M.S.Sinclair | st A.C.Gilchrist | 2 |
| 761 | N.J.Astle | c J.N.Gillespie | 2 |

Australia v New Zealand, Bellerive Oval, Hobart, 22, 23, 24, 25, 26, November 2001

| 762 | M.D.Bell | cw A.C.Gilchrist | 1 |

Australia v New Zealand, W.A.C.A. Ground, Perth, 30, November, 1, 2, 3, 4, December 2001

| 763 | L.Vincent | c M.E.Waugh | 1 |
| 764 | S.P.Fleming | b | 2 |

Australia v South Africa, Adelaide Oval, 14, 15, 16, 17, 18, December 2001

765	H.H.Gibbs	st A.C.Gilchrist	1
766	L.Klusener	b	1
767	S.M.Pollock	cw A.C.Gilchrist	1
768	M.V.Boucher	c J.L.Langer	1
769	M.Ntini	c R.T.Ponting	1
770	G.Kirsten	c R.T.Ponting	2
771	S.M.Pollock	c R.T.Ponting	2
772	C.W.Henderson	c R.T.Ponting	2

Australia v South Africa, Melbourne Cricket Ground, 26, 27, 28, 29, December 2001

773	H.H.Dippenaar	c M.L.Hayden	2
774	N.D.McKenzie	cw A.C.Gilchrist	2
775	M.V.Boucher	c M.E.Waugh	2

Australia v South Africa, Sydney Cricket Ground, 2, 3, 4, 5, January 2002

776	N.D.McKenzie	b	1
777	J.L.Ontong	lbw	1
778	M.V.Boucher	c R.T.Ponting	1
779	J.H.Kallis	cw A.C.Gilchrist	2
780	J.L.Ontong	lbw	2
781	A.A.Donald	c B.Lee	2

Australians v South Africa A, North West Cricket Stadium, Potchefstroom, 17, 18, 19, February 2002

| 782 | D.M.Benkenstein | c M.L.Hayden | 1 |
| 783 | A.J.Hall | c M.E.Waugh | 1 |

Australia v South Africa, Wanderers Stadium, Johannesburg, 22, 23, 24, February 2002

784	H.H.Gibbs	lbw	1
785	A.Nel	lbw	1
786	A.G.Prince	b	2
787	H.H.Gibbs	st A.C.Gilchrist	2
788	H.H.Dippenaar	lbw	2
789	M.V.Boucher	b	2

Australia v South Africa, Newlands, Cape Town, 8, 9, 10, 11, 12, March 2002

790	N.D.McKenzie	b	1
791	M.Ntini	c M.E.Waugh	1
792	H.H.Gibbs	c R.T.Ponting	2
793	G.C.Smith	cw A.C.Gilchrist	2
794	J.H.Kallis	lbw	2
795	A.G.Prince	c R.T.Ponting	2
796	M.Ntini	c J.L.Langer	2
797	D.Pretorius	c M.E.Waugh	2

Australia v South Africa, Kingsmead, Durban, 15, 16, 17, 18, March 2002

798	J.H.Kallis	c & b	1
799	A.G.Prince	c B.Lee	1
800	M.V.Boucher	c & b	1
801	M.Ntini	c G.D.McGrath	1
802	N.D.McKenzie	c M.L.Hayden	2
803	A.G.Prince	c M.E.Waugh	2

Australia v Pakistan, P Saravanamuttu Stadium, Colombo, 3, 4, 5, 6, 7, October 2002

804	Abdur Razzaq	cw A.C.Gilchrist	1
805	Misbah-ul Haq	c M.E.Waugh	1
806	Faisal Iqbal	c M.E.Waugh	1
807	Saqlain Mushtaq	lbw	1
808	Waqar Younis	lbw	1
809	Rashid Latif	c D.R.Martyn	1
810	Shoaib Akhtar	c G.D.McGrath	1
811	Imran Nazir	c G.D.McGrath	2
812	Abdur Razzaq	lbw	2
813	Misbah-ul Haq	c S.R.Waugh	2
814	Younis Khan	lbw	2

Australia v Pakistan, Sharjah Cricket Association Stadium, 11, 12, October 2002

815	Faisal Iqbal	lbw	1
816	Abdur Razzaq	c D.R.Martyn	1
817	Saqlain Mushtaq	lbw	1
818	Waqar Younis	lbw	1
819	Imran Nazir	cw A.C.Gilchrist	2
820	Faisal Iqbal	c M.E.Waugh	2
821	Shoaib Akhtar	c S.R.Waugh	2
822	Waqar Younis	lbw	2

Australia v Pakistan, Sharjah Cricket Association Stadium, 19, 20, 21, 22, October 2002

823	Imran Farhat	lbw	1
824	Faisal Iqbal	cw A.C.Gilchrist	1
825	Rashid Latif	c M.E.Waugh	1
826	Mohammad Sami	lbw	1
827	Danish Kaneria	st A.C.Gilchrist	1
828	Misbah-ul Haq	lbw	2
829	Rashid Latif	lbw	2
830	Saqlain Mushtaq	lbw	2

Victoria v Tasmania, Melbourne Cricket Ground, 30, 31, October, 1, 2, November 2002

831	J.Cox	c I.J.Harvey	1
832	D.J.Marsh	cw D.S.Berry	1
833	M.J.di Venuto	b	2
834	S.G.Clingeleffer	c I.J.Harvey	2
835	S.B.Tubb	c sub	2

Australia v England, Brisbane Cricket Ground, Woolloongabba, 7, 8, 9, 10, November 2002

836	M.J.Hoggard	c M.L.Hayden	1
837	A.J.Stewart	c M.L.Hayden	2
838	M.A.Butcher	c R.T.Ponting	2
839	A.R.Caddick	c D.S.Lehmann	2

Victoria v Western Australia, W.A.C.A. Ground, Perth, 14, 15, 16, November 2002

840	C.J.L.Rogers	c C.L.White	1

Australia v England, Adelaide Oval, 21, 22, 23, 24, November 2002

841	R.W.T.Key	c R.T.Ponting	1

842	N.Hussain	cw A.C.Gilchrist	1
843	R.K.J.Dawson	lbw	1
844	A.R.Caddick	b	1
845	M.P.Vaughan	c G.D.McGrath	2
846	A.J.Stewart	lbw	2
847	S.J.Harmison	lbw	2

**Australia v England, W.A.C.A. Ground, Perth,
29, 30, November, 1, December 2002**

848	A.J.Tudor	c D.R.Martyn	1
849	N.Hussain	cw A.C.Gilchrist	2
850	C.White	st A.C.Gilchrist	2

**Victoria v Tasmania, Melbourne Cricket Ground,
16, 17, 18, 19, February 2004**

851	S.R.Watson	c M.H.W.Inness	1
852	M.J.di Venuto	c M.P.Mott	1
853	D.J.Marsh	b	2
854	S.P.Kremerskothen	c M.H.W.Inness	2
855	M.G.Dighton	st D.S.Berry	2
856	X.J.Doherty	st D.S.Berry	2

**Australians v Sri Lanka Board President's XI, Colombo Cricket Club Ground,
2, 3, 4, March 2004**

857	P.D.R.L.Perera	st W.A.Seccombe	1
858	R.P.Arnold	c B.A.Williams	2
859	K.S.Lokuarachchi	lbw	2

**Australia v Sri Lanka, Galle International Stadium,
8, 9, 10, 11, 12, March 2004**

860	S.T.Jayasuriya	lbw	1
861	H.P.Tillakaratne	lbw	1
862	U.D.U.Chandana	cw A.C.Gilchrist	1
863	H.D.P.K.Dharmasena	c M.L.Hayden	1
864	M.Muralidaran	c & b	1
865	M.S.Atapattu	c M.L.Hayden	2
866	T.M.Dilshan	lbw	2
867	D.P.M.D.Jayawardene	c M.L.Hayden	2
868	H.P.Tillakaratne	c A.Symonds	2
869	H.D.P.K.Dharmasena	c M.L.Hayden	2

Australia v Sri Lanka, Asgiriya Stadium, Kandy, 16, 17, 18, 19, 20, March 2004

870	D.P.M.D.Jayawardene	c A.Symonds	1
871	T.M.Dilshan	lbw	1
872	H.P.Tillakaratne	cw A.C.Gilchrist	1
873	K.S.Lokuarachchi	c M.S.Kasprowicz	1
874	M.Muralidaran	c A.Symonds	1
875	K.C.Sangakkara	c & b	2
876	H.P.Tillakaratne	c R.T.Ponting	2
877	T.M.Dilshan	b	2
878	W.P.U.J.C.Vaas	c J.L.Langer	2
879	K.S.Lokuarachchi	lbw	2

Australia v Sri Lanka, Sinhalese Sports Club Ground, Colombo, 24, 25, 26, 27, 28, March 2004

880	W.P.U.J.C.Vaas	b	1
881	H.M.R.K.B.Herath	c D.R.Martyn	1
882	K.C.Sangakkara	b	2
883	T.M.Dilshan	c D.R.Martyn	2
884	D.N.T.Zoysa	b	2
885	W.P.U.J.C.Vaas	lbw	2

Hampshire v Durham, The Rose Bowl, Southampton, 16, 17, 18, 19, April 2004

886	M.J.North	c B.V.Taylor	1
887	R.D.King	lbw	1
888	N.Peng	b	2
889	G.M.Hamilton	b	2
890	G.D.Bridge	b	2
891	L.E.Plunkett	c C.T.Tremlett	2
892	R.D.King	b	2

Hampshire v Leicestershire, The Rose Bowl, Southampton, 28, 29, 30, April, 1, May 2004

893	J.K.Maunders	b	1
894	J.L.Sadler	lbw	1
895	B.J.Hodge	c M.J.Clarke	2
896	P.A.J.DeFreitas	c M.J.Clarke	2

Hampshire v Derbyshire, The Rose Bowl, Southampton, 7, 8, 9, 10, May 2004

897	S.D.Stubbings	c M.J.Brown	1
898	A.I.Gait	c D.A.Kenway	2

Hampshire v Nottinghamshire, The Rose Bowl, Southampton, 2, 3, June 2004

899	P.J.Franks	c M.J.Clarke	1
900	G.J.Smith	c A.D.Mascarenhas	1

Hampshire v Essex, County Ground, Chelmsford, 9, 10, 11, June 2004

901	A.Habib	lbw	1
902	R.S.Bopara	c M.J.Brown	1

Australia v Sri Lanka, Marrara Cricket Ground, Darwin, 1, 2, 3, July 2004

903	U.D.U.Chandana	cw A.C.Gilchrist	1
904	W.P.U.J.C.Vaas	c M.L.Hayden	1
905	S.L.Malinga	c J.N.Gillespie	1

Australia v Sri Lanka, Cazaly's Stadium, Cairns, 9, 10, 11, 12, 13, July 2004

906	K.C.Sangakkara	c J.N.Gillespie	1
907	T.M.Dilshan	c M.S.Kasprowicz	1
908	U.D.U.Chandana	st A.C.Gilchrist	1
909	S.T.Jayasuriya	cw A.C.Gilchrist	2
910	R.S.Kaluwitharana	c D.S.Lehmann	2
911	K.C.Sangakkara	b	2
912	U.D.U.Chandana	st A.C.Gilchrist	2

Hampshire v Nottinghamshire, Trent Bridge, Nottingham, 23, 24, 25, 26, July 2004

913	R.J.Warren	lbw	1
914	K.P.Pietersen	c M.J.Brown	1

Hampshire v Glamorgan, Sophia Gardens, Cardiff, 29, 30, 31, July 2004

915	R.D.B.Croft	b	1
916	A.G.Wharf	lbw	1
917	M.S.Kasprowicz	lbw	1
918	D.L.Hemp	b	2
919	M.J.Powell	c M.J.Clarke	2
920	M.P.Maynard	st N.Pothas	2
921	J.Hughes	b	2
922	M.S.Kasprowicz	c M.J.Clarke	2
923	D.A.Cosker	cw N.Pothas	2

Hampshire v Essex, The Rose Bowl, Southampton, 3, 4, 5, August 2004

924	A.Habib	c D.A.Kenway	1
925	J.S.Foster	c M.J.Brown	1
926	A.R.Adams	st N.Pothas	1
927	D.Gough	lbw	1
928	A.Flower	cw N.Pothas	2

Hampshire v Glamorgan, The Rose Bowl, Southampton, 11, 12, 13, 14, August 2004

929	M.T.G.Elliott	st N.Pothas	2
930	D.L.Hemp	b	2
931	M.P.Maynard	c M.J.Clarke	2
932	J.Hughes	b	2

Hampshire v Somerset, County Ground, Taunton, 18, 19, 20, 21, August 2004

933	J.Cox	cw N.Pothas	2
934	J.D.Francis	c S.M.Katich	2
935	J.C.Hildreth	c L.R.Prittipaul	2
936	R.L.Johnson	b	2
937	A.W.Laraman	cw N.Pothas	2
938	R.J.Turner	lbw	2

Hampshire v Durham, Riverside Ground, Chester-le-Street, 24, 25, 26, 27, August 2004

939	G.J.Muchall	lbw	1
940	P.Mustard	st N.Pothas	1
941	N.Killeen	c D.A.Kenway	1
942	K.J.Coetzer	cw N.Pothas	2

Hampshire v Leicestershire, Grace Road, Leicester, 1, 2, 3, 4, September 2004

943	D.G.Brandy	b	1
944	D.I.Stevens	cw N.Pothas	2
945	O.D.Gibson	b	2
946	J.L.Sadler	c J.P.Crawley	2

Australia v India, M Chinnaswamy Stadium, Bangalore, 6, 7, 8, 9, 10, October 2004

947	V.V.S.Laxman	b	1
948	I.K.Pathan	cw A.C.Gilchrist	1
949	V.V.S.Laxman	lbw	2
950	P.A.Patel	lbw	2

Australia v India, MA Chidambaram Stadium, Chepauk, Chennai, 14, 15, 16, 17, 18, October 2004

951	Yuvraj Singh	cw A.C.Gilchrist	1
952	I.K.Pathan	c M.L.Hayden	1
953	V.K.Sehwag	c M.J.Clarke	1
954	P.A.Patel	cw A.C.Gilchrist	1
955	A.Kumble	b	1
956	Harbhajan Singh	c & b	1

Australia v India, Vidarbha Cricket Association Ground, Nagpur, 26, 27, 28, 29, October 2004

957	V.V.S.Laxman	c M.J.Clarke	1
958	P.A.Patel	c M.L.Hayden	1
959	V.K.Sehwag	c M.J.Clarke	2
960	Zaheer Khan	c D.R.Martyn	2

Australia v New Zealand, Brisbane Cricket Ground, Woolloongabba, 18, 19, 20, 21, November 2004

961	C.D.McMillan	cw A.C.Gilchrist	1
962	B.B.McCullum	st A.C.Gilchrist	1
963	K.D.Mills	c M.L.Hayden	1
964	C.S.Martin	c R.T.Ponting	1
965	S.B.Styris	lbw	2
966	J.D.P.Oram	c M.L.Hayden	2
967	D.L.Vettori	c M.L.Hayden	2
968	C.S.Martin	lbw	2

Australia v New Zealand, Adelaide Oval, 26, 27, 28, 29, 30, November 2004

969	J.E.C.Franklin	lbw	1
970	S.B.Styris	c M.J.Clarke	2
971	C.S.Martin	c R.T.Ponting	2

Australia v Pakistan, W.A.C.A. Ground, Perth, 16, 17, 18, 19, December 2004

972	Younis Khan	c J.N.Gillespie	1
973	Abdur Razzaq	b	1
974	Mohammad Khalil	b	1

Australia v Pakistan, Melbourne Cricket Ground, 26, 27, 28, 29, December 2004

975	Yousuf Youhana	st A.C.Gilchrist	1
976	Mohammad Sami	lbw	1
977	Shoaib Akhtar	st A.C.Gilchrist	1

978	Yousuf Youhana	c R.T.Ponting	2
979	Kamran Akmal	lbw	2
980	Shoaib Malik	c J.N.Gillespie	2

Australia v Pakistan, Sydney Cricket Ground,

2, 3, 4, 5, January 2005

981	Yasir Hameed	c M.J.Clarke	1
982	Yasir Hameed	lbw	2
983	Kamran Akmal	c M.L.Hayden	2
984	Naved-ul-Hasan	lbw	2
985	Shoaib Akhtar	c D.R.Martyn	2

Victoria v Western Australia, W.A.C.A. Ground, Perth, 16, 17, 18, January 2005

| 986 | M.W.Goodwin | lbw | 1 |

Victoria v South Australia, Melbourne Cricket Ground, 28, 29, 30, 31, January 2005

987	D.J.Harris	st P.J.Roach	1
988	L.Williams	c C.L.White	1
989	D.J.Cullen	c & b	1
990	C.J.Ferguson	c J.Moss	2

Victoria v Tasmania, Melbourne Cricket Ground, 24, 25, 26, 27, February 2005

991	X.J.Doherty	lbw	1
992	D.A.McNees	b	1
993	D.G.Wright	st A.J.Crosthwaite	1
994	G.J.Bailey	c C.L.White	2
995	M.G.Bevan	c C.L.White	2

Victoria v Queensland, Melbourne Cricket Ground, 3, 4, 5, 6, March 2005

| 996 | C.A.Philipson | c G.C.Rummans | 1 |

Australia v New Zealand, Jade Stadium, Christchurch, 10, 11, 12, 13, March 2005

997	S.P.Fleming	lbw	1
998	H.J.H.Marshall	b	1
999	C.D.McMillan	c S.M.Katich	2
1000	H.J.H.Marshall	b	2
1001	D.L.Vettori	lbw	2
1002	I.E.O'Brien	lbw	2
1003	C.S.Martin	lbw	2

Australia v New Zealand, Basin Reserve, Wellington, 18, 19, 20, 21, 22, March 2005

1004	B.B.McCullum	c M.J.Clarke	1
1005	C.D.McMillan	b	1
1006	D.L.Vettori	c D.R.Martyn	1

Australia v New Zealand, Eden Park, Auckland, 26, 27, 28, 29, March 2005

1007	H.J.H.Marshall	c R.T.Ponting	1
1008	J.E.C.Franklin	c S.M.Katich	1
1009	P.J.Wiseman	c J.N.Gillespie	1
1010	B.B.McCullum	lbw	2
1011	N.J.Astle	c S.M.Katich	2
1012	J.E.C.Franklin	c R.T.Ponting	2
1013	D.L.Vettori	c G.D.McGrath	2

Hampshire v Gloucestershire, The Rose Bowl, Southampton, 13, 14, 15, 16, April 2005

1014	CM.Spearman	lbw	1
1015	J.M.M.Averis	c D.A.Kenway	1
1016	T.H.C.Hancock	c S.M.Katich	1
1017	C.G.Taylor	lbw	2
1018	T.H.C.Hancock	c S.M.Katich	2
1019	M.A.Hardinges	lbw	2

Hampshire v Sussex, County Ground, Hove, 20, 21, 22, 23, April 2005

1020	C.J.Adams	c & b	1
1021	M.J.Prior	lbw	1
1022	M.J.Prior	lbw	2
1023	R.S.C.Martin-Jenkins	lbw	2
1024	R.J.Kirtley	lbw	2
1025	J.D.Lewry	b	2

Hampshire v Middlesex, The Rose Bowl, Southampton, 6, 7, 8, 9, May 2005

1026	E.C.Joyce	c & b	1
1027	O.A.Shah	st N.Pothas	1
1028	C.B.Keegan	lbw	1
1029	A.J.Strauss	b	2
1030	E.C.Joyce	c K.P.Pietersen	2
1031	E.T.Smith	b	2
1032	B.J.M.Scott	lbw	2

Hampshire v Kent, St Lawrence Ground, Canterbury, 11, 12, 13, 14, May 2005

1033	D.P.Fulton	c T.S.Burrows	1
1034	S.J.Cook	b	1
1035	M.M.Patel	lbw	1
1036	R.W.T.Key	c K.P.Pietersen	2
1037	G.O.Jones	b	2
1038	S.J.Cook	b	2

Hampshire v Glamorgan, The Rose Bowl, Southampton, 20, 21, 22, 23, May 2005

1039	M.A.Wallace	b	1
1040	D.D.Cherry	lbw	2

Hampshire v Warwickshire, Stratford-upon-Avon Cricket Club Ground, 25, 26, May 2005

1041	A.G.R.Loudon	b	1
1042	I.J.L.Trott	lbw	1
1043	D.R.Brown	b	1
1044	T.Frost	c K.P.Pietersen	1
1045	J.O.Troughton	b	1
1046	H.H.Streak	cw N.Pothas	1

Hampshire v Nottinghamshire, Trent Bridge, Nottingham, 1, 2, 3, 4, June 2005

1047	C.M.W.Read	st J.P.Crawley	2
1048	R.J.Sidebottom	b	2

Hampshire v Surrey, The Rose Bowl, Southampton, 15, 16, 17, June 2005

1049	R.S.Clinton	c G.A.Lamb	1
1050	J.Ormond	c G.A.Lamb	1

Hampshire v Middlesex, John Walker's Ground, Southgate, 8, 9, 10, 11, July 2005

1051	B.L.Hutton	c S.D.Udal	1
1052	P.N.Weekes	c A.D.Mascarenhas	1
1053	B.L.Hutton	c M.J.Brown	2
1054	B.J.M.Scott	c S.D.Udal	2

Australia v England, Lord's Cricket Ground, St John's Wood, 21, 22, 23, 24, July 2005

1055	M.J.Hoggard	c M.L.Hayden	1
1056	K.P.Pietersen	c D.R.Martyn	1

1057	M.E.Trescothick	c M.L.Hayden	2
1058	I.R.Bell	lbw	2
1059	A.Flintoff	cw A.C.Gilchrist	2
1060	S.J.Harmison	lbw	2

Australia v England, Edgbaston, Birmingham, 4, 5, 6, 7, August 2005

1061	A.J.Strauss	b	1
1062	A.F.Giles	lbw	1
1063	S.J.Harmison	b	1
1064	M.J.Hoggard	lbw	1
1065	A.J.Strauss	b	2
1066	K.P.Pietersen	cw A.C.Gilchrist	2
1067	I.R.Bell	cw A.C.Gilchrist	2
1068	A.Flintoff	b	2
1069	A.F.Giles	c M.L.Hayden	2
1070	S.J.Harmison	c R.T.Ponting	2

Australia v England, Old Trafford, Manchester, 11, 12, 13, 14, 15, August 2005

1071	M.E.Trescothick	cw A.C.Gilchrist	1
1072	A.Flintoff	c J.L.Langer	1
1073	A.F.Giles	c M.L.Hayden	1
1074	S.P.Jones	b	1

Australia v England, Trent Bridge, Nottingham, 25, 26, 27, 28, August 2005

1075	A.J.Strauss	c M.L.Hayden	1
1076	A.F.Giles	lbw	1
1077	S.J.Harmison	st A.C.Gilchrist	1
1078	M.J.Hoggard	cw A.C.Gilchrist	1
1079	M.E.Trescothick	c R.T.Ponting	2
1080	M.P.Vaughan	c M.L.Hayden	2
1081	A.J.Strauss	c M.J.Clarke	2
1082	G.O.Jones	c M.S.Kasprowicz	2

Australia v England, The Oval, Kennington, 8, 9, 10, 11, 12, September 2005

1083	M.E.Trescothick	c M.L.Hayden	1
1084	M.P.Vaughan	c M.J.Clarke	1
1085	I.R.Bell	lbw	1
1086	K.P.Pietersen	b	1
1087	A.J.Strauss	c S.M.Katich	1

1088	A.F.Giles	lbw	1
1089	A.J.Strauss	c S.M.Katich	2
1090	M.E.Trescothick	lbw	2
1091	A.Flintoff	c & b	2
1092	P.D.Collingwood	c R.T.Ponting	2
1093	A.F.Giles	b	2
1094	S.J.Harmison	c M.L.Hayden	2

Hampshire v Glamorgan, Sophia Gardens, Cardiff, 15, 16, 17, 18, September 2005

1095	R.N.Grant	c S.M.Katich	1
1096	M.J.Powell	c & b	1
1097	A.G.Wharf	lbw	1
1098	D.S.Harrison	lbw	1
1099	D.D.Cherry	lbw	2

Hampshire v Nottinghamshire, The Rose Bowl, Southampton, 21, 22, 23, September 2005

1100	S.P.Fleming	c J.H.K.Adams	2

Australia v ICC World XI, Sydney Cricket Ground, 14, 15, 16, 17, October 2005

1101	V.K.Sehwag	c S.M.Katich	1
1102	J.H.Kallis	c M.L.Hayden	1
1103	M.V.Boucher	cw A.C.Gilchrist	1
1104	R.S.Dravid	c M.L.Hayden	2
1105	B.C.Lara	cw A.C.Gilchrist	2
1106	M.V.Boucher	c M.L.Hayden	2

Australia v West Indies, Brisbane Cricket Ground, Woolloongabba, 3, 4, 5, 6, November 2005

1107	S.Chanderpaul	c N.W.Bracken	1
1108	D.B.Powell	cw A.C.Gilchrist	1
1109	F.H.Edwards	b	1
1110	C.D.Collymore	c M.J.Clarke	1
1111	J.J.C.Lawson	lbw	1

Australia v West Indies, Bellerive Oval, Hobart, 17, 18, 19, 20, 21, November 2005

1112	B.C.Lara	cw A.C.Gilchrist	2
1113	M.N.Samuels	c B.J.Hodge	2
1114	D.J.J.Bravo	b	2
1115	C.D.Collymore	cw A.C.Gilchrist	2

Australia v West Indies, Adelaide Oval, 25, 26, 27, 28, 29, November 2005

1116	F.H.Edwards	c M.L.Hayden	1
1117	W.W.Hinds	st A.C.Gilchrist	2
1118	D.B.Powell	b	2
1119	B.C.Lara	c M.L.Hayden	2
1120	S.Chanderpaul	c B.J.Hodge	2
1121	D.R.Smith	lbw	2
1122	D.C.Ramdin	cw A.C.Gilchrist	2

Australia v South Africa, W.A.C.A. Ground, Perth, 16, 17, 18, 19, 20, December 2005

1123	A.B.de Villiers	b	1
1124	A.G.Prince	lbw	1
1125	M.V.Boucher	c M.L.Hayden	1
1126	A.B.de Villiers	c B.J.Hodge	2
1127	A.G.Prince	lbw	2
1128	J.M.Kemp	c R.T.Ponting	2

Australia v South Africa, Melbourne Cricket Ground, 26, 27, 28, 29, 30, December 2005

1129	A.G.Prince	c R.T.Ponting	1
1130	N.Boje	b	1
1131	A.B.de Villiers	st A.C.Gilchrist	2
1132	H.H.Gibbs	b	2
1133	M.V.Boucher	c R.T.Ponting	2
1134	A.G.Prince	c M.L.Hayden	2

Australia v South Africa, Sydney Cricket Ground, 2, 3, 4, 5, 6, January 2006

1135	A.G.Prince	lbw	1
1136	A.Nel	c B.J.Hodge	1

Victoria v South Australia, Adelaide Oval, 2, 3, 4, February 2006

1137	C.J.Borgas	lbw	1
1138	C.J.Ferguson	c & b	1
1139	S.W.Tait	st A.J.Crosthwaite	1
1140	D.S.Lehmann	st A.J.Crosthwaite	2

Victoria v Tasmania, Junction Oval, Melbourne, 13, 14, 15, 16, February 2006

1141	G.J.Bailey	lbw	1
1142	T.R.Birt	st A.J.Crosthwaite	1

Victoria v Queensland, Junction Oval, Melbourne, 2, 3, 4, 5, March 2006

1143	J.P.Maher	c C.L.White	1
1144	M.L.Love	c C.L.White	1
1145	C.T.Perren	c C.L.White	1
1146	M.L.Hayden	lbw	1
1147	C.D.Hartley	cw N.S.Pilon	1
1148	A.A.Noffke	c C.L.White	1
1149	D.J.Doran	c B.J.Hodge	1
1150	M.L.Hayden	lbw	2
1151	C.T.Perren	c C.L.White	2
1152	J.P.Maher	b	2

Australia v South Africa, Newlands, Cape Town, 16, 17, 18, March 2006

1153	G.C.Smith	lbw	2
1154	J.A.Rudolph	b	2
1155	M.Ntini	c M.S.Kasprowicz	2

Australia v South Africa, Kingsmead, Durban, 24, 25, 26, 27, 28, March 2006

1156	A.G.Prince	c A.Symonds	1
1157	J.A.Rudolph	c M.E.K.Hussey	1
1158	A.B.de Villiers	st A.C.Gilchrist	2
1159	G.C.Smith	c J.L.Langer	2
1160	J.H.Kallis	lbw	2
1161	J.A.Rudolph	c J.L.Langer	2
1162	A.Nel	c M.L.Hayden	2
1163	M.Ntini	lbw	2

Australia v South Africa, Wanderers Stadium, Johannesburg, 31, March, 1, 2, 3, 4, April 2006

1164	J.A.Rudolph	c M.L.Hayden	1
1165	H.H.Gibbs	c D.R.Martyn	2
1166	A.G.Prince	c A.Symonds	2
1167	N.Boje	c A.Symonds	2

Australia v Bangladesh, Narayanganj Osmani Stadium, Fatullah, 9, 10, 11, 12, 13, April 2006

1168	Mohammad Rafique	lbw	2
1169	Mashrafe Bin Mortaza	b	2
1170	Enamul Haque	lbw	2

Australia v Bangladesh, Bir Shrestha Shahid Ruhul Amin Stadium, Chittagong,
16, 17, 18, 19, 20, April 2006

1171	Mohammad Ashraful	c M.L.Hayden	1
1172	Aftab Ahmed	cw A.C.Gilchrist	1
1173	Shahadat Hossain	c J.N.Gillespie	1
1174	Habibul Bashar	c M.L.Hayden	2
1175	Rajin Saleh	c R.T.Ponting	2
1176	Mohammad Ashraful	b	2
1177	Shahriar Nafees	cw A.C.Gilchrist	2
1178	Mashrafe Bin Mortaza	c J.N.Gillespie	2

Hampshire v Middlesex, The Rose Bowl, Southampton,
3, 4, 5, May 2006

1179	E.T.Smith	b	2
1180	A.J.Strauss	lbw	2
1181	P.N.Weekes	c J.H.K.Adams	2
1182	B.J.M.Scott	lbw	2
1183	C.E.W.Silverwood	c A.D.Mascarenhas	2
1184	M.M.Betts	c S.M.Ervine	2
1185	J.Louw	b	2

Hampshire v Warwickshire, Edgbaston, Birmingham,
9, 10, 11, 12, May 2006

1186	M.J.Powell	c M.A.Carberry	1
1187	D.R.Brown	cw N.Pothas	1
1188	H.H.Streak	lbw	1
1189	N.M.Carter	b	1
1190	J.O.Troughton	b	1
1191	I.J.Westwood	c S.M.Ervine	2
1192	J.O.Troughton	b	2

Hampshire v Kent, The Rose Bowl, Southampton,
24, 25, 26, 27, May 2006

1193	J.M.Kemp	b	1
1194	N.J.O'Brien	c J.T.A.Bruce	1
1195	M.M.Patel	lbw	1
1196	R.H.Joseph	b	1
1197	R.W.T.Key	b	2

Hampshire v Yorkshire, Headingley, Leeds,
31, May, 1, 2, 3, June 2006

| 1198 | C.White | c G.A.Lamb | 1 |

1199	G.L.Brophy	c J.H.K.Adams	1
1200	J.N.Gillespie	cw N.Pothas	1
1201	T.T.Bresnan	lbw	1
1202	D.S.Lehmann	c G.A.Lamb	2
1203	G.L.Brophy	cw N.Pothas	2
1204	A.McGrath	c R.J.Logan	2

Hampshire v Nottinghamshire, The Rose Bowl, Southampton, 7, 8, 9, June 2006

1205	D.J.Bicknell	c S.M.Ervine	2
1206	J.E.R.Gallian	c & b	2
1207	C.E.Shreck	lbw	2

Hampshire v Durham, The Rose Bowl, Southampton, 20, 21, 22, June 2006

| 1208 | G.J.Muchall | lbw | 2 |

Hampshire v Nottinghamshire, Trent Bridge, Nottingham, 14, 15, 16, 17, July 2006

1209	J.E.R.Gallian	b	1
1210	R.J.Sidebottom	c C.C.Benham	1
1211	S.P.Fleming	c D.J.Thornely	1
1212	D.Alleyne	c C.C.Benham	2

Hampshire v Yorkshire, The Rose Bowl, Southampton, 26, 27, 28, July 2006

1213	J.J.Sayers	c J.H.K.Adams	2
1214	M.J.Lumb	cw N.Pothas	2
1215	S.A.Patterson	lbw	2

Hampshire v Kent, St Lawrence Ground, Canterbury, 2, 3, 4, 5, August 2006

1216	G.O.Jones	lbw	1
1217	T.Henderson	c S.M.Ervine	1
1218	M.J.Saggers	b	1

Hampshire v Middlesex, Lord's Cricket Ground, St John's Wood, 8, 9, 10, 11, August 2006

1219	J.W.M.Dalrymple	lbw	1
1220	S.B.Styris	lbw	1
1221	O.A.Shah	lbw	1
1222	C.E.W.Silverwood	b	1

Hampshire v Sussex, County Ground, Hove, 31, August, 1, 2, 3, September 2006

1223	M.W.Goodwin	cw N.Pothas	1
1224	R.S.C.Martin-Jenkins	lbw	1
1225	M.J.Prior	cw N.Pothas	1
1226	Mushtaq Ahmed	cw N.Pothas	1
1227	Yasir Arafat	st N.Pothas	1
1228	J.D.Lewry	b	1

Hampshire v Durham, Riverside Ground, Chester-le-Street, 7, 8, 9, September 2006

1229	P.Mustard	c D.J.Thornely	1
1230	O.D.Gibson	c J.H.K.Adams	1
1231	D.M.Benkenstein	c sub	2
1232	P.Mustard	c D.J.Thornely	2
1233	C.D.Thorp	c & b	2
1234	N.Killeen	c C.C.Benham	2
1235	M.L.Lewis	c M.A.Carberry	2

Hampshire v Lancashire, The Rose Bowl, Southampton, 20, 21, 22, 23, September 2006

1236	M.B.Loye	c M.J.Brown	2

Victoria v Western Australia, W.A.C.A. Ground, Perth, 15, 16, 17, 18, October 2006

1237	S.E.Marsh	lbw	1

Victoria v South Australia, Adelaide Oval, 27, 28, 29, 30, October 2006

1238	M.J.Cosgrove	c & b	1
1239	G.A.Manou	c C.L.White	1
1240	C.J.Borgas	b	1
1241	C.B.Bailey	lbw	1
1242	P.C.Rofe	lbw	1
1243	C.J.Borgas	c C.L.White	2

Victoria v Tasmania, Melbourne Cricket Ground, 14, 15, 16, 17, November 2006

1244	B.Geeves	c & b	1
1245	B.W.Hilfenhaus	lbw	1
1246	A.R.Griffith	c N.Jewell	1

***Australia v England, Brisbane Cricket Ground, Woolloongabba,
23, 24, 25, 26, 27, November 2006***

1247	I.R.Bell	lbw	2
1248	A.N.Cook	c M.E.K.Hussey	2
1249	P.D.Collingwood	st A.C.Gilchrist	2
1250	A.Flintoff	c J.L.Langer	2

***Australia v England, Adelaide Oval,
1, 2, 3, 4, 5, December 2006***

1251	G.O.Jones	c D.R.Martyn	1
1252	A.J.Strauss	c M.E.K.Hussey	2
1253	K.P.Pietersen	b	2
1254	A.F.Giles	c M.L.Hayden	2
1255	M.J.Hoggard	b	2

***Australia v England, W.A.C.A. Ground, Perth,
14, 15, 16, 17, 18, December 2006***

1256	M.J.Hoggard	c M.L.Hayden	1
1257	I.R.Bell	c J.L.Langer	2
1258	A.Flintoff	b	2
1259	S.J.Harmison	lbw	2
1260	M.S.Panesar	b	2

***Australia v England, Melbourne Cricket Ground,
26, 27, 28, December 2006***

1261	A.J.Strauss	b	1
1262	C.M.W.Read	c R.T.Ponting	1
1263	S.J.Harmison	c M.J.Clarke	1
1264	K.P.Pietersen	c A.Symonds	1
1265	M.S.Panesar	c A.Symonds	1
1266	S.I.Mahmood	lbw	2
1267	S.J.Harmison	lbw	2

***Australia v England, Sydney Cricket Ground,
2, 3, 4, 5, January 2007***

1268	M.S.Panesar	lbw	1
1269	A.Flintoff	st A.C.Gilchrist	2

How Warne captured his wickets:

Caught in field	553	43.58%
Leg before wicket	251	19.78%
Bowled	223	17.57%
Caught by wicket-keeper	120	9.46%

Stumped	81	6.38%
Caught and bowled	41	3.23%
Total	1269	100.00%

Warne's wickets:

14 A.J.Stewart

11 N.Hussain, A.G.Prince

10 M.A.Atherton, A.J.Strauss, G.P.Thorpe

9 M.V.Boucher, M.A.Butcher, A.R.Caddick, R.S.Dravid, A.F.Giles, S.J.Harmison, M.E.Trescothick

8 S.Chanderpaul, W.J.Cronje, P.A.J.DeFreitas, S.P.Fleming, D.Gough, B.C.Lara, C.D.McMillan, D.J.Richardson, Saqlain Mushtaq

7 N.J.Astle, A.Flintoff, H.H.Gibbs, J.H.Kallis, M.Ntini, D.L.Vettori

6 M.G.Bevan, T.M.Dilshan, S.B.Doull, G.A.Gooch, M.J.Hoggard, C.L.Hooper, V.V.S.Laxman, B.M.McMillan, K.P.Pietersen, S.M.Pollock, M.R.Ramprakash, H.P.Tillakaratne, W.P.U.J.C.Vaas, C.A.Walsh

5 Abdur Razzaq, J.Angel, Azhar Mahmood, I.R.Bell, C.L.Cairns, U.D.U.Chandana, Ijaz Ahmed, Inzamamul Haq, G.Kirsten, Rashid Latif, R.A.Smith, A.J.Tudor, Waqar Younis, Wasim Akram

4 J.C.Adams, Basit Ali, K.C.G.Benjamin, I.R.Bishop, N.Boje, J.Cox, R.D.B.Croft, D.J.Cullinan, A.B.de Villiers, M.J.di Venuto, Faisal Iqbal, M.W.Goodwin, A.Habib, C.Z.Harris, M.L.Hayden, D.L.Hemp, D.P.M.D.Jayawardene, A.H.Jones, G.O.Jones, R.W.T.Key, M.J.McCague, N.D.McKenzie, J.P.Maher, C.S.Martin, D.N.Patel, J.A.Rudolph, K.R.Rutherford, R.G.Samuels, K.C.Sangakkara, Shoaib Akhtar, H.H.Streak, M.A.Taylor, P.C.R.Tufnell, M.P.Vaughan, M.E.Waugh, C.White

3 Aamer Sohail, C.J.Adams, P.R.Adams, Akram Raza, C.E.L.Ambrose, K.L.T.Arthurton, C.J.Borgas, P.A.de Silva, P.S.de Villiers, A.A.Donald, P.A.Emery,D.A.Fitzgerald, J.E.C.Franklin, M.W.Gatting, T.H.C.Hancock, W.J.Holdsworth, A.J.Hollioake, R.S.Kaluwitharana, M.S.Kasprowicz,S.M.Katich, P.N.Kirsten, M.N.Lathwell, D.S.Lehmann, K.S.Lokuarachchi, B.B.McCullum, H.J.H.Marshall, C.R.Matthews, M.P.Maynard, Misbah-ul Haq, T.M.Moody, M.Muralidaran, P.Mustard, A.Nel, P.A.Nixon, M.J.North, J.Ormond, M.B.Owens, M.S.Panesar, A.C.Parore, P.A.Patel, M.J.Prior, Rameez Raja, S.Ramesh, J.N.Rhodes, R.B.Richardson, Saeed Anwar, B.J.M.Scott, J.C.Scuderi, W.A.Seccombe, V.K.Sehwag, O.A.Shah, J.D.Siddons, E.T.Smith, G.C.Smith, N.J.Speak, S.B.Styris, M.L.Su'a, P.M.Such, S.R.Tendulkar, J.O.Troughton, S.D.Udal, P.N.Weekes, K.C.Wessels, G.P.Wickramasinghe, P.J.Wiseman

2 Aaqib Javed, G.I.Allott, M.S.Atapattu, A.M.Bacher, G.J.Bailey,
J.N.Batty, W.K.M.Benjamin, D.M.Benkenstein, M.M.Betts,
T.E.Blain, E.A.Brandes, J.A.Brayshaw, G.L.Brophy, D.R.Brown,
D.Byas, D.D.Cherry, P.D.Collingwood, C.D.Collymore, S.J.Cook,
J.P.Crawley, H.D.P.K.Dharmasena, S.S.Dighe, H.H.Dippenaar,
X.J.Doherty, F.H.Edwards, G.M.Fellows, C.J.Ferguson, A.Flower,
N.A.Folland, D.P.Fulton, J.E.R.Gallian, S.C.Ganguly, O.D.Gibson,
D.R.Gilbert, A.C.Gilchrist, G.M.Hamilton, Harbhajan Singh,
B.C.Hollioake, P.C.L.Holloway, A.G.Huckle, J.Hughes, B.L.Hutton,
Imran Nazir, S.T.Jayasuriya, E.C.Joyce, B.P.Julian, Kamran Akmal,
J.M.Kemp, N.Killeen, R.D.King, L.Klusener, J.L.Langer, C.C.Lewis,
J.D.Lewry, A.McGrath, R.J.J.McLean, D.E.Malcolm, D.R.Martyn,
D.J.Marsh, R.S.C.Martin-Jenkins, Mashrafe Bin Mortaza,
D.D.Masters, G.D.Mendis, Mohammad Akram, Mohammad
Ashraful, Mohammad Sami, Mohsin Kamal, D.K.Morrison,
G.J.Muchall, T.A.Munton, Mushtaq Ahmed, A.A.Noffke, J.L.Ontong,
M.M.Patel, I.K.Pathan, B.P.Patterson, C.T.Perren, D.J.Pipe,
B.A.Pocock, D.B.Powell, M.J.Powell(Gm), J.V.Paranjpe,
A.Ranatunga, J.D.Ratcliffe, C.M.W.Read, S.J.Rhodes, P.E.Robinson,
R.C.Russell, J.L.Sadler, R.J.Sidebottom, N.S.Sidhu,
C.E.W.Silverwood, P.V.Simmons, M.S.Sinclair, M.J.Slater, B.F.Smith
J.Srinath, D.I.Stevens, S.D.Stubbings, P.L.Symcox, A.Symonds,
R.J.Tucker, R.J.Turner, M.R.J.Veletta, M.J.Walker, T.R.Ward, A.P.Wells,
A.G.Wharf, G.J.Whittall, S.C.Williams, Yasir Hameed, Younis Khan,
B.A.Young, S.Young, Yousuf Youhana, T.J.Zoehrer, D.N.T.Zoysa

1 A.R.Adams, Aftab Ahmed, U.Afzaal, A.B.Agarkar, P.Aldred,
D.Alleyne, H.A.G.Anthony, S.D.Anurasiri, R.P.Arnold, K.J.Arnott,
J.M.Arthur, Ata-ur-Rehman, I.D.Austin, J.M.M.Averis, M.Azharuddin,
C.B.Bailey, M.D.Bailey, T.J.Barsby, T.H.Bayliss, M.D.Bell,
J.E.Benjamin, D.J.Bicknell, T.R.Birt, I.D.Blackwell, G.S.Blewett,
D.C.Boon, R.S.Bopara, A.R.Border, D.G.Brandy, D.J.J.Bravo,
T.T.Bresnan, G.D.Bridge, B.C.Broad, A.D.Brown, C.O.Browne,
S.J.E.Brown, M.L.Bruyns, M.G.Burmester, R.Q.Cake,
A.D.R.Campbell, S.L.Campbell, N.M.Carter, M.E.Cassar,
G.Chapple, R.Chee Quee, V.P.Clarke, S.G.Clingeleffer, R.S.Clinton,
K.J.Coetzer, A.N.Cook, S.H.Cook, M.J.Cosgrove, D.A.Cosker,
P.A.Cottey, G.R.Cowdrey, M.D.Crowe, B.A.Cruse, D.J.Cullen,
A.C.Cummins, R.J.Cunliffe, D.B.D'Oliveira, J.M.Dakin, A.Dale,
J.A.Daley, J.W.M.Dalrymple, Danish Kaneria, R.P.Davis, R.I.Dawson,
R.K.J.Dawson, R.P.de Groen, S.I.de Saram, K.J.Dean, D.M.Dempsey,
M.G.Dighton, D.J.Doran, B.J.Drew, S.C.Ecclestone, M.T.G.Elliott,
Enamul Haque, I.D.Fisher, M.V.Fleming, G.W.Flower, G.I.Foley,
J.S.Foster, N.A.Foster, J.D.Francis, P.J.Franks, T.Frost, A.I.Gait,
I.S.Gallage, B.Geeves, S.P.George, J.N.Gillespie, R.N.Grant,
A.R.Griffith, T.R.Gripper, Habibul Bashar, A.J.Hall, M.A.Hardinges,
R.A.Harper, A.J.Harris, D.J.Harris, D.S.Harrison, C.D.Hartley,
U.C.Hathurusingha, A.N.Hayhurst, R.C.Haynes, I.A.Healy,
C.W.Henderson, T.Henderson, H.M.R.K.B.Herath, R.P.Hewage,

G.A.Hick, D.J.Hickey, J.C.Hildreth, B.W.Hilfenhaus, D.F.Hills,
W.W.Hinds, B.J.Hodge, R.I.C.Holder, N.P.Hough, D.L.Houghton,
A.C.Hudson, G.A.Hughes, M.E.K.Hussey, Imran Farhat,
K.C.Jackson, R.D.Jacobs, M.P.Jarvis, H.A.P.W.Jayawardene,
N.C.Johnson, R.L.Johnson, D.M.Jones, P.S.Jones, S.P.Jones,
L.A.Joseph, R.H.Joseph, V.G.Kambli, H.H.Kanitkar, S.J.Karppinen,
C.B.Keegan, W.S.Kendall, D.A.Kenway, G.J.Kersey, R.J.Kirtley,
S.P.Kremerskothen, K.M.Krikken, G.J.Kruis, A.Kumble, S.J.Lacey,
G.A.Lamb, A.W.Laraman, M.P.Lavender, S.G.Law, J.J.C.Lawson,
S.Lee, J.J.B.Lewis, M.L.Lewis, R.N.Lewis, G.D.Lloyd, A.L.Logie,
A.G.R.Loudon, J.Louw, M.L.Love, G.B.T.Lovell, M.B.Loye, M.J.Lumb,
M.A.Lynch, N.C.McGarrell, S.C.G.MacGill, G.D.McGrath
P.E.McIntyre, N.A.M.McLean, G.I.Macmillan, D.A.McNees,
M.A.W.R.Madurasinghe, S.I.Mahmood, S.L.Malinga,
G.A.Manou, Manzoor Akhtar, G.R.Marsh, S.E.Marsh, J.A.H.Marshall,
A.D.Mascarenhas, C.D.Matthews, G.R.J.Matthews, J.K.Maunders,
J.D.Middlebrook, K.D.Mills, Mohammad Khalil, Mohammad
Rafique, Moin Khan, N.R.Mongia, R.R.Montgomerie, B.D.Moore
Gordon, R.F.Morris, M.P.Mott, A.J.Murphy, J.R.Murray,
A.A.Muzumdar, Naved-ul-Hasan, P.C.Nobes, I.E.O'Brien,
N.J.O'Brien, J.D.P.Oram, K.A.Parsons, S.A.Patterson, N.Peng,
M.M.D.N.R.G.Perera, P.D.R.L.Perera, C.A.Philipson, W.Phillip,
N.C.Phillips, A.R.K.Pierson, B.T.Player, L.E.Plunkett, J.C.Pooley,
S.C.Pope, R.R.Powar, M.J.Powell(Wa), M.S.K.Prasad, D.Pretorius,
A.J.Pycroft, P.J.L.Radley, Rajin Saleh, D.C.Ramdin, D.C.Rampersad,
B.A.Reid, S.J.Renshaw, M.H.Richardson, P.C.Rofe, C.J.L.Rogers,
A.S.Rollins, J.S.Roos, M.J.Saggers, Saleem Malik, M.N.Samuels,
J.J.Sayers, K.F.Semple, Shahadat Hossain, Shahriar Nafees,
R.J.Shastri, S.F.Shephard, A.Sheriyar, Shoaib Malik, C.E.Shreck,
L.P.C.Silva, M.G.Sinclair, M.P.Smethurst, A.M.Smith, D.Smith,
D.R.Smith, G.J.Smith, R.P.Snell, CM.Spearman, M.P.Speight,
D.J.Spencer, A.M.Stuart, S.W.Tait, D.Taljard, C.J.Tavaré, C.G.Taylor,
S.D.Thomas, C.D.Thorp, P.D.Trego, I.J.L.Trott, S.B.Tubb, R.G.Twose,
A.P.van Troost, L.Vincent, M.A.Wallace, M.J.Walsh, D.M.Ward,
I.J.Ward, R.J.Warren, Wasim Jaffer, S.L.Watkin, D.J.Watson,
S.R.Watson, W.Watson, S.R.Waugh, V.J.Wells, I.J.Westwood,
L.J.Wharton, J.J.Whitaker, B.N.Wigney, J.R.Wileman, D.Williams,
L.Williams, W.K.Wishart, K.A.Wong, J.Wood, A.J.Wright, D.G.Wright,
J.G.Wright, Yasir Arafat, Yuvraj Singh, Zaheer Khan, Zahid Fazal.

How Warne was dismissed in first class cricket:

Caught in field......................172 ....51.19%
Leg before wicket..................46 ....13.69%
Caught by wicket-keeper.......45 ....13.39%
Bowled ....33 ....9.82%
Stumped..............................16 ....4.76%
Run out...............................13 ....3.87%
Caught and bowled ....10 ....2.98%
Hit wicket..............................1 ....0.30%

Total.................................336 ....100.00%

Bowlers Who Claimed Warne's Wicket:

9   D.L.Vettori

8   I.R.Bishop, A.R.Caddick

6   A.Flintoff, Harbhajan Singh, A.Kumble, C.A.Walsh

5   C.E.L.Ambrose, J.Angel, D.Gough, C.L.Hooper, S.M.Pollock,
    Saqlain Mushtaq

4   Danish Kaneria, A.A.Donald, A.R.C.Fraser

3   Aamer Sohail, P.R.Adams, R.D.B.Croft, M.A.Ealham, J.N.Gillespie,
    S.J.Harmison, C.W.Henderson, H.M.R.K.B.Herath, M.Muralidaran,
    M.Ntini, Shoaib Akhtar, W.P.U.J.C.Vaas

2   S.D.Anurasiri, N.Boje, D.R.Brown, C.L.Cairns, U.D.U.Chandana,
    P.A.J.DeFreitas, P.S.De Villiers, D.A.Freedman, A.F.Giles,
    A.R.Griffith, M.J.Hoggard, P.W.Jackson, B.P.Julian, S.P.Jones,
    S.J.Lacey, S.Lee, M.J.McCague, P.E.McIntyre, D.E.Malcolm,
    C.R.Matthews, J.D.Middlebrook, D.K.Morrison, A.Nel, M.M.Patel,
    L.E.Plunkett, D.B.Powell, C.E.Shreck, J.Srinath, S.B.Styris,
    R.L.Sanghvi, C.D.Thorp, R.J.Tucker, S.L.Venkatapathy Raju, Wasim
    Akram, M.E.Waugh

1   Abdul Razzaq, A.R.Adams, J.C.Adams, A.B.Agarkar, W.S.Andrews,
    NJ.Astle, S.V.Bahutule, A.A.Barnett, K.C.G.Benjamin, M.M.Betts,
    D.J.J.Bravo, T.T.Bresnan, S.J.E.Brown, M.A.Butcher, R.K.Chauhan,
    P.T.Collins, C.D.Collymore, D.A.Cosker, W.J.Cronje, J.H.Dawes,
    R.K.J.Dawson, X.J.Doherty, D.J.Doran, K.P.Dutch, J.E.Emburey,
    Enamul Haque, M.V.Fleming, J.E.C.Franklin, P.J.Franks,
    A.P.R.Gidman, A.J.Hall, J.C.Hallett, G.M.Hamilton, R.J.Harris,
    A.K.Heal, N.C.Johnson, R.H.Joseph, J.H.Kallis, Kapil Dev,
    M.Kartik, M.S.Kasprowicz, J.M.Kemp, R.D.King, S.P.Kirby, R.J.Kirtley,
    L.Klusener, N.M.Kulkarni, S.R.Lampitt, C.K.Langeveldt,
    A.W.Laraman, S.G.Law, M.A.K.Lawson, C.C.Lewis, J.Lewis,
    M.L.Lewis, R.J.Logan, K.S.Lokuarachchi, A.G.R.Loudon, J.Louw,
    G.D.McGrath, B.M.McMillan, B.E.McNamara, D.L.Maddy,

S.L.Malinga, Manzoor Akhtar, R.S.C.Martin-Jenkins, D.D.Masters,
C.R.Miller, D.J.Millns, Mohammad Akram, Mohammad Ali,
Mohammad Rafique, Mohsin Kamal, A.D.Mullally, Mushtaq Ahmed,
M.V.Nagamootoo, G.R.Napier, S.B.O'Connor, A.H.Omarshah,
M.S.Panesar, N.O.Perry, K.R.Pushpakumara, C.T.Peploe,
A.R.K.Pierson, C.Pringle, C.P.H.Ramanayake, M.J.Rawnsley,
J.A.Rennie, G.D.Rose, I.D.K.Salisbury, J.E.K.Schofield, B.N.Schultz,
J.C.Scuderi, R.J.Sidebottom, P.R.Sleep, A.M.Smith, J.N.Snape,
J.P.Stephenson, S.C.Storey, H.H.Streak, A.M.Stuart, P.M.Such,
P.L.Symcox, S.R.Tendulkar, S.D.Thomas, A.J.Tudor, P.C.R.Tufnell,
A.P.van Troost, H.R.J.Trump, D.R.Tuffey, J.F.Venter, Waqar
Younis, D.J.Wates, S.R.Watson, V.J.Wells, B.M.White, M.R.Whitney,
G.P.Wickramasinghe, K.I.W.Wijegunawardene, B.A.Williams,
R.C.Williams, P.Wilson, W.K.Wishart, Yasir Arafat, S.Young,
D.N.T.Zoysa.

SHANE WARNE'S TEST RECORD

BATTING AND FIELDING RECORD IN EACH SERIES

Series (Opp)	M	I	NO	Runs	HS	Avge	100s	50s	0s	C
1991-92I	2	4	1	28	20	9.33	0	0	1	1
1992-93SL	2	3	0	66	35	22.00	0	0	0	1
1992-93W	4	7	0	42	14	6.00	0	0	2	3
1992-93N	3	4	2	49	22*	24.50	0	0	0	1
1993E	6	5	2	113	37	37.66	0	0	0	4
1993-94N	3	2	1	85	74*	85.00	0	1	0	4
1993-94SA	3	4	1	16	11	5.33	0	0	1	2
1993-94SA	3	5	0	41	15	8.20	0	0	0	0
1994-95P	3	4	0	69	33	17.25	0	0	1	2
1994-95E	5	10	1	60	36*	6.66	0	0	3	5
1994-95W	4	5	0	28	11	5.60	0	0	2	2
1995-96P	3	4	1	39	27*	13.00	0	0	0	0
1995-96SL	3	1	0	33	33	33.00	0	0	0	5
1996-97W	5	7	0	128	30	18.28	0	0	0	6
1996-97SA	3	5	0	42	18	8.40	0	0	1	3
1997E	6	10	0	188	53	18.80	0	1	3	2
1997-98N	3	3	0	71	36	23.66	0	0	0	0
1997-98SA	3	5	1	27	12	6.75	0	0	1	5
1997-98I	3	5	0	105	35	21.00	0	0	0	0
1998-99E	1	2	1	10	8	10.00	0	0	0	2
1998-99W	3	6	0	138	32	23.00	0	0	0	3
1999-2000SL	3	4	0	6	6	1.50	0	0	3	2
1999-2000Z	1	1	0	6	6	6.00	0	0	0	0
1999-2000P	3	4	1	99	86	33.00	0	1	1	4
1999-2000I	3	3	0	88	86	29.33	0	1	1	3
1999-2000N	3	4	0	36	12	9.00	0	0	0	4
2000-01I	3	5	0	50	39	10.00	0	0	3	2
2001E	5	4	0	13	8	3.25	0	0	2	6
2001-02N	3	4	0	201	99	50.25	0	2	0	4
2001-02SA	3	4	0	85	41	21.25	0	0	0	2
2001-02SA	3	5	1	129	63	32.25	0	1	0	5
2002-03P	3	4	0	30	19	7.50	0	0	2	2
2002-03E	3	3	0	117	57	39.00	0	1	0	1
2003-04SL	3	6	0	79	32	13.16	0	0	2	3
2004-05SL	2	4	0	9	4	2.25	0	0	0	4
2004-05I	3	5	0	38	31	7.60	0	0	1	4
2004-05N	2	2	1	63	53*	63.00	0	1	0	4

Series (Opp)	M	I	NO	Runs	HS	Avge	100s	50s	0s	C
2004-05P	3	3	0	38	16	12.66	0	0	0	5
2004-05N	3	3	1	53	50*	26.50	0	1	0	1
2005E	5	9	0	249	90	27.66	0	1	2	5
2005-06W	3	3	0	48	47	16.00	0	0	1	5
2005-06SA	3	5	1	38	24	9.50	0	0	1	1
2005-06SA	3	4	0	82	36	20.50	0	0	0	1
2005-06B	2	2	0	11	6	5.50	0	0	0	1
2006-07E	5	5	1	196	71	49.00	0	1	0	5
TOTAL	144	197	17	3142	99	17.45	0	12	34	125

BATTING AND FIELDING RECORD IN EACH INNINGS

	I	NO	Runs	HS	Avge	100s	50s	0s	C
1st Innings	136	11	2411	99	19.28	0	11	23	71
2nd Innings	61	6	731	53	13.29	0	1	11	54
TOTAL	144	197	17	3142	99	17.45	0	12	34	125

BATTING AND FIELDING RECORD AGAINST EACH COUNTRY

Opponent	M	I	NO	Runs	HS	Avge	100s	50s	0s	C
Bangladesh	2	2	0	11	6	5.50	0	0	0	1
England	36	48	5	946	90	22.00	0	4	10	30
India	14	22	1	309	86	14.71	0	1	6	10
New Zealand	20	22	5	558	99	32.82	0	5	0	18
Pakistan	15	19	2	275	86	16.17	0	1	4	13
South Africa	24	37	4	460	63	13.93	0	1	4	19
Sri Lanka	13	18	0	193	35	10.72	0	0	5	15
West Indies	19	28	0	384	47	13.71	0	0	5	19
Zimbabwe	1	1	0	6	6	6.00	0	0	0	0
TOTAL	144	197	17	3142	99	17.45	0	12	34	125

Bangladesh	M	I	NO	Runs	HS	Avge	100s	50s	0s	C
2005-06B	2	2	0	11	6	5.50	0	0	0	1

England	M	I	NO	Runs	HS	Avge	100s	50s	0s	C
1993E	6	5	2	113	37	37.66	0	0	0	4
1994-95E	5	10	1	60	36*	6.66	0	0	3	5

	M	I	NO	Runs	HS	Avge	100s	50s	0s	C
1997E	6	10	0	188	53	18.80	0	1	3	2
1998-99E	1	2	1	10	8	10.00	0	0	0	2
2001E	5	4	0	13	8	3.25	0	0	2	6
2002-03E	3	3	0	117	57	39.00	0	1	0	1
2005E	5	9	0	249	90	27.66	0	1	2	5
2006-07E	5	5	1	196	71	49.00	0	1	0	5
In Australia	14	20	3	383	71	22.52	0	2	3	13
In England	22	28	2	563	90	21.65	0	2	7	17
TOTAL	36	48	5	946	90	22.00	0	4	10	30

India	M	I	NO	Runs	HS	Avge	100s	50s	0s	C
1991-92I	2	4	1	28	20	9.33	0	0	1	1
1997-98I	3	5	0	105	35	21.00	0	0	0	0
1999-2000I	3	3	0	88	86	29.33	0	1	1	3
2000-01I	3	5	0	50	39	10.00	0	0	3	2
2004-05I	3	5	0	38	31	7.60	0	0	1	4
In Australia	5	7	1	116	86	19.33	0	1	2	4
In India	9	15	0	193	39	12.86	0	0	4	6
TOTAL	14	22	1	309	86	14.71	0	1	6	10

New Zealand	M	I	NO	Runs	HS	Avge	100s	50s	0s	C
1992-93N	3	4	2	49	22*	24.50	0	0	0	1
1993-94N	3	2	1	85	74*	85.00	0	1	0	4
1997-98N	3	3	0	71	36	23.66	0	0	0	0
1999-2000N	3	4	0	36	12	9.00	0	0	0	4
2001-02N	3	4	0	201	99	50.25	0	2	0	4
2004-05N	2	2	1	63	53*	63.00	0	1	0	4
2004-05N	3	3	1	53	50*	26.50	0	1	0	1
In Australia	11	11	2	420	99	46.66	0	4	0	12
In New Zealand	9	11	3	138	50*	17.25	0	1	0	6
TOTAL	20	22	5	558	99	32.82	0	5	0	18

Pakistan	M	I	NO	Runs	HS	Avge	100s	50s	0s	C
1994-95P	3	4	0	69	33	17.25	0	0	1	2
1995-96P	3	4	1	39	27*	13.00	0	0	0	0
1999-2000P	3	4	1	99	86	33.00	0	1	1	4
2002-03P	3	4	0	30	19	7.50	0	0	2	2
2004-05P	3	3	0	38	16	12.66	0	0	0	5
In Australia	9	11	2	176	86	19.55	0	1	1	9
In Pakistan	3	4	0	69	33	17.25	0	0	1	2
In Sri Lanka	1	2	0	0	0	0.00	0	0	2	0
In U.A.E.	2	2	0	30	19	15.00	0	0	0	2
TOTAL	15	19	2	275	86	16.17	0	1	4	13

South Africa	M	I	NO	Runs	HS	Avge	100s	50s	0s	C
1993-94SA	3	4	1	16	11	5.33	0	0	1	2
1993-94SA	3	5	0	41	15	8.20	0	0	0	0
1996-97SA	3	5	0	42	18	8.40	0	0	1	3
1997-98SA	3	5	1	27	12	6.75	0	0	1	5
2001-02SA	3	4	0	85	41	21.25	0	0	0	2
2001-02SA	3	5	1	129	63	32.25	0	1	0	5
2005-06SA	3	5	1	38	24	9.50	0	0	1	1
2005-06SA	3	4	0	82	36	20.50	0	0	0	1
In Australia	12	18	3	166	0	11.06	0	0	3	10
In South Africa	12	19	1	294	36	16.33	0	1	1	9
TOTAL	24	37	4	460	63	13.93	0	1	4	19

Sri Lanka	M	I	NO	Runs	HS	Avge	100s	50s	0s	C
1992-93SL	2	3	0	66	35	22.00	0	0	0	1
1995-96SL	3	1	0	33	33	33.00	0	0	0	5
1999-2000SL	3	4	0	6	6	1.50	0	0	3	2
2003-04SL	3	6	0	79	32	13.16	0	0	2	3
2004-05SL	2	4	0	9	4	2.25	0	0	0	4

In Australia	5	5	0	42	33	8.40	0	0	0	9
In Sri Lanka	8	13	0	151	32	11.61	0	0	5	6
TOTAL	13	18	0	193	35	10.72	0	0	5	15

West Indies	M	I	NO	Runs	HS	Avge	100s	50s	0s	C
1992-93W	4	7	0	42	14	6.00	0	0	2	3
1994-95W	4	5	0	28	11	5.60	0	0	2	2
1996-97W	5	7	0	128	30	18.28	0	0	0	6
1998-99W	3	6	0	138	32	23.00	0	0	0	3
2005-06W	3	3	0	48	47	16.00	0	0	1	5
In Australia	12	17	0	218	47	12.82	0	0	3	14
In West Indies	7	11	0	166	32	15.09	0	0	2	5
TOTAL	19	28	0	384	47	13.71	0	0	5	19

Zimbabwe	M	I	NO	Runs	HS	Avge	100s	50s	0s	C
1999-2000Z	1	1	0	6	6	6.00	0	0	0	0

BATTING AND FIELDING RECORD IN EACH COUNTRY

Country	M	I	NO	Runs	HS	Avge	100s	50s	0s	C
Australia	68	89	11	1521	99	19.50	0	8	12	71
Bangladesh	2	2	0	11	6	5.50	0	0	0	1
England	22	28	2	563	90	21.65	0	2	7	17
India	9	15	0	193	39	12.86	0	0	4	6
New Zealand	9	11	3	138	50*	17.25	0	1	0	6
Pakistan	3	4	0	69	33	17.25	0	0	1	2
South Africa	12	19	1	294	63	16.33	0	1	1	9
Sri Lanka	9	15	0	151	35	10.06	0	0	7	6
U.A.E.	2	2	0	30	19	15.00	0	0	0	2
West Indies	7	11	0	166	32	15.09	0	0	2	5
Zimbabwe	1	1	0	6	6	6.00	0	0	0	0
TOTAL	144	197	17	3142	99	17.45	0	12	34	125

Australia	M	I	NO	Runs	HS	Avge	100s	50s	0s	C
1991-92I	2	4	1	28	20	9.33	0	0	1	1
1992-93W	4	7	0	42	14	6.00	0	0	2	3
1993-94N	3	2	1	85	74*	85.00	0	1	0	4
1993-94SA	3	4	1	16	11	5.33	0	0	1	2
1994-95E	5	10	1	60	36*	6.66	0	0	3	5
1995-96P	3	4	1	39	27*	13.00	0	0	0	0
1995-96SL	3	1	0	33	33	33.00	0	0	0	5
1996-97W	5	7	0	128	30	18.28	0	0	0	6
1997-98N	3	3	0	71	36	23.66	0	0	0	0
1997-98SA	3	5	1	27	12	6.75	0	0	1	5
1998-99E	1	2	1	10	8	10.00	0	0	0	2
1999-2000P	3	4	1	99	86	33.00	0	1	1	4
1999-2000I	3	3	0	88	86	29.33	0	1	1	3
2001-02N	3	4	0	201	99	50.25	0	2	0	4
2001-02SA	3	4	0	85	41	21.25	0	0	0	2
2002-03E	3	3	0	117	57	39.00	0	1	0	1
2004-05SL	2	4	0	9	4	2.25	0	0	0	4
2004-05N	2	2	1	63	53*	63.00	0	1	0	4
2004-05P	3	3	0	38	16	12.66	0	0	0	5
2005-06W	3	3	0	48	47	16.00	0	0	1	5
2005-06SA	3	5	1	38	24	9.50	0	0	1	1
2006-07E	5	5	1	196	71	49.00	0	1	0	5
TOTAL	68	89	11	1521	99	19.50	0	8	12	71

Bangladesh	M	I	NO	Runs	HS	Avge	100s	50s	0s	C
2005-06B	2	2	0	11	6	5.50	0	0	0	1

England	M	I	NO	Runs	HS	Avge	100s	50s	0s	C
1993E	6	5	2	113	37	37.66	0	0	0	4
1997E	6	10	0	188	53	18.80	0	1	3	2
2001E	5	4	0	13	8	3.25	0	0	2	6
2005E	5	9	0	249	90	27.66	0	1	2	5
TOTAL	22	28	2	563	90	21.65	0	2	7	17

India	M	I	NO	Runs	HS	Avge	100s	50s	0s	C
1997-98I	3	5	0	105	35	21.00	0	0	0	0
2000-01I	3	5	0	50	39	10.00	0	0	3	2
2004-05I	3	5	0	38	31	7.60	0	0	1	4
TOTAL	9	15	0	193	39	12.86	0	0	4	6

New Zealand	M	I	NO	Runs	HS	Avge	100s	50s	0s	C
1992-93N	3	4	2	49	22*	24.50	0	0	0	1
1999-2000N	3	4	0	36	12	9.00	0	0	0	4
2004-05N	3	3	1	53	50*	26.50	0	1	0	1
TOTAL	9	11	3	138	50*	17.25	0	1	0	6

Pakistan	M	I	NO	Runs	HS	Avge	100s	50s	0s	C
1994-95P	3	4	0	69	33	17.25	0	0	1	2

South Africa	M	I	NO	Runs	HS	Avge	100s	50s	0s	C
1993-94SA	3	5	0	41	15	8.20	0	0	0	0
1996-97SA	3	5	0	42	18	8.40	0	0	1	3
2001-02SA	3	5	1	129	63	32.25	0	1	0	5
2005-06SA	3	4	0	82	36	20.50	0	0	0	1
TOTAL	12	19	1	294	63	16.33	0	1	1	9

Sri Lanka	M	I	NO	Runs	HS	Avge	100s	50s	0s	C
1992-93SL	2	3	0	66	35	22.00	0	0	0	1
1999-2000SL	3	4	0	6	6	1.50	0	0	3	2
2002-03P	1	2	0	0	0	0.00	0	0	2	0
2003-04SL	3	6	0	79	32	13.16	0	0	2	3
TOTAL	9	15	0	151	35	10.06	0	0	7	6

U.A.E.	M	I	NO	Runs	HS	Avge	100s	50s	0s	C
2002-03P	2	2	0	30	19	15.00	0	0	0	2

West Indies	M	I	NO	Runs	HS	Avge	100s	50s	0s	C
1994-95W	4	5	0	28	11	5.60	0	0	2	2
1998-99W	3	6	0	138	32	23.00	0	0	0	3
TOTAL	7	11	0	166	32	15.09	0	0	2	5

Zimbabwe	M	I	NO	Runs	HS	Avge	100s	50s	0s	C
1999-2000Z	1	1	0	6	6	6.00	0	0	0	0

BATTING AND FIELDING RECORD ON EACH GROUND

Australia	M	I	NO	Runs	HS	Avge	100s	50s	0s	C
Adelaide	13	19	3	329	86	20.56	0	2	5	14
Brisbane	11	12	1	365	86	33.18	0	3	1	15
Cairns	1	2	0	6	4	3.00	0	0	0	3
Darwin	1	2	0	3	2	1.50	0	0	0	1
Hobart	6	6	2	112	70	28.00	0	1	1	6
Melbourne	11	15	2	113	40*	8.69	0	0	2	7
Perth	12	16	0	329	99	20.56	0	1	1	15
Sydney	13	17	3	264	71	18.85	0	1	2	10
TOTAL	68	89	11	1521	99	19.50	0	8	12	71

Bangladesh	M	I	NO	Runs	HS	Avge	100s	50s	0s	C
Fatullah	1	2	0	11	6	5.50	0	0	0	0
Chittagong	1					-	0	0	0	1
TOTAL	2	2	0	11	6	5.50	0	0	0	1

England	M	I	NO	Runs	HS	Avge	100s	50s	0s	C
Birmingham	4	6	0	147	47	24.50	0	0	0	3
Leeds	3	2	0	0	0	0.00	0	0	2	2
Lord's	4	4	0	35	28	8.75	0	0	1	4
Manchester	3	5	1	195	90	48.75	0	2	0	1
Nottingham	4	6	1	100	45	20.00	0	0	3	0
The Oval	4	5	0	86	37	17.20	0	0	1	7
TOTAL	22	28	2	563	90	21.65	0	2	7	17

India	M	I	NO	Runs	HS	Avge	100s	50s	0s	C
Bangalore	2	3	0	65	33	21.66	0	0	0	0
Chennai	3	6	0	67	35	11.16	0	0	2	2
Kolkata	2	4	0	20	11	5.00	0	0	2	0
Mumbai	1	1	0	39	39	39.00	0	0	0	1
Nagpur	1	1	0	2	2	2.00	0	0	0	3
TOTAL	9	15	0	193	39	12.86	0	0	4	6

New Zealand	M	I	NO	Runs	HS	Avge	100s	50s	0s	C
Auckland	3	5	1	25	12	6.25	0	0	0	2
Christchurch	2	2	1	24	22*	24.00	0	0	0	0
Hamilton	1	1	0	10	10	10.00	0	0	0	1
Wellington	3	3	1	79	50*	39.50	0	1	0	3
TOTAL	9	11	3	138	50*	17.25	0	1	0	6

Pakistan	M	I	NO	Runs	HS	Avge	100s	50s	0s	C
Karachi	1	2	0	22	22	11.00	0	0	1	1
Lahore	1	1	0	33	33	33.00	0	0	0	0
Rawalpindi	1	1	0	14	14	14.00	0	0	0	1
TOTAL	3	4	0	69	33	17.25	0	0	1	2

South Africa	M	I	NO	Runs	HS	Avge	100s	50s	0s	C
Cape Town	3	4	1	96	63	32.00	0	1	0	1
Centurion	1	2	0	12	12	6.00	0	0	1	0
Durban	3	5	0	89	36	17.80	0	0	0	3
Johannesburg	4	6	0	76	36	12.66	0	0	0	2
Port Elizabeth	1	2	0	21	18	10.50	0	0	0	3
TOTAL	12	19	1	294	63	16.33	0	1	1	9

Sri Lanka	M	I	NO	Runs	HS	Avge	100s	50s	0s	C
Colombo,PSS	1	2	0	0	0	0.00	0	0	2	0
Colombo,SSC	3	5	0	91	35	18.20	0	0	2	3
Galle	2	3	0	23	23	7.66	0	0	2	2
Kandy	2	4	0	30	18	7.50	0	0	1	1
Moratuwa	1	1	0	7	7	7.00	0	0	0	0
TOTAL	9	15	0	151	35	10.06	0	0	7	6

U.A.E.	M	I	NO	Runs	HS	Avge	100s	50s	0s	C
Sharjah	2	2	0	30	19	15.00	0	0	0	2

West Indies	M	I	NO	Runs	HS	Avge	100s	50s	0s	C
Bridgetown	2	3	0	51	32	17.00	0	0	0	2
Kingston	2	3	0	47	24	15.66	0	0	1	1
Port-of-Spain	2	4	0	57	25	14.25	0	0	1	2
St John's	1	1	0	11	11	11.00	0	0	0	0
TOTAL	7	11	0	166	32	15.09	0	0	2	5

Zimbabwe	M	I	NO	Runs	HS	Avge	100s	50s	0s	C
Harare	1	1	0	6	6	6.00	0	0	0	0

The following bowlers captured Warne's wicket:

9 D.L.Vettori(N)

8 I.R.Bishop(W)

6 A.R.Caddick(E), A.Kumble(I), C.A.Walsh(W)

5 C.E.L.Ambrose(W), D.Gough(E), Harbhajan Singh(I), S.M.Pollock(SA)

4 A.A.Donald(SA), A.R.C.Fraser(E)

3 Aamer Sohail(P), P.R.Adams(SA), M.A.Ealham(E), A.Flintoff(E), S.J.Harmison(E), M.Muralidaran(SL), M.Ntini(SA), Saqlain Mushtaq(P), Shoaib Akhtar(P), W.P.U.J.C.Vaas(SL)

2 S.D.Anurasiri(SL), N.Boje(SA), C.L.Cairns(N), U.D.U.Chandana(SL), Danish Kaneria(P), P.A.J.DeFreitas(E), P.S.de Villiers(SA), A.F.Giles(E), H.M.R.K.B.Herath(SL), C.L.Hooper(W), S.P.Jones(E), D.E.Malcolm(E), C.R.Matthews(SA), D.K.Morrison(N), A.Nel(SA), M.S.Panesar(E), D.B.Powell(W), J.Srinath(I), S.L.Venkatapathy Raju(I), Wasim Akram(P)

1 Abdur Razzaq(P), A.B.Agarkar(I), N.J.Astle(N), K.C.G.Benjamin(W), D.J.J.Bravo(W), M.A.Butcher(E), R.K.Chauhan(I), P.T.Collins(W), R.D.B.Croft(E), W.J.Cronje(SA), R.K.J.Dawson(E), J.E.Emburey(E), Enamul Haque[2](B), J.E.C.Franklin(N), C.W.Henderson(SA), M.J.Hoggard(E), J.H.Kallis(SA), Kapil Dev(I), M.Kartik(I), J.M.Kemp(SA), L.Klusener(SA), C.K.Langeveldt(SA), C.C.Lewis(E), B.M.McMillan(SA), S.L.Malinga(SL), Mohammad Rafique(B), Mohsin Kamal(P), Mushtaq Ahmed(P), S.B.O'Connor(N), N.O.Perry(W), C.P.H.Ramanayake(SL), R.L.Sanghvi(I), B.N.Schultz(SA), H.H.Streak(Z), P.M.Such(E), P.L.Symcox(SA), S.R.Tendulkar(I), P.C.R.Tufnell(E), Waqar Younis(P), G.P.Wickramasinghe(SL), D.N.T.Zoysa(SL)

The details of Warne's dismissals are:

Caught .... 85 .... 47.22%
Leg before wicket .... 30 .... 16.67%
Caught by wicket-keeper .... 29 .... 16.11%
Bowled .... 12 .... 6.67%
Caught and bowled .... 11 .... 6.11%
Run out .... 6 .... 3.33%
Stumped .... 6 .... 3.33%
Hit wicket .... 1 .... 0.56%

TOTAL .... 180 .... 100.00%

BOWLING RECORD IN EACH SERIES

Series (Opp)	M	Balls	Mdns	Runs	Wkts	Avge	5wi	10wm	Best
1991-92I	2	408	9	228	1	228.00	0	0	1/150
1992-93SL	2	229	8	158	3	52.66	0	0	3/11
1992-93W	4	650	23	313	10	31.30	1	0	7/52
1992-93N	3	954	73	256	17	15.05	0	0	4/8
1993E	6	2639	178	877	34	25.79	1	0	5/82
1993-94N	3	909	49	305	18	16.94	1	0	6/31
1993-94SA	3	1051	63	307	18	17.05	2	1	7/56
1993-94SA	3	1145	69	336	15	22.40	0	0	4/86
1994-95P	3	1090	50	504	18	28.00	2	0	6/136
1994-95E	5	1537	84	549	27	20.33	2	1	8/71
1994-95W	4	828	35	406	15	27.06	0	0	4/70
1995-96P	3	690	52	198	19	10.42	1	1	7/23
1995-96SL	3	988	43	433	12	36.08	0	0	4/71
1996-97W	5	1303	56	594	22	27.00	0	0	4/95
1996-97SA	3	798	47	282	11	25.63	0	0	4/43
1997E	6	1423	69	577	24	24.04	1	0	6/48
1997-98N	3	1024	36	476	19	25.05	1	0	5/88
1997-98SA	3	1123	51	417	20	20.85	2	1	6/34
1997-98I	3	1002	37	540	10	54.00	0	0	4/85
1998-99E	1	234	7	110	2	55.00	0	0	1/43
1998-99W	3	503	18	268	2	134.00	0	0	1/70
1999-2000SL	3	337	20	115	8	14.37	1	0	5/52
1999-2000Z	1	319	13	137	6	22.83	0	0	3/68
1999-2000P	3	779	37	370	12	30.83	1	0	5/110
1999-2000I	3	762	35	335	8	41.87	0	0	4/92
1999-2000N	3	776	33	414	15	27.60	0	0	4/68
2000-01I	3	913	31	505	10	50.50	0	0	4/47

Series (Opp)	M	Balls	Mdns	Runs	Wkts	Avge	5wi	10wm	Best
2001E	5	1172	41	580	31	18.70	3	1	7/165
2001-02N	3	746	19	430	6	71.66	0	0	3/89
2001-02SA	3	1041	35	473	17	27.82	1	0	5/113
2001-02SA	3	972	38	442	20	22.10	1	0	6/161
2002-03P	3	744	29	342	27	12.66	2	1	7/94
2002-03E	3	787	29	347	14	24.78	0	0	4/93
2003-04SL	3	1008	37	521	26	20.03	4	2	5/43
2004-05SL	2	605	24	280	10	28.00	0	0	4/70
2004-05I	3	840	27	421	14	30.07	1	0	6/125
2004-05N	2	572	17	256	11	23.27	0	0	4/15
2004-05P	3	747	24	402	14	28.71	0	0	4/111
2004-05N	3	789	25	374	17	22.00	1	0	5/39
2005E	5	1517	37	797	40	19.92	3	2	6/46
2005-06W	3	794	27	366	16	22.87	2	0	6/80
2005-06SA	3	1032	45	462	14	33.00	0	0	4/74
2005-06SA	3	766	19	423	15	28.20	1	0	6/86
2005-06B	2	524	12	300	11	27.27	1	0	5/113
2006-07E	5	1448	43	698	23	30.34	1	0	5/39
TOTAL	144	40518	1754	17924	702	25.53	37	10	8/71

BOWLING RECORD IN EACH INNINGS

	M	Balls	Mdns	Runs	Wkts	Avge	5wi	10wm	Best
1st Innings		21354	874	9766	346	28.22	18		7/23
2nd Innings		19164	880	8158	356	22.91	19		8/71
TOTAL	144	40518	1754	17924	702	25.53	37	10	8/71

BOWLING RECORD AGAINST EACH COUNTRY

Opponent	M	Balls	Mdns	Runs	Wkts	Avge	5wi	10wm	Best
Bangladesh	2	524	12	300	11	27.27	1	0	5/113
England	36	10757	488	4535	195	23.25	11	4	8/71
India	14	3925	139	2029	43	47.18	1	0	6/125
New Zealand	20	5770	252	2511	103	24.37	3	0	6/31
Pakistan	15	4050	192	1816	90	20.17	6	2	7/23
South Africa	24	7928	367	3142	130	24.16	7	2	7/56
Sri Lanka	13	3167	132	1507	59	25.54	5	2	5/43
West Indies	19	4078	159	1947	65	29.95	3	0	7/52
Zimbabwe	1	319	13	137	6	22.83	0	0	3/68
TOTAL	144	40518	1754	17924	702	25.53	37	10	8/71

Bangladesh	M	Balls	Mdns	Runs	Wkts	Avge	5wi	10wm	Best
2005-06B	2	524	12	300	11	27.27	1	0	5/113

England	M	Balls	Mdns	Runs	Wkts	Avge	5wi	10wm	Best
1993E	6	2639	178	877	34	25.79	1	0	5/82
1994-95E	5	1537	84	549	27	20.33	2	1	8/71
1997E	6	1423	69	577	24	24.04	1	0	6/48
1998-99E	1	234	7	110	2	55.00	0	0	1/43
2001E	5	1172	41	580	31	18.70	3	1	7/165
2002-03E	3	787	29	347	14	24.78	0	0	4/93
2005E	5	1517	37	797	40	19.92	3	2	6/46
2006-07E	5	1448	43	698	23	30.34	1	0	5/39
In Australia	14	4006	163	1704	66	25.81	3	1	8/71
In England	22	6751	325	2831	129	21.94	8	3	7/165
TOTAL	36	10757	488	4535	195	23.25	11	4	8/71

India	M	Balls	Mdns	Runs	Wkts	Avge	5wi	10wm	Best
1991-92I	2	408	9	228	1	228.00	0	0	1/150
1997-98I	3	1002	37	540	10	54.00	0	0	4/85
1999-2000I	3	762	35	335	8	41.87	0	0	4/92
2000-01I	3	913	31	505	10	50.50	0	0	4/47
2004-05I	3	840	27	421	14	30.07	1	0	6/125
In Australia	5	1170	44	563	9	62.55	0	0	4/92
In India	9	2755	95	1466	34	43.11	1	0	6/125
TOTAL	14	3925	139	2029	43	47.18	1	0	6/125

New Zealand	M	Balls	Mdns	Runs	Wkts	Avge	5wi	10wm	Best
1992-93N	3	954	73	256	17	15.05	0	0	4/8
1993-94N	3	909	49	305	18	16.94	1	0	6/31
1997-98N	3	1024	36	476	19	25.05	1	0	5/88
1999-2000N	3	776	33	414	15	27.60	0	0	4/68
2001-02N	3	746	19	430	6	71.66	0	0	3/89
2004-05N	2	572	17	256	11	23.27	0	0	4/15
2004-05N	3	789	25	374	17	22.00	1	0	5/39
In Australia	11	3251	121	1467	54	27.16	2	0	6/31
In New Zealand	9	2519	131	1044	49	21.30	1	0	5/39
TOTAL	20	5770	252	2511	103	24.37	3	0	6/31

Pakistan	M	Balls	Mdns	Runs	Wkts	Avge	5wi	10wm	Best
1994-95P	3	1090	50	504	18	28.00	2	0	6/136
1995-96P	3	690	52	198	19	10.42	1	1	7/23
1999-2000P	3	779	37	370	12	30.83	1	0	5/110
2002-03P	3	744	29	342	27	12.66	2	1	7/94
2004-05P	3	747	24	402	14	28.71	0	0	4/111
In Australia	9	2216	113	970	45	21.55	2	1	7/23
In Pakistan	3	1090	50	504	18	28.00	2	0	6/136
In Sri Lanka	1	330	10	188	11	17.09	1	1	7/94
In U.A.E.	2	414	19	154	16	9.62	1	0	5/74
TOTAL	15	4050	192	1816	90	20.17	6	2	7/23

South Africa	M	Balls	Mdns	Runs	Wkts	Avge	5wi	10wm	Best
1993-94SA	3	1051	63	307	18	17.05	2	1	7/56
1993-94SA	3	1145	69	336	15	22.40	0	0	4/86
1996-97SA	3	798	47	282	11	25.63	0	0	4/43
1997-98SA	3	1123	51	417	20	20.85	2	1	6/34
2001-02SA	3	1041	35	473	17	27.82	1	0	5/113
2001-02SA	3	972	38	442	20	22.10	1	0	6/161
2005-06SA	3	1032	45	462	14	33.00	0	0	4/74
2005-06SA	3	766	19	423	15	28.20	1	0	6/86
In Australia	12	4247	194	1659	69	24.04	5	2	7/56
In South Africa	12	3681	173	1483	61	24.31	2	0	6/86
TOTAL	24	7928	367	3142	130	24.16	7	2	7/56

Sri Lanka	M	Balls	Mdns	Runs	Wkts	Avge	5wi	10wm	Best
1992-93SL	2	229	8	158	3	52.66	0	0	3/11
1995-96SL	3	988	43	433	12	36.08	0	0	4/71
1999-2000SL	3	337	20	115	8	14.37	1	0	5/52
2003-04SL	3	1008	37	521	26	20.03	4	2	5/43
2004-05SL	2	605	24	280	10	28.00	0	0	4/70
In Australia	5	1593	67	713	22	32.40	0	0	4/70
In Sri Lanka	8	1574	65	794	37	21.45	5	2	5/43
TOTAL	13	3167	132	1507	59	25.54	5	2	5/43

West Indies	M	Balls	Mdns	Runs	Wkts	Avge	5wi	10wm	Best
1992-93W	4	650	23	313	10	31.30	1	0	7/52
1994-95W	4	828	35	406	15	27.06	0	0	4/70
1996-97W	5	1303	56	594	22	27.00	0	0	4/95
1998-99W	3	503	18	268	2	134.00	0	0	1/70
2005-06W	3	794	27	366	16	22.87	2	0	6/80
In Australia	12	2747	106	1273	48	26.52	3	0	7/52
In West Indies	7	1331	53	674	17	39.64	0	0	4/70
TOTAL	19	4078	159	1947	65	29.95	3	0	7/52

Zimbabwe	M	Balls	Mdns	Runs	Wkts	Avge	5wi	10wm	Best
1999-2000Z	1	319	13	137	6	22.83	0	0	3/68

BOWLING RECORD IN EACH COUNTRY

Country	M	Balls	Mdns	Runs	Wkts	Avge	5wi	10wm	Best
Australia	68	19230	808	8349	313	26.67	15	4	8/71
Bangladesh	2	524	12	300	11	27.27	1	0	5/113
England	22	6751	325	2831	129	21.94	8	3	7/165
India	9	2755	95	1466	34	43.11	1	0	6/125
New Zealand	9	2519	131	1044	49	21.30	1	0	5/39
Pakistan	3	1090	50	504	18	28.00	2	0	6/136
South Africa	12	3681	173	1483	61	24.31	2	0	6/86
Sri Lanka	9	1904	75	982	48	20.45	6	3	7/94
U.A.E.	2	414	19	154	16	9.62	1	0	5/74
West Indies	7	1331	53	674	17	39.64	0	0	4/70
Zimbabwe	1	319	13	137	6	22.83	0	0	3/68
TOTAL	144	40518	1754	17924	702	25.53	37	10	8/71

Australia	M	Balls	Mdns	Runs	Wkts	Avge	5wi	10wm	Best
1991-92I	2	408	9	228	1	228.00	0	0	1/150
1992-93W	4	650	23	313	10	31.30	1	0	7/52
1993-94N	3	909	49	305	18	16.94	1	0	6/31
1993-94SA	3	1051	63	307	18	17.05	2	1	7/56
1994-95E	5	1537	84	549	27	20.33	2	1	8/71
1995-96P	3	690	52	198	19	10.42	1	1	7/23

1995-96SL	3	988	43	433	12	36.08	0	0	4/71
1996-97W	5	1303	56	594	22	27.00	0	0	4/95
1997-98N	3	1024	36	476	19	25.05	1	0	5/88
1997-98SA	3	1123	51	417	20	20.85	2	1	6/34
1998-99E	1	234	7	110	2	55.00	0	0	1/43
1999-2000P	3	779	37	370	12	30.83	1	0	5/110
1999-2000I	3	762	35	335	8	41.87	0	0	4/92
2001-02N	3	746	19	430	6	71.66	0	0	3/89
2001-02SA	3	1041	35	473	17	27.82	1	0	5/113
2002-03E	3	787	29	347	14	24.78	0	0	4/93
2004-05SL	2	605	24	280	10	28.00	0	0	4/70
2004-05N	2	572	17	256	11	23.27	0	0	4/15
2004-05P	3	747	24	402	14	28.71	0	0	4/111
2005-06W	3	794	27	366	16	22.87	2	0	6/80
2005-06SA	3	1032	45	462	14	33.00	0	0	4/74
2006-07E	5	1448	43	698	23	30.34	1	0	5/39
TOTAL	68	19230	808	8349	313	26.67	15	4	8/71

Bangladesh	M	Balls	Mdns	Runs	Wkts	Avge	5wi	10wm	Best
2005-06B	2	524	12	300	11	27.27	1	0	5/113

England	M	Balls	Mdns	Runs	Wkts	Avge	5wi	10wm	Best
1993E	6	2639	178	877	34	25.79	1	0	5/82
1997E	6	1423	69	577	24	24.04	1	0	6/48
2001E	5	1172	41	580	31	18.70	3	1	7/165
2005E	5	1517	37	797	40	19.92	3	2	6/46
TOTAL	22	6751	325	2831	129	21.94	8	3	7/165

India	M	Balls	Mdns	Runs	Wkts	Avge	5wi	10wm	Best
1997-98I	3	1002	37	540	10	54.00	0	0	4/85
2000-01I	3	913	31	505	10	50.50	0	0	4/47
2004-05I	3	840	27	421	14	30.07	1	0	6/125
TOTAL	9	2755	95	1466	34	43.11	1	0	6/125

New Zealand	M	Balls	Mdns	Runs	Wkts	Avge	5wi	10wm	Best
_1992-93N_	3	954	73	256	17	15.05	0	0	4/8
_1999-2000N_	3	776	33	414	15	27.60	0	0	4/68
_2004-05N_	3	789	25	374	17	22.00	1	0	5/39
TOTAL	9	2519	131	1044	49	21.30	1	0	5/39

Pakistan	M	Balls	Mdns	Runs	Wkts	Avge	5wi	10wm	Best
_1994-95P_	3	1090	50	504	18	28.00	2	0	6/136

South Africa	M	Balls	Mdns	Runs	Wkts	Avge	5wi	10wm	Best
_1993-94SA_	3	1145	69	336	15	22.40	0	0	4/86
_1996-97SA_	3	798	47	282	11	25.63	0	0	4/43
_2001-02SA_	3	972	38	442	20	22.10	1	0	6/161
_2005-06SA_	3	766	19	423	15	28.20	1	0	6/86
TOTAL	12	3681	173	1483	61	24.31	2	0	6/86

Sri Lanka	M	Balls	Mdns	Runs	Wkts	Avge	5wi	10wm	Best
_1992-93SL_	2	229	8	158	3	52.66	0	0	3/11
_1999-2000SL_	3	337	20	115	8	14.37	1	0	5/52
_2002-03P_	1	330	10	188	11	17.09	1	1	7/94
_2003-04SL_	3	1008	37	521	26	20.03	4	2	5/43
TOTAL	9	1904	75	982	48	20.45	6	3	7/94

U.A.E.	M	Balls	Mdns	Runs	Wkts	Avge	5wi	10wm	Best
_2002-03P_	2	414	19	154	16	9.62	1	0	5/74

West Indies	M	Balls	Mdns	Runs	Wkts	Avge	5wi	10wm	Best
_1994-95W_	4	828	35	406	15	27.06	0	0	4/70
_1998-99W_	3	503	18	268	2	134.00	0	0	1/70
TOTAL	7	1331	53	674	17	39.64	0	0	4/70

Zimbabwe	M	Balls	Mdns	Runs	Wkts	Avge	5wi	10wm	Best
_1999-2000Z_	1	319	13	137	6	22.83	0	0	3/68

BOWLING RECORD ON EACH GROUND

Australia	M	Balls	Mdns	Runs	Wkts	Avge	5wi	10wm	Best
Adelaide	13	4065	177	1705	56	30.44	2	0	6/80
Brisbane	11	3320	162	1381	68	20.30	3	2	8/71
Cairns	1	450	21	199	7	28.42	0	0	4/70
Darwin	1	155	3	81	3	27.00	0	0	3/20
Hobart	6	1373	50	621	28	22.17	3	0	6/31
Melbourne	11	3138	129	1284	56	22.92	3	0	7/52
Perth	12	2855	109	1349	37	36.45	0	0	4/83
Sydney	13	3874	157	1729	58	29.81	4	2	7/56
TOTAL	68	19230	808	8349	313	26.67	15	4	8/71

Bangladesh	M	Balls	Mdns	Runs	Wkts	Avge	5wi	10wm	Best
Fatullah	1	198	5	140	3	46.66	0	0	3/28
Chittagong	1	326	7	160	8	20.00	1	0	5/113
TOTAL	2	524	12	300	11	27.27	1	0	5/113

England	M	Balls	Mdns	Runs	Wkts	Avge	5wi	10wm	Best
Birmingham	4	1141	57	544	25	21.76	3	1	6/46
Leeds	3	716	36	268	3	89.33	0	0	1/43
Lord's	4	944	41	372	19	19.57	0	0	4/57
Manchester	3	1152	66	421	21	20.04	1	0	6/48
Nottingham	4	1290	65	514	29	17.72	1	0	6/33
The Oval	4	1508	60	712	32	22.25	3	2	7/165
TOTAL	22	6751	325	2831	129	21.94	8	3	7/165

India	M	Balls	Mdns	Runs	Wkts	Avge	5wi	10wm	Best
Bangalore	2	720	27	379	9	42.11	0	0	3/106
Chennai	3	933	30	513	13	39.46	1	0	6/125
Kolkata	2	577	10	364	3	121.33	0	0	2/65
Mumbai	1	300	18	107	5	21.40	0	0	4/47
Nagpur	1	225	10	103	4	25.75	0	0	2/47
TOTAL	9	2755	95	1466	34	43.11	1	0	6/125

New Zealand	M	Balls	Mdns	Runs	Wkts	Avge	5wi	10wm	Best
Auckland	3	783	38	350	18	19.44	0	0	4/8
Christchurch	2	612	28	237	14	16.92	1	0	5/39
Hamilton	1	270	16	106	3	35.33	0	0	2/61
Wellington	3	854	49	351	14	25.07	0	0	4/68
TOTAL	9	2519	131	1044	49	21.30	1	0	5/39

Pakistan	M	Balls	Mdns	Runs	Wkts	Avge	5wi	10wm	Best
Karachi	1	379	22	150	8	18.75	1	0	5/89
Lahore	1	431	14	240	9	26.66	1	0	6/136
Rawalpindi	1	280	14	114	1	114.00	0	0	1/58
TOTAL	3	1090	50	504	18	28.00	2	0	6/136

South Africa	M	Balls	Mdns	Runs	Wkts	Avge	5wi	10wm	Best
Cape Town	3	1217	57	465	17	27.35	1	0	6/161
Centurion	1	216	11	89	0	-	0	0	0/89
Durban	3	953	41	399	18	22.16	1	0	6/86
Johannesburg	4	1047	52	448	21	21.33	0	0	4/43
Port Elizabeth	1	248	12	82	5	16.40	0	0	3/62
TOTAL	12	3681	173	1483	61	24.31	2	0	6/86

Sri Lanka	M	Balls	Mdns	Runs	Wkts	Avge	5wi	10wm	Best
Colombo,PSS	1	330	10	188	11	17.09	1	1	7/94
Colombo,SSC	3	607	24	336	9	37.33	0	0	4/92
Galle	2	516	26	193	13	14.84	2	1	5/43
Kandy	2	385	12	225	15	15.00	3	1	5/52
Moratuwa	1	66	3	40	0	-	0	0	0/40
TOTAL	9	1904	75	982	48	20.45	6	3	7/94

U.A.E.	M	Balls	Mdns	Runs	Wkts	Avge	5wi	10wm	Best
Sharjah	2	414	19	154	16	9.62	1	0	5/74

West Indies	M	Balls	Mdns	Runs	Wkts	Avge	5wi	10wm	Best
Bridgetown	2	470	13	260	6	43.33	0	0	3/64
Kingston	2	472	22	236	7	33.71	0	0	4/70
Port-of-Spain	2	179	9	77	1	77.00	0	0	1/16
St John's	1	210	9	101	3	33.66	0	0	3/83
TOTAL	7	1331	53	674	17	39.64	0	0	4/70

Zimbabwe	M	Balls	Mdns	Runs	Wkts	Avge	5wi	10wm	Best
Harare	1	319	13	137	6	22.83	0	0	3/68

Warne dismissed the following batsmen:

14 A.J.Stewart(E)

11 N.Hussain(E), A.G.Prince(SA)

10 M.A.Atherton(E)

9 A.F.Giles(E), S.J.Harmison(E), G.P.Thorpe(E)

8 A.R.Caddick(E), W.J.Cronje(SA), C.D.McMillan(N), D.J.Richardson(SA), A.J.Strauss(E), M.E.Trescothick(E)

7 N.J.Astle(N), M.V.Boucher(SA), M.A.Butcher(E), R.S.Dravid(I), A.Flintoff(E), H.H.Gibbs(SA), D.Gough(E), D.L.Vettori(N)

6 S.B.Doull(N), S.P.Fleming(N), G.A.Gooch(E), M.J.Hoggard(E), J.H.Kallis(SA), B.C.Lara(W), B.M.McMillan(SA), M.Ntini(SA), S.M.Pollock(SA), H.P.Tillakaratne(SL), W.P.U.J.C.Vaas(SL), C.A.Walsh(W)

5 Abdur Razzaq(P), I.R.Bell(E), C.L.Cairns(N), U.D.U.Chandana(SL), S.Chanderpaul(W), T.M.Dilshan(SL), Inzamamul Haq(P), G.Kirsten(SA), V.V.S.Laxman(I), K.P.Pietersen(E), M.R.Ramprakash(E), Rashid Latif(P), Saqlain Mushtaq(P), Waqar Younis(P), Wasim Akram(P)

4 Azhar Mahmood(P), Basit Ali(P), K.C.G.Benjamin(W), I.R.Bishop(W), D.J.Cullinan(SA), P.A.J.DeFreitas(E), A.B.de Villiers(SA) Faisal Iqbal(P), C.L.Hooper(W), D.P.M.D.Jayawardene(SL), A.H.Jones(N), N.D.McKenzie(SA), C.S.Martin(N), D.N.Patel(N), J.A.Rudolph(SA), K.R.Rutherford(N), R.G.Samuels(W), K.C.Sangakkara(SL), Shoaib Akhtar(P), R.A.Smith(E), P.C.R.Tufnell(E)

3 Aamer Sohail(P), J.C.Adams(W), P.R.Adams(SA), Akram Raza(P), C.E.L.Ambrose(W), K.L.T.Arthurton(W), P.A.de Silva(SL), P.S.de Villiers(SA), A.A.Donald(SA), J.E.C.Franklin(N), M.W.Gatting(E), C.Z.Harris(N), Ijaz Ahmed(P), R.S.Kaluwitharana(SL), P.N.Kirsten(SA), B.B.McCullum(N), H.J.H.Marshall(N), C.R.Matthews(SA), Misbah-ul-Haq(P), M.Muralidaran(SL), A.Nel(SA), M.S.Panesar(E), A.C.Parore(N), P.A.Patel(I), Rameez Raja(P), S.Ramesh(I), J.N.Rhodes(SA), Saeed Anwar(P), G.C.Smith(SA), M.L.Su'a(N), P.M.Such(E), S.R.Tendulkar(I), A.J.Tudor(E), M.P.Vaughan(E), K.C.Wessels(SA), C.White(E), G.P.Wickramasinghe(SL), P.J.Wiseman(N)

2 Aaqib Javed(P), G.I.Allott(N), M.S.Atapattu(SL), A.M.Bacher(SA), W.K.M.Benjamin(W), T.E.Blain(N), N.Boje(SA), P.D.Collingwood(E) C.D.Collymore(W), J.P.Crawley(E), R.D.B.Croft(E), H.D.P.K.Dharmasena(SL), H.H.Dippenaar(SA), S.C.Ganguly(I), Harbhajan Singh(I), Imran Nazir(P), S.T.Jayasuriya(SL), G.O.Jones(E), Kamran Akmal(P), L.Klusener(SA), C.C.Lewis(E), K.S.Lokuarachchi(SL), M.J.McCague(E), D.E.Malcolm(E), Mashrafe Bin Mortaza(B), Mohammad Akram(P), Mohammad Sami(P), D.K.Morrison(N), J.L.Ontong(SA), M.B.Owens(N), I.K.Pathan(I), B.A.Pocock(N), D.B.Powell(W), A.Ranatunga(SL), S.J.Rhodes(E), R.B.Richardson(W), V.K.Sehwag(I), N.S.Sidhu(I), M.S.Sinclair(N), J.Srinath(I),

H.H.Streak(Z), S.B.Styris(N), P.L.Symcox(SA), G.J.Whittall(Z), Tasir Hameed(P), B.A.Young(N), Younis Khan(P), Yousuf Youhana(P), D.N.T.Zoysa(SL)

1 Aftab Ahmed(B), U.Afzaal(E), A.B.Agarkar(I), S.D.Anurasiri(SL), M.Azharuddin(I), M.D.Bell(N), D.J.J.Bravo(W), C.O.Browne(W), S.L.Campbell(W), A.N.Cook(E), M.D.Crowe(N), Danish Kaneria(P), R.K.J.Dawson(E), R.P.de Groen(N), S.S.Dighe(I), Enamul Haque(B), N.A.Foster(E), M.W.Goodwin(Z), T.R.Gripper(Z), Habibul Bashar(B), U.C.Hathurusingha(SL), C.W.Henderson(SA), H.M.KR.K.B.Herath(SL), G.A.Hick(E), W.W.Hinds(W), A.J.Hollioake(E), B.C.Hollioake(E), A.C.Hudson(SA), Imran Farhat(P), R.D.Jacobs(W), S.P.Jones(E), H.H.Kanitkar(I), J.M.Kemp(SA), R.W.T.Key(E), A.Kumble(I), M.N.Lathwell(E), J.J.C.Lawson(W), A.W.R.Madurasinghe(SL), S.I.Mahmood(E), S.L.Malinga(SL), M.P.Maynard(E), K.D.Mills(N), Mohammad Khalil(P), Mohammad Rafique(B), Mohsin Kamal(P), Moin Khan(P), N.R.Mongia(I), J.R.Murray(W), Mushtaq Ahmed(P), Naved-ul-Hasan(P), I.E.O'Brien(N), J.D.P.Oram(N), J.Ormond(E), M.S.K.Prasad(I), D.Pretorius(SA), Rahin Saleh(B), C.M.W.Read(E), M.H.Richardson(N), Saleem Malik(P), M.N.Samuels(W), Shahadat Hossain(B), Shahriar Nafees(B), R.J.Shastri(I), Shoaib Malik(P), P.V.Simmons(W), D.R.Smith(W), R.P.Snell(SA), R.G.Twose(N), L.Vincent(N), S.L.Watkin(E), W.Watson(N), D.Williams(W), S.C.Williams(W), J.G.Wright(N), Yuvraj Singh(I), Zaheer Khan(I), Zahid Fazal(P).

Details of Warne's wickets in Tests:

Caught	320	45.59%
Leg before wicket	138	19.66%
Bowled	116	16.52%
Caught by wicket-keeper	71	10.11%
Stumped	36	5.13%
Caught and bowled	21	2.99%
TOTAL	702	100.00%

WARNE'S FIVE WICKETS IN AN INNINGS

1	7/52	v	West Indies	Melbourne	1992-93
2	5/82	v	England	Birmingham	1993
3	6/31	v	New Zealand	Hobart	1993-94
4	7/56)	v	South Africa	Sydney	1993-94
5	5/72)				
6	5/89	v	Pakistan	Karachi	1994-95
7	6/136	v	Pakistan	Lahore	1994-95
8	8/71	v	England	Brisbane	1994-95
9	6/64	v	England	Melbourne	1994-95

10	7/23	v	Pakistan	Brisbane	1995-96
11	6/48	v	England	Manchester	1997
12	5/88	v	New Zealand	Hobart	1997-98
13	5/75)	v	South Africa	Sydney	1997-98
14	6/34)				
15	5/52	v	Sri Lanka	Kandy	1999-2000
16	5/110	v	Pakistan	Hobart	1999-2000
17	5/71	v	England	Birmingham	2001
18	6/33	v	England	Nottingham	2001
19	7/165	v	England	The Oval	2001
20	5/113	v	South Africa	Adelaide	2001-02
21	6/161	v	South Africa	Cape Town	2001-02
22	7/94	v	Pakistan	Colombo,PSS	2002-03
23	5/74	v	Pakistan	Sharjah	2002-03
24	5/116	v	Sri Lanka	Galle	2003-04
25	5/43	v	Sri Lanka	Galle	2003-04
26	5/65)	v	Sri Lanka	Kandy	2003-04
27	5/90)				
28	6/125	v	India	Chennai	2004-05
29	5/39	v	New Zealand	Christchurch	2004-05
30	6/46	v	England	Birmingham	2005
31	6/122)	v	England	The Oval	2005
32	6/124)				
33	5/48	v	West Indies	Brisbane	2005-06
34	6/80	v	West Indies	Adelaide	2005-06
35	6/86	v	South Africa	Durban	2005-06
36	5/113	v	Bangladesh	Chittagong	2005-06
37	5/39	v	England	Melbourne	2006-07

WARNE'S TEN WICKETS IN A TEST

12/128	(7/56 + 5/72)	v	South Africa	Sydney	1993-94
11/110	(3/39 + 8/71)	v	England	Brisbane	1994-95
11/77	(7/23 + 4/54)	v	Pakistan	Brisbane	1995-96
11/109	(5/75 + 6/34)	v	South Africa	Sydney	1997-98
11/188	(7/94 + 4/94)	v	Pakistan	Colombo (PSS)	2002-03
11/229	(7/165 + 4/64)	v	England	Brisbane	2002-03
10/159	(5/116 + 5/43)	v	Sri Lanka	Galle	2003-04
10/155	(5/65 + 5/90)	v	Sri Lanka	Kandy	2003-04
10/162	(4/116 + 6/46)	v	England	Birmingham	2005
12/246	(6/122 + 6/124)	v	England	The Oval	2005

SHANE WARNE'S TEST RECORD MATCH BY MATCH

1 *Australia v India, 3rd Test, Sydney Cricket Ground, January 2, 3, 4, 5, 6, 1992*

1st innings	cw C.S.Pandit b Kapil Dev.....20.....45.0/ 7/150/1	
	R.J.Shastri	c D.M.Jones
2nd innings	not out.....1	

2 *Australia v India, 4th Test, Adelaide Oval, January 25, 26, 27, 28, 29, 1992*

1st innings	st C.S.Pandit b S.L.Venkatapathy Raju.....7.....7.0/ 1/ 18/0
2nd innings	cw C.S.Pandit b J.Srinath.....0.....16.0/ 1/ 60/0 ..c1

3 *Australia v Sri Lanka, 1st Test, Sinhalese Sports Club Ground, Colombo, August 17, 18, 19, 21, 22, 1992*

1st innings	c and b S.D.Anurasiri.....24.....22.0/ 2/107/0 ..c1	
2nd innings	b S.D.Anurasiri.....35.....5.1/ 3/ 11/3	
2	G.P.Wickramasinghe	c M.E.Waugh
3	S.D.Anurasiri	c M.E.Waugh
4	M.A.W.R.Madurasinghe	c G.R.J.Matthews

4 *Australia v Sri Lanka, 3rd Test, Tyrone Fernando Stadium, Moratuwa, September 8, 9, 10, 12, 13, 1992*

1st innings	c A.P.Gurusinha b C.P.H.Ramanayake.....7.....11.0/ 3/ 40/0
2nd innings	dnb

5 *Australia v West Indies, 2nd Test, Melbourne Cricket Ground, 26, 27, 28, 29, 30, December 1992*

1st innings	c J.C.Adams b I.R.Bishop.....1.....24.0/ 7/ 65/1	
5	C.E.L.Ambrose	c C.J.McDermott
2nd innings	c K.L.T.Arthurton b C.E.L.Ambrose.....5.....23.2/ 8/ 52/7	
6	R.B.Richardson	b
7	K.L.T.Arthurton	st I.A.Healy
8	C.L.Hooper	c M.R.Whitney
9	P.V.Simmons	c D.C.Boon
10	D.Williams	c M.E.Waugh

| 11 | I.R.Bishop | c M.A.Taylor |
| 12 | C.A.Walsh | c M.G.Hughes |

6 Australia v West Indies, 3rd Test, Sydney Cricket Ground, January 2, 3, 4, 5, 6, 1993

1st innings				
13	c P.V.Simmons b C.L.Hooper		14 ...... 41.0/ 6/116/1 ..c1
	C.L.Hooper	b	
2nd innings	dnb		

7 Australia v West Indies, 4th Test, Adelaide Oval, January 23, 24, 25, 26, 1993

1st innings	lbw b C.L.Hooper		0 ...... 2.0/ 0/ 11/0
2nd innings	lbw b I.R.Bishop		9 ...... 6.0/ 2/ 18/1 ..c1
14	R.B.Richardson	cw I.A.Healy	

8 Australia v West Indies, 5th Test, Western Australia Cricket Association Ground, Perth, January 30, 31, February 1, 1993

| 1st innings | run out | 13 ...... 12.0/ 0/ 51/0 ..c1 |
| 2nd innings | cw J.R.Murray b C.E.L.Ambrose | 0 |

9 Australia v New Zealand, 1st Test, Lancaster Park, Christchurch, February 25, 26, 27, 28, 1993

1st innings	not out		22 ..... 22.0/12/ 23/3
15	K.R.Rutherford	b	
16	J.G.Wright	lbw	
17	M.B.Owens	lbw	
2nd innings	dnb		26.0/ 7/ 63/4
18	C.L.Cairns	c M.A.Taylor	
19	A.C.Parore	c D.C.Boon	
20	D.N.Patel	b	
21	K.R.Rutherford	cw I.A.Healy	

10 Australia v New Zealand, 2nd Test, Basin Reserve, Wellington, March 4, 5, 6, 7, 8, 1993

1st innings	c M.J.Greatbatch b D.K.Morrison		22 ...... 29.0/ 9/ 59/2
22	W.Watson	c M.A.Taylor	
23	M.B.Owens	b	
2nd innings	dnb		40.0/25/ 49/2

| 24 | A.H.Jones | lbw |
| 25 | T.E.Blain | cw I.A.Healy |

11 Australia v New Zealand, 3rd Test, Eden Park, Auckland, March 12, 13, 14, 15, 16, 1993

1st innings	not out.........3...... 15.0/12/ 8/4
26	K.R.Rutherford	st I.A.Healy
27	D.N.Patel	cw I.A.Healy
28	C.Z.Harris	c M.A.Taylor
29	M.L.Su'a	c S.R.Waugh
2nd innings	c A.H.Jones b D.K.Morrison.........2...... 27.0/ 8/ 54/2
30	M.D.Crowe	c J.L.Langer
31	A.H.Jones	b

12 Australia v England, 1st Test, Old Trafford, Manchester, June 3, 4, 5, 6, 7, 1993

1st innings	not out.........15..... 24.0/10/ 51/4
32	M.W.Gatting	b
33	R.A.Smith	c M.A.Taylor
34	G.A.Gooch	c B.P.Julian
35	A.R.Caddick	cw I.A.Healy
2nd innings	dnb......... 49.0/26/ 86/4 ..c1
36	M.A.Atherton	c M.A.Taylor
37	R.A.Smith	b
38	A.J.Stewart	cw I.A.Healy
39	C.C.Lewis	c M.A.Taylor

13 Australia v England, 2nd Test, Lord's Cricket Ground, St John's Wood, London, June 17, 18, 19, 20, 21, 1993

1st innings	dnb......... 35.0/12/ 57/4
40	C.C.Lewis	lbw
41	N.A.Foster	c A.R.Border
42	M.A.Atherton	b
43	P.M.Such	c M.A.Taylor
2nd innings	dnb......... 48.5/17/102/4
44	G.A.Gooch	cw I.A.Healy

45	M.W.Gatting	lbw
46	P.M.Such	b
47	P.C.R.Tufnell	b

14 Australia v England, 3rd Test, Trent Bridge, Nottingham, July 1, 2, 3, 5, 6, 1993

1st innings not out ....35 ...... 40.0/17/ 74/3

48	M.A.Atherton	c D.C.Boon
49	A.J.Stewart	c M.E.Waugh
50	N.Hussain	c D.C.Boon

2nd innings dnb 50.0/21/108/3

51	R.A.Smith	cw I.A.Healy
52	M.N.Lathwell	lbw
53	G.A.Gooch	c M.A.Taylor

15 Australia v England, 4th Test, Headingley, Leeds, July 22, 23, 24, 25, 26, 1993

1st innings dnb 23.0/ 9/ 43/1

| 54 | M.J.McCague | c M.A.Taylor |

2nd innings dnb 40.0/16/ 63/0

16 Australia v England, 5th Test, Edgbaston, Birmingham, August 5, 6, 7, 8, 9, 1993

1st innings cw A.J.Stewart b J.E.Emburey ...... 10 ...... 21.0/ 7/ 63/1 ..c1

| 55 | A.J.Stewart | c & b |

2nd innings dnb 49.0/23/ 82/5

56	M.A.Atherton	c A.R.Border
57	R.A.Smith	lbw
58	G.A.Gooch	b
59	A.J.Stewart	lbw
60	G.P.Thorpe	st I.A.Healy

17 Australia v England, 6th Test, The Oval, Kennington, London, August 19, 20, 21, 22, 23, 1993

1st innings cw A.J.Stewart b A.R.C.Fraser ...... 16 ...... 20.0/ 5/ 70/2 ..c1

| 61 | M.P.Maynard | b |
| 62 | N.Hussain | c M.A.Taylor |

2nd innings lbw b A.R.C.Fraser ...... 37 ...... 40.0/15/ 78/3 ..c1

63	G.A.Gooch	cw I.A.Healy
64	S.L.Watkin	lbw
65	P.M.Such	lbw

18   Australia v New Zealand, 1st Test, Western Australia Cricket Association Ground, Perth, November 12, 13, 14, 15, 16, 1993

1st innings	c D.N.Patel b C.L.Cairns	11 ..... 37.1/ 6/ 90/1
66	C.L.Cairns	b
2nd innings	dnb	13.0/ 6/ 23/0

19   Australia v New Zealand, 2nd Test, Bellerive Oval, Hobart, November 26, 27, 28, 29, 1993

1st innings	dnb	18.0/ 5/ 36/3 ..c1
67	D.N.Patel	c M.A.Taylor
68	M.L.Su'a	c M.A.Taylor
69	S.B.Doull	lbw
2nd innings	dnb	19.5/ 9/ 31/6 ..c1
70	B.A.Pocock	st I.A.Healy
71	K.R.Rutherford	b
72	M.L.Su'a	b
73	D.K.Morrison	b
74	T.E.Blain	c & b
75	S.B.Doull	c T.B.A.May

20   Australia v New Zealand, 3rd Test, Brisbane Cricket Ground, Woolloongabba, December 3, 4, 5, 6, 7, 1993

1st innings	not out	74 ..... 28.3/12/ 66/4 ..c1
76	A.H.Jones	b
77	C.L.Cairns	c & b
78	D.K.Morrison	cw I.A.Healy
79	R.P.de Groen	c A.R.Border
2nd innings	dnb	35.0/11/ 59/4 ..c1
80	A.H.Jones	c A.R.Border
81	B.A.Young	b
82	D.N.Patel	b

83   S.B.Doull   c M.A.Taylor

21   *Australia v South Africa, 1st Test, Melbourne Cricket Ground, December 26, 27, 28, 29, 30, 1993*

1st innings   lbw b P.S.de Villiers ...... 0 ..... 31.0/ 8/ 63/1

84   W.J.Cronje   c D.C.Boon

2nd innings   dnb

22   *Australia v South Africa, 2nd Test, Sydney Cricket Ground, January 2, 3, 4, 5, 6, 1994*

1st innings   c J.N.Rhodes b P.L.Symcox ...... 11 ...... 27.0/ 8/ 56/7 ..c1

85	D.J.Cullinan	b
86	J.N.Rhodes	lbw
87	G.Kirsten	st I.A.Healy
88	D.J.Richardson	c M.A.Taylor
89	K.C.Wessels	c & b
90	C.R.Matthews	c M.A.Taylor
91	P.L.Symcox	b

2nd innings   run out ...... 1 ...... 42.0/17/ 72/5

92	K.C.Wessels	b
93	D.J.Cullinan	lbw
94	C.R.Matthews	c M.E.Waugh
95	P.S.de Villiers	lbw
96	A.A.Donald	cw I.A.Healy

23   *Australia v South Africa, 3rd Test, Adelaide Oval, January 28, 29, 30, 31, February 1, 1994*

1st innings   not out ...... 4 ...... 44.2/15/ 85/1

97   P.N.Kirsten   c M.E.Waugh

2nd innings   dnb ...... 30.5/15/ 31/4 ..c1

98	W.J.Cronje	lbw
99	G.Kirsten	b
100	B.M.McMillan	lbw
101	R.P.Snell	c & b

24 Australia v South Africa, 1st Test, New Wanderers Stadium, Johannesburg, March 4, 5, 6, 7, 8, 1994

1st innings	lbw b C.R.Matthews		15 ..... 14.0/ 4/ 42/1
102	D.J.Richardson	lbw	
2nd innings	lbw b B.M.McMillan		1 ..... 44.5/14/ 86/4
103	A.C.Hudson	b	
104	K.C.Wessels	c A.R.Border	
105	D.J.Richardson	c A.R.Border	
106	B.M.McMillan	b	

25 Australia v South Africa, 2nd Test, Newlands, Cape Town, March 17, 18, 19, 20, 21, 1994

1st innings	c B.M.McMillan b P.S.de Villiers		11 ..... 47.0/18/ 78/3
107	P.N.Kirsten	lbw	
108	B.M.McMillan	b	
109	P.S.de Villiers	c M.A.Taylor	
2nd innings	dnb		30.0/13/ 38/3
110	G.Kirsten	lbw	
111	P.N.Kirsten	c M.A.Taylor	
112	P.S.de Villiers	lbw	

26 Australia v South Africa, 3rd Test, Kingsmead, Durban, March 25, 26, 27, 28, 29, 1994

1st innings	c K.C.Wessels b C.R.Matthews		2 ..... 55.0/20/ 92/4
113	W.J.Cronje	c S.R.Waugh	
114	J.N.Rhodes	lbw	
115	D.J.Richardson	c P.R.Reiffel	
116	C.R.Matthews	lbw	
2nd innings	c B.M.McMillan b A.A.Donald		12

27 Australia v Pakistan, 1st Test, National Stadium, Karachi, September 28, 29, 30, October 1, 2, 1994

1st innings	cw Rashid Latif b Aamer Sohail		22 ..... 27.0/10/ 61/3
117	Aamer Sohail	c M.G.Bevan	
118	Inzamamul Haq	c M.A.Taylor	
119	Rashid Latif	c M.A.Taylor	

2nd innings lbw b Waqar Younis .... 0 ...... 36.1/12/ 89/5 ..c1
120 Zahid Fazal c D.C.Boon
121 Akram Raza lbw
122 Wasim Akram c & b
123 Basit Ali lbw
124 Waqar Younis cw I.A.Healy

28   Australia v Pakistan, 2nd Test, Rawalpindi Cricket Stadium, October 5, 6, 7, 8, 9, 1994

1st innings c and b Aamer Sohail .... 14 ..... 21.4/ 8/ 58/1 ..c1
125 Inzamamul Haq lbw

2nd innings dnb 25.0/ 6/ 56/0

29   Australia v Pakistan, 3rd Test, Gaddafi Stadium, Lahore, November 1, 2, 3, 4, 5, 1994

1st innings c and b Mohsin Kamal .... 33 ..... 41.5/12/136/6
126 Saeed Anwar b
127 Basit Ali c M.E.Waugh
128 Ijaz Ahmed c D.C.Boon
129 Akram Raza b
130 Aaqib Javed c M.E.Waugh
131 Mohsin Kamal lbw

2nd innings dnb 30.0/ 2/104/3
132 Aamer Sohail st P.A.Emery
133 Akram Raza lbw
134 Aaqib Javed b

30   Australia v England, 1st Test, Brisbane Cricket Ground, Woolloongabba, November 25, 26, 27, 28, 29, 1994

1st innings cw S.J.Rhodes b D.Gough .... 2 ..... 21.2/ 7/ 39/3 ..c1
135 G.P.Thorpe c & b
136 P.A.J.DeFreitas cw I.A.Healy
137 P.C.R.Tufnell c M.A.Taylor

2nd innings c sub b P.A.J.DeFreitas .... 0 ..... 50.2/22/ 71/8
138 A.J.Stewart b
139 M.A.Atherton lbw

140	G.P.Thorpe	b
141	G.A.Hick	cw I.A.Healy
142	G.A.Gooch	cw I.A.Healy
143	P.A.J.DeFreitas	b
144	M.J.McCague	lbw
145	D.Gough	c M.E.Waugh

31 Australia v England, 2nd Test, Melbourne Cricket Ground, December 24, 26, 27, 28, 29, 1994

1st innings	c G.A.Hick b D.Gough	6 ...... 27.4/ 8/ 64/6 ..c1
146	M.A.Atherton	lbw
147	G.P.Thorpe	c M.E.Waugh
148	M.W.Gatting	c S.R.Waugh
149	S.J.Rhodes	c M.E.Waugh
150	A.J.Stewart	c & b
151	P.A.J.DeFreitas	st I.A.Healy
2nd innings	c P.A.J.DeFreitas b D.Gough	0 ...... 13.0/ 6/ 16/3
152	P.A.J.DeFreitas	lbw
153	D.Gough	cw I.A.Healy
154	D.E.Malcolm	c D.C.Boon

32 Australia v England, 3rd Test, Sydney Cricket Ground, January 1, 2, 3, 4, 5, 1995

1st innings	c M.W.Gatting b A.R.C.Fraser	0 ...... 36.0/10/ 88/1
155	D.E.Malcolm	b
2nd innings	not out	36 ...... 16.0/ 2/ 48/0

33 Australia v England, 4th Test, Adelaide Oval, January 26, 27, 28, 29, 30, 1995

1st innings	c G.P.Thorpe b A.R.C.Fraser	7 ...... 31.0/ 9/ 72/2
156	G.P.Thorpe	c M.A.Taylor
157	J.P.Crawley	b
2nd innings	lbw b C.C.Lewis	2 ...... 30.5/ 9/ 82/2 ..c1
158	S.J.Rhodes	c D.W.Fleming
159	P.C.R.Tufnell	lbw

34 Australia v England, 5th Test, Western Australia Cricket Association Ground, Perth, February 3, 4, 5, 6, 7, 1995

1st innings cw S.J.Rhodes b P.A.J.DeFreitas ......1 ...... 23.0/ 8/ 58/2 ..c2
160 G.P.Thorpe st I.A.Healy
161 M.R.Ramprakash b
2nd innings c C.C.Lewis b D.E.Malcolm ......6......7.0/ 3/ 11/0

35 Australia v West Indies, 1st Test, Kensington Oval, Bridgetown, Barbados, March 31, April 1, 2, 1995

1st innings c J.C.Adams b C.A.Walsh ......6......12.0/ 2/ 57/2 ..c1
162 W.K.M.Benjamin c M.A.Taylor
163 C.A.Walsh c S.R.Waugh
2nd innings dnb......26.3/ 5/ 64/3
164 S.L.Campbell c S.R.Waugh
165 J.R.Murray c S.R.Waugh
166 K.C.G.Benjamin b

36 Australia v West Indies, 2nd Test, Antigua Recreation Ground, St John's, Antigua, April 8, 9, 10, 12, 13, 1995

1st innings c K.L.T.Arthurton b C.A.Walsh......11 ...... 28.0/ 9/ 83/3
167 S.C.Williams c D.C.Boon
168 J.C.Adams lbw
169 K.L.T.Arthurton c M.A.Taylor
2nd innings dnb......7.0/ 0/ 18/0

37 Australia v West Indies, 3rd Test, Queen's Park Oval, Port of Spain, Trinidad, April 21, 22, 23, 1995

1st innings b C.E.L.Ambrose......0 ...... 12.0/ 5/ 16/1
170 W.K.M.Benjamin c M.J.Slater
2nd innings c C.L.Hooper b C.A.Walsh......11 ...... 3.5/ 0/ 26/0 ..c1

38 Australia v West Indies, 4th Test, Sabina Park, Kingston, Jamaica, April 29, 30, May 1, 3, 1995

1st innings c B.C.Lara b K.C.G.Benjamin......0 ...... 25.0/ 6/ 72/2
171 B.C.Lara cw I.A.Healy
172 C.O.Browne c D.C.Boon

2nd innings

173	K.L.T.Arthurton	lbw	
174	C.E.L.Ambrose	st I.A.Healy	
175	C.A.Walsh	c G.S.Blewett	
176	K.C.G.Benjamin	c M.A.Taylor	
	dnb		23.4/ 8/ 70/4

39   Australia v Pakistan, 1st Test, Brisbane Cricket Ground, Woolloongabba, November 9, 10, 11, 13, 1995

1st innings   cw Moin Khan b Aamer Sohail ..... 5 ...... 16.1/ 9/ 23/7

177	Rameez Raja	c M.A.Taylor
178	Aamer Sohail	st I.A.Healy
179	Inzamamul Haq	c S.R.Waugh
180	Moin Khan	c C.J.McDermott
181	Basit Ali	c M.A.Taylor
182	Wasim Akram	c D.C.Boon
183	Mohammad Akram	c G.S.Blewett

2nd innings   dnb 27.5/10/ 54/4

184	Wasim Akram	c M.J.Slater
185	Saleem Malik	c C.J.McDermott
186	Waqar Younis	lbw
187	Mohammad Akram	lbw

40   Australia v Pakistan, 2nd Test, Bellerive Oval, Hobart, November 17, 18, 19, 20, 21, 1995

1st innings   not out 27
2nd innings   dnb

41   Australia v Pakistan, 3rd Test, Sydney Cricket Ground, November 30, December 1, 2, 3, 4, 1995

1st innings   cw Rashid Latif b Wasim Akram ..... 2 ...... 34.0/20/ 55/4

188	Rameez Raja	c M.J.Slater
189	Inzamamul Haq	cw I.A.Healy
190	Ijaz Ahmed	c G.D.McGrath
191	Mushtaq Ahmed	c C.J.McDermott

2nd innings   c Saqlain Mushtaq b Mushtaq Ahmed ..... 5 ...... 37.0/13/ 66/4

192	Ijaz Ahmed	lbw

193	Rameez Raja	c M.E.Waugh
194	Basit Ali	b
195	Rashid Latif	lbw

42 Australia v Sri Lanka, 1st Test, Western Australia Cricket Association Ground, Perth, December 8, 9, 10, 11, 1995

1st innings dnb .... 27.0/ 7/ 75/3 ..c2
196	P.A.de Silva	c & b
197	R.S.Kaluwitharana	c M.A.Taylor
198	W.P.U.J.C.Vaas	cw I.A.Healy

2nd innings .... 29.4/ 6/ 96/3 ..c1
199	P.A.de Silva	c R.T.Ponting
200	W.P.U.J.C.Vaas	cw I.A.Healy
201	H.P.Tillakaratne	c R.T.Ponting

43 Australia v Sri Lanka, 2nd Test, Melbourne Cricket Ground, December 26, 27, 28, 29, 30, 1995

1st innings dnb .... 18.0/ 5/ 49/1 ..c1
202	H.P.Tillakaratne	c M.A.Taylor

2nd innings dnb .... 37.0/10/ 71/4 ..c1
203	U.C.Hathurusingha	lbw
204	R.S.Kaluwitharana	st I.A.Healy
205	G.P.Wickramasinghe	st I.A.Healy
206	M.Muralidaran	c M.A.Taylor

44 Australia v Sri Lanka, 3rd Test, Adelaide Oval, January 25, 26, 27, 28, 29, 1996

1st innings c K.R.Pushpakumara b G.P.Wickramasinghe ....33 .....26.0/ 4/ 74/0
2nd innings dnb 27.0/11/ 68/1
207	G.P.Wickramasinghe	b

45 Australia v West Indies, 1st Test, Brisbane Cricket Ground, Woolloongabba, November 22, 23, 24, 25, 26, 1996

1st innings c and b I.R.Bishop ....24 ..... 27.0/ 3/ 88/2 ..c1
208	I.R.Bishop	lbw
209	K.C.G.Benjamin	lbw

2nd innings

	dnb		41.0/16/ 92/2 ..c1
210	R.G.Samuels	c M.A.Taylor	
211	J.C.Adams	lbw	

46   Australia v West Indies, 2nd Test, Sydney Cricket Ground, November 29, 30, December 1, 2, 3, 1996

1st innings   cw C.O.Browne b I.R.Bishop .... 28 ...... 35.2/13/ 65/3 ..c1

212	C.L.Hooper	lbw
213	S.Chanderpaul	c & b
214	I.R.Bishop	c M.T.G.Elliott

2nd innings   dnb 27.4/ 5/ 95/4

215	R.G.Samuels	b
216	S.Chanderpaul	b
217	K.C.G.Benjamin	c M.A.Taylor
218	C.A.Walsh	c G.D.McGrath

47   Australia v West Indies, 3rd Test, Melbourne Cricket Ground, December 26, 27, 28, 1996

1st innings   c S.L.Campbell b I.R.Bishop .... 10 ...... 28.1/ 3/ 72/3 ..c1

219	R.G.Samuels	c M.A.Taylor
220	C.E.L.Ambrose	b
221	C.A.Walsh	c M.E.Waugh

2nd innings   c J.C.Adams b C.E.L.Ambrose .... 18 ...... 3.0/ 0/ 17/0

48   Australia v West Indies, 4th Test, Adelaide Oval, January 25, 26, 27, 28, 1997

1st innings   c C.L.Hooper b I.R.Bishop .... 9 ...... 16.0/ 4/ 42/3 ..c1

222	B.C.Lara	c G.S.Blewett
223	S.Chanderpaul	c M.A.Taylor
224	J.C.Adams	c & b

2nd innings   dnb 20.0/ 4/ 68/3

225	C.L.Hooper	lbw
226	I.R.Bishop	c M.G.Bevan
227	B.C.Lara	cw I.A.Healy

49 Australia v West Indies, 5th Test, Western Australia Cricket Association Ground, Perth, February 1, 2, 3, 1997

1st innings cw C.O.Browne b I.R.Bishop .... 9 ..... 19.0/ 8/ 55/2 ..c1
228 B.C.Lara cw I.A.Healy
229 R.G.Samuels c M.E.Waugh
2nd innings c P.V.Simmons b I.R.Bishop 30

50 Australia v South Africa, 1st Test, New Wanderers Stadium, Johannesburg, February 28, March 1, 2, 3, 4, 1997

1st innings b W.J.Cronje .... 9 ...27.4/ 9/ 68/2
230 W.J.Cronje c M.E.Waugh
231 P.R.Adams lbw
2nd innings dnb 28.0/15/ 43/4
232 G.Kirsten b
233 D.J.Cullinan cw I.A.Healy
234 J.N.Rhodes lbw
235 J.H.Kallis b

51 Australia v South Africa, 2nd Test, St George's Park, Port Elizabeth, March 14, 15, 16, 17, 1997

1st innings lbw b P.R.Adams .... 18 ..... 23.4/ 5/ 62/3 ..c2
236 D.J.Richardson c G.D.McGrath
237 B.M.McMillan c S.R.Waugh
238 A.A.Donald c & b
2nd innings lbw b J.H.Kallis .... 3 ..... 17.4/ 7/ 20/2 ..c1
239 S.M.Pollock lbw
240 P.R.Adams c M.A.Taylor

52 Australia v South Africa, 3rd Test, Centurion Park, Centurion, March 21, 22, 23, 24, 1997

1st innings lbw b B.N.Schultz .... 0 ......36.0/11/ 89/0
2nd innings lbw b A.A.Donald 12

53 Australia v England, 1st Test, Edgbaston, Birmingham, June 5, 6, 7, 8, 1997

1st innings c D.E.Malcolm b A.R.Caddick .... 47 .....35.0/ 8/110/1
241 N.Hussain cw I.A.Healy

2nd innings   c and b M.A.Ealham .... 32 ...... 7.3/ 0/ 27/0

54   Australia v England, 2nd Test, Lord's Cricket Ground, St John's Wood, London, June 19, 20, 21, 22, 23, 1997

1st innings   c N.Hussain b D.Gough .... 0 .... 2.0/ 0/ 9/0
2nd innings   dnb .... 19.0/ 4/ 47/2 ..c1

242   N.Hussain   c & b
243   M.A.Butcher   b

55   Australia v England, 3rd Test, Old Trafford, Manchester, July 3, 4, 5, 6, 7, 1997

1st innings   cw A.J.Stewart b M.A.Ealham .... 3 ...... 30.0/14/ 48/6

244   A.J.Stewart   c M.A.Taylor
245   G.P.Thorpe   c M.A.Taylor
246   N.Hussain   cw I.A.Healy
247   J.P.Crawley   cw I.A.Healy
248   D.Gough   lbw
249   A.R.Caddick   c M.E.Waugh

2nd innings   cw A.J.Stewart b A.R.Caddick .... 53 ...... 30.4/ 8/ 63/3

250   A.J.Stewart   b
251   G.P.Thorpe   cw I.A.Healy
252   A.R.Caddick   c J.N.Gillespie

56   Australia v England, 4th Test, Headingley, Leeds, July 24, 25, 26, 27, 28, 1997

1st innings   c G.P.Thorpe b M.A.Ealham .... 0 .... 1.0/ 0/ 2/0
2nd innings   dnb .... 21.0/ 6/ 53/1 ..c1

253   N.Hussain   c J.N.Gillespie

57   Australia v England, 5th Test, Trent Bridge, Nottingham, August 7, 8, 9, 10, 1997

1st innings   c G.P.Thorpe b D.E.Malcolm .... 0 ...... 32.0/ 8/ 86/4

254   M.A.Atherton   cw I.A.Healy
255   A.J.Stewart   cw I.A.Healy
256   N.Hussain   b
257   G.P.Thorpe   c G.S.Blewett

2nd innings   c G.P.Thorpe b R.D.B.Croft .... 20 ...... 16.0/ 4/ 43/3

258	B.C.Hollioake	lbw
259	R.D.B.Croft	c G.D.McGrath
260	A.R.Caddick	lbw

58 *Australia v England, 6th Test, The Oval, Kennington, London, August 21, 22, 23, 1997*

1st innings b A.R.Caddick..30......17.0/ 8/ 32/2

261	A.J.Hollioake	b
262	P.C.R.Tufnell	c G.S.Blewett

2nd innings c P.J.Martin b P.C.R.Tufnell.....................3......26.0/ 9/ 57/2

263	N.Hussain	c M.T.G.Elliott
264	M.R.Ramprakash	st I.A.Healy

59 *Australia v New Zealand, 1st Test, Brisbane Cricket Ground, Woolloongabba, November 7, 8, 9, 10, 11, 1997*

1st innings c S.P.Fleming b D.L.Vettori...............21......42.0/13/106/4

265	B.A.Pocock	c M.A.Taylor
266	C.D.McMillan	lbw
267	A.C.Parore	c M.A.Taylor
268	C.Z.Harris	b

2nd innings dnb...25.0/ 6/ 54/3

269	C.Z.Harris	b
270	D.L.Vettori	c M.A.Taylor
271	G.I.Allott	lbw

60 *Australia v New Zealand, 2nd Test, Western Australia Cricket Association Ground, Perth, November 20, 21, 22, 23, 1997*

1st innings c S.B.O'Connor b D.L.Vettori...............36......22.4/ 3/ 83/4

272	S.P.Fleming	c G.S.Blewett
273	C.L.Cairns	c M.E.Waugh
274	S.B.Doull	c M.A.Taylor
275	G.I.Allott	b

2nd innings dnb...26.0/ 4/ 64/2

276	D.L.Vettori	c M.A.Taylor
277	S.P.Fleming	c G.S.Blewett

61   *Australia v New Zealand, 3rd Test, Bellerive Oval, Hobart, November 27, 28, 29, 30, December 1, 1997*

1st innings: st A.C.Parore b D.L.Vettori............14......27.0/ 4/ 81/1

278	R.G.Twose	lbw

2nd innings: dnb............28.0/ 6/ 88/5

279	C.L.Cairns	st I.A.Healy
280	S.P.Fleming	st I.A.Healy
281	B.A.Young	c R.T.Ponting
282	C.D.McMillan	c M.A.Taylor
283	A.C.Parore	c M.T.G.Elliott

62   *Australia v South Africa, 1st Test, Melbourne Cricket Ground, December 26, 27, 28, 29, 30, 1997*

1st innings: c and b S.M.Pollock............1.....42.0/15/ 64/3

284	W.J.Cronje	c G.S.Blewett
285	S.M.Pollock	lbw
286	L.Klusener	lbw

2nd innings: c P.L.Symcox b A.A.Donald............10......44.0/11/ 97/3

287	A.M.Bacher	c M.A.Taylor
288	D.J.Cullinan	b
289	B.M.McMillan	c M.A.Taylor

63   *Australia v South Africa, 2nd Test, Sydney Cricket Ground, January 2, 3, 4, 5, 1998*

1st innings: lbw b S.M.Pollock............12.....32.1/ 8/ 75/5

290	S.M.Pollock	c M.A.Taylor
291	D.J.Richardson	b
292	W.J.Cronje	c M.A.Taylor
293	P.L.Symcox	cw I.A.Healy
294	P.R.Adams	c S.R.Waugh

2nd innings: dnb............21.0/ 9/ 34/6 ..c1

295	W.J.Cronje	c R.T.Ponting
296	H.H.Gibbs	c G.S.Blewett
297	B.M.McMillan	b
298	S.M.Pollock	c M.A.Taylor

| 299 | D.J.Richardson | c & b |
| 300 | J.H.Kallis | b |

64   *Australia v South Africa, 3rd Test, Adelaide Oval, January 30, 31, February 1, 2, 3, 1998*

1st innings
301	cw D.J.Richardson b S.M.Pollock		0 ...... 33.0/ 6/ 95/2 ..c3
	W.J.Cronje	b	
302	D.J.Richardson	c M.A.Taylor	4 ...... 15.0/ 2/ 52/1 ..c1

2nd innings
| 303 | not out | | |
| | A.M.Bacher | c S.C.G.MacGill | |

65   *Australia v India, 1st Test, M.A.Chidambaram Stadium, Chepauk, Chennai,*
March 6, 7, 8, 9, 10, 1998

1st innings
304	c S.R.Tendulkar b A.Kumble		17 ...... 35.0/11/ 85/4
305	S.R.Tendulkar	c M.A.Taylor	
306	M.Azharuddin	c P.R.Reiffel	
307	J.Srinath	c M.A.Taylor	
	R.S.Dravid	c G.R.Robertson	

2nd innings
| 308 | c A.Kumble b R.K.Chauhan | | 35 ...... 30.0/ 7/122/1 |
| | R.S.Dravid | cw I.A.Healy | |

66   *Australia v India, 2nd Test, Eden Gardens, Calcutta, March 18, 19, 20, 21, 1998*

1st innings   c M.Azharuddin b A.Kumble ...... 11 ...... 42.0/ 4/147/0
2nd innings   c and b A.Kumble 9

67   *Australia v India, 3rd Test, M.Chinnaswamy Stadium, Bangalore, March 25, 26, 27, 28, 1998*

1st innings
309	c Harbhajan Singh b S.L.Venkatapathy Raju		33 ...... 35.0/ 9/106/3
	N.S.Sidhu	b	
310	R.S.Dravid	b	
311	N.R.Mongia	c R.T.Ponting	

2nd innings
	dnb		25.0/ 6/ 80/2
312	V.V.S.Laxman	c R.T.Ponting	
313	N.S.Sidhu	c D.S.Lehmann	

68   *Australia v England, 5th Test, Sydney Cricket Ground, January 2, 3, 4, 5, 1999*

1st innings   not out ...... 2 ...... 20.0/ 4/ 67/1 ..c2

314	M.A.Butcher	lbw	
2nd innings 315	c M.R.Ramprakash b P.M.Such	8..... 19.0/ 3/ 43/1	
	M.A.Butcher	st I.A.Healy	

69   Australia v West Indies, 1st Test, Queen's Park Oval, Port-of-Spain, Trinidad, March 5, 6, 7, 8, 1999

1st innings	c S.L.Campbell b C.E.L.Ambrose	21..... 14.0/ 4/ 35/0
2nd innings	b C.A.Walsh	25...........c1

70   Australia v West Indies, 2nd Test, Sabina Park, Kingston, Jamaica, March 13, 14, 15, 16, 1999

1st innings 316	c D.R.E.Joseph b P.T.Collins	24..... 30.0/ 8/ 94/1 ..c1
	R.D.Jacobs c J.N.Gillespie	
2nd innings	c D.R.E.Joseph b C.A.Walsh	23

71   Australia v West Indies, 3rd Test, Kensington Oval, Bridgetown, Barbados, March 26, 27, 28, 29, 30, 1999

1st innings 317	c B.C.Lara b N.O.Perry	13...... 15.5/ 2/ 70/1 ..c1
	C.A.Walsh c M.J.Slater	
2nd innings	lbw b C.A.Walsh	32.....24.0/ 4/ 69/0

72   Australia v Sri Lanka, 1st Test, Asgiriya Stadium, Kandy, September 9, 10, 11, 1999

1st innings 318	c M.S.Atapattu b D.N.T.Zoysa	0...... 16.0/ 4/ 52/5
	D.P.M.D.Jayawardene c R.T.Ponting	
319	A.Ranatunga cw I.A.Healy	
320	U.D.U.Chandana c sub	
321	P.A.de Silva c R.T.Ponting	
322	D.N.T.Zoysa c C.R.Miller	
2nd innings	run out	6....... 6.5/ 3/ 18/0

73   Australia v Sri Lanka, 2nd Test, Galle International Stadium, September 22, 23, 24, 25, 26, 1999

1st innings 323	c M.S.Atapattu b H.M.R.K.B.Herath	0...... 25.0/11/ 29/3 ..c1
	M.S.Atapattu cw I.A.Healy	
324	D.P.M.D.Jayawardene c G.S.Blewett	
325	A.Ranatunga c C.R.Miller	
2nd innings	dnb	3.2/ 1/ 5/0

74 Australia v Sri Lanka, 3rd Test, Sinhalese Sports Club, Colombo, September 30, October 1, 2, 3, 4, 1999

1st innings	lbw b W.P.U.J.C.Vaas	0	5.0/ 1/ 11/0 ..c1
2nd innings	dnb		

75 Australia v Zimbabwe, Only Test, Harare Sports Club, October 14, 15, 16, 17, 1999

1st innings	cw A.Flower b H.H.Streak	6	23.0/ 2/ 69/3
326	T.R.Gripper	lbw	
327	H.H.Streak	c M.E.Waugh	
328	G.J.Whittall	cw I.A.Healy	
			30.1/11/ 68/3
2nd innings	dnb......		
329	G.J.Whittall	c M.E.Waugh	
330	H.H.Streak	lbw	
331	M.W.Goodwin	c S.R.Waugh	

76 Australia v Pakistan, 1st Test, Brisbane Cricket Ground, Woolloongabba, November 5, 6, 7, 8, 9, 1999

1st innings	c Mushtaq Ahmed b Wasim Akram......	86......	28.1/11/ 73/1 ..c1
332	Saeed Anwar	c M.E.Waugh	
			25.0/ 8/ 80/2
2nd innings	dnb......		
333	Abdur Razzaq	c R.T.Ponting	
334	Azhar Mahmood	st A.C.Gilchrist	

77 Australia v Pakistan, 2nd Test, Bellerive Oval, Hobart, November 18, 19, 20, 21, 22, 1999

1st innings	b Saqlain Mushtaq......	0	16.0/ 6/ 45/3 ..c1
335	Azhar Mahmood	b	
336	Saqlain Mushtaq	lbw	
337	Wasim Akram	cw A.C.Gilchrist	
2nd innings	not out......	0	45.4/11/110/5
338	Saqlain Mushtaq	lbw	
339	Saeed Anwar	b	
340	Azhar Mahmood	lbw	
341	Wasim Akram	c G.S.Blewett	
342	Inzamamul Haq	c M.E.Waugh	

78   *Australia v Pakistan, 3rd Test, Western Australia Cricket Association Ground, Perth, November 26, 27, 28, 1999*

1st innings	cw Moin Khan b Saqlain Mushtaq		13	2.0/ 0/ 6/0 ...c1
2nd innings	dnb	b		13.0/ 1/ 56/1 ..c1
343	Azhar Mahmood			

79   *Australia v India, 1st Test, Adelaide Oval, December 10, 11, 12, 13, 14, 1999*

1st innings	lbw b A.Kumble		86	42.0/12/ 92/4
344	R.S.Dravid	c J.L.Langer		
345	S.R.Tendulkar	c J.L.Langer		
346	S.C.Ganguly	st A.C.Gilchrist		
347	M.S.K.Prasad	b		
2nd innings	c R.S.Dravid b J.Srinath		0	10.0/ 6/ 21/2
348	R.S.Dravid	cw A.C.Gilchrist		
349	S.Ramesh	lbw		

80   *Australia v India, 2nd Test, Melbourne Cricket Ground, December 26, 27, 28, 29, 30, 1999*

1st innings	c M.S.K.Prasad b A.B.Agarkar		2	24.0/ 5/ 77/1
350	H.H.Kanitkar	lbw		
2nd innings	dnb			26.0/ 7/ 63/1 ..c2
351	S.R.Tendulkar	lbw		

81   *Australia v India, 3rd Test, Sydney Cricket Ground, January 2, 3, 4, 2000*

1st innings	dnb			12.0/ 4/ 22/0
2nd innings	dnb			13.0/ 1/ 60/0 ..c1

82   *Australia v New Zealand, 1st Test, Eden Park, Auckland, March 11, 12, 13, 14, 15, 2000*

1st innings	c S.P.Fleming b D.L.Vettori		7	22.0/ 4/ 68/3
352	M.S.Sinclair	lbw		
353	N.J.Astle	c M.E.Waugh		
354	C.D.McMillan	lbw		
2nd innings	c P.J.Wiseman b D.L.Vettori		12	20.3/ 5/ 80/2 ..c2
355	N.J.Astle	b		
356	P.J.Wiseman	cw A.C.Gilchrist		

83 *Australia v New Zealand, 2nd Test, Basin Reserve, Wellington, March 24, 25, 26, 27, 2000*

1st innings lbw b D.L.Vettori .... 7 ..... 14.5/ 1/ 68/4 ..c1
357 c C.R.Miller S.P.Fleming
358 c M.E.Waugh N.J.Astle
359 c J.L.Langer D.L.Vettori
360 c M.J.Slater S.B.Doull

2nd innings dnb.. 27.0/ 7/ 92/3
361 b N.J.Astle
362 c M.E.Waugh C.D.McMillan
363 c S.R.Waugh S.B.Doull

84 *Australia v New Zealand, 3rd Test, WestpacTrust Park, Hamilton, March 31, April 1, 2, 3, 2000*

1st innings lbw b S.B.O'Connor.. 10 ..... 20.0/ 5/ 45/1 ..c1
364 b P.J.Wiseman

2nd innings dnb.. 25.0/11/ 61/2
365 cw A.C.Gilchrist N.J.Astle
366 c M.E.Waugh C.D.McMillan

85 *Australia v India, 1st Test, Wankhede Stadium, Mumbai, February 27, 28, March 1, 2001*

1st innings c S.R.Tendulkar b R.L.Sanghvi.. 39 ..... 22.0/ 7/ 47/4 ..c1
367 c M.L.Hayden S.C.Ganguly
368 c & b A.B.Agarkar
369 c M.E.Waugh J.Srinath
370 c S.R.Waugh Harbhajan Singh

2nd innings dnb.. 28.0/11/ 60/1
371 b R.S.Dravid

86 *Australia v India, 2nd Test, Eden Gardens, Kolkata, March 11, 12, 13, 14, 15, 2001*

1st innings c S.Ramesh b Harbhajan Singh.. 0 ..... 20.1/ 3/ 65/2
372 b R.S.Dravid
373 c M.L.Hayden V.V.S.Laxman

2nd innings lbw b S.R.Tendulkar.. 0 ..... 34.0/ 3/152/1
374 c M.E.Waugh S.Ramesh

87   *Australia v India, 3rd Test, M.A.Chidambaram Stadium, Chepauk, Chennai, March 18, 19, 20, 21, 22, 2001*

1st innings   c S.S.Das b Harbhajan Singh ...... 0 ...... 42.0/ 7/140/2
- 375   S.Ramesh   c R.T.Ponting
- 376   S.S.Dighe   lbw

2nd innings   lbw b Harbhajan Singh ...... 11 ...... 6.0/ 0/ 41/0 ..c1

88   *Australia v England, 1st Test, Edgbaston, Birmingham, July 5, 6, 7, 8, 2001*

1st innings   c M.A.Atherton b M.A.Butcher ...... 8 ...... 19.0/ 4/ 71/5 ..c1
- 377   M.A.Butcher   c R.T.Ponting
- 378   U.Afzaal   b
- 379   C.White   lbw
- 380   A.F.Giles   cw A.C.Gilchrist
- 381   D.Gough   c J.N.Gillespie

2nd innings   dnb ...... 10.1/ 4/ 29/3 ..c1
- 382   M.E.Trescothick   c M.E.Waugh
- 383   D.Gough   lbw
- 384   A.F.Giles   c M.E.Waugh

89   *Australia v England, 2nd Test, Lord's Cricket Ground, St John's Wood, London, July 19, 20, 21, 22, 2001*

1st innings   cw A.J.Stewart b A.R.Caddick ...... 5 ...... 5.3/ 0/ 16/2
- 385   A.R.Caddick   b
- 386   D.Gough   b

2nd innings   dnb ...... 20.0/ 4/ 58/1 ..c1
- 387   M.A.Atherton   b

90   *Australia v England, 3rd Test, Trent Bridge, Nottingham, August 2, 3, 4, 2001*

1st innings   lbw b A.R.Caddick ...... 0 ...... 16.0/ 4/ 37/2
- 388   A.J.Tudor   lbw
- 389   R.D.B.Croft   c R.T.Ponting

2nd innings   dnb 18.0/ 5/ 33/6
- 390   M.E.Trescothick   cw A.C.Gilchrist
- 391   M.A.Atherton   cw A.C.Gilchrist

392	A.J.Stewart	b
393	M.R.Ramprakash	st A.C.Gilchrist
394	C.White	c S.R.Waugh
395	A.J.Tudor	c R.T.Ponting

91   *Australia v England, 4th Test, Headingley, Leeds, August 6, 17, 18, 19, 20, 2001*

1st innings	cw A.J.Stewart b D.Gough	0	......	16.0/ 2/ 49/0 ..c1
2nd innings	dnb			18.2/ 3/ 58/1
396	M.R.Ramprakash	c M.E.Waugh		

92   *Australia v England, 5th Test, The Oval, Kennington, London, August 23, 24, 25, 26, 27, 2001*

1st innings	dnb		44.2/ 7/165/7
397	M.A.Atherton	b	
398	M.E.Trescothick	b	
399	M.A.Butcher	c J.L.Langer	
400	A.J.Stewart	cw A.C.Gilchrist	
401	A.R.Caddick	lbw	
402	J.Ormond	b	
403	D.Gough	st A.C.Gilchrist	
2nd innings	dnb		28.0/ 8/ 64/4 ..c2
404	M.A.Butcher	c S.R.Waugh	
405	N.Hussain	lbw	
406	M.R.Ramprakash	c M.L.Hayden	
407	A.J.Stewart	b	

93   *Australia v New Zealand, 1st Test, Brisbane Cricket Ground, Woolloongabba, November 8, 9, 10, 11, 12, 2001*

1st innings	c M.S.Sinclair b C.L.Cairns	22	......	18.0/ 2/ 61/0 ..c1
2nd innings	dnb			18.0/ 2/ 89/3
408	M.H.Richardson	lbw		
409	M.S.Sinclair	st A.C.Gilchrist		
410	N.J.Astle	c J.N.Gillespie		

94   Australia v New Zealand, 2nd Test, Bellerive Oval, Hobart, November 22, 23, 24, 25, 26, 2001

1st innings	411	b N.J.Astle	70 ...... 24.2/ 3/ 70/1 ..c1
		cw A.C.Gilchrist M.D.Bell	
2nd innings		dnb	

95   Australia v New Zealand, 3rd Test, Western Australia Cricket Association Ground, Perth, November 30, December 1, 2, 3, 4, 2001

1st innings	412	c M.H.Richardson b D.L.Vettori	99 ...... 43.0/ 9/135/1
		L.Vincent c M.E.Waugh	
2nd innings	413	run out	10 ...... 21.0/ 3/ 75/1 ..c2
		S.P.Fleming b	

96   Australia v South Africa, 1st Test, Adelaide Oval, December 14, 15, 16, 17, 18, 2001

1st innings	414	b L.Klusener	41 ...... 39.4/ 9/113/5
		H.H.Gibbs st A.C.Gilchrist	
	415	L.Klusener b	
	416	S.M.Pollock cw A.C.Gilchrist	
	417	M.V.Boucher c J.L.Langer	
	418	M.Ntini c R.T.Ponting	
2nd innings		b C.W.Henderson	6 ...... 29.0/ 7/ 57/3 ..c2
	419	G.Kirsten c R.T.Ponting	
	420	S.M.Pollock c R.T.Ponting	
	421	C.W.Henderson c R.T.Ponting	

97   Australia v South Africa, 2nd Test, Melbourne Cricket Ground, December 26, 27, 28, 29, 2001

1st innings		c G.Kirsten b A.A.Donald	1 ...... 19.0/ 3/ 56/0
2nd innings		dnb	24.0/ 3/ 68/3
	422	H.H.Dippenaar c M.L.Hayden	
	423	N.D.McKenzie cw A.C.Gilchrist	
	424	M.V.Boucher c M.E.Waugh	

98   Australia v South Africa, 3rd Test, Sydney Cricket Ground, January 2, 3, 4, 5, 2002

| 1st innings | 425 | b S.M.Pollock | 37 ...... 19.0/ 5/ 47/3 |
| | | N.D.McKenzie   b | |

426   J.L.Ontong   lbw
427   M.V.Boucher   c R.T.Ponting
2nd innings   dnb 42.5/ 8/132/3
428   J.H.Kallis   cw A.C.Gilchrist
429   J.L.Ontong   lbw
430   A.A.Donald   c B.Lee

99   Australia v South Africa, 1st Test, New Wanderers Stadium, Johannesburg, February 22, 23, 24, 2002

1st innings   c N.D.McKenzie b N.Boje .... 12 .... 9.0/ 0/ 26/2 ..c2
431   H.H.Gibbs   lbw
432   A.Nel   lbw
2nd innings   dnb 12.0/ 3/ 44/4
433   A.G.Prince   b
434   H.H.Gibbs   st A.C.Gilchrist
435   H.H.Dippenaar   lbw
436   M.V.Boucher   b

100   Australia v South Africa, 2nd Test, Newlands, Cape Town, March 8, 9, 10, 11, 12, 2002

1st innings   c J.H.Kallis b P.R.Adams .... 63 ...... 28.0/10/ 70/2 ..c1
437   N.D.McKenzie   b
438   M.Ntini   c M.E.Waugh
2nd innings   not out .... 15 ..... 70.0/15/161/6
439   H.H.Gibbs   c R.T.Ponting
440   G.C.Smith   cw A.C.Gilchrist
441   J.H.Kallis   lbw
442   A.G.Prince   c R.T.Ponting
443   M.Ntini   c J.L.Langer
444   D.Pretorius   c M.E.Waugh

101   Australia v South Africa, 3rd Test, Kingsmead, Durban, March 15, 16, 17, 18, 2002

1st innings   cw M.V.Boucher b M.Ntini ...... 26 ..... 13.0/ 4/ 33/4 ..c2
445   J.H.Kallis   c & b
446   A.G.Prince   c B.Lee

447	M.V.Boucher	c & b		
448	M.Ntini	c G.D.McGrath		
2nd innings	c N.D.McKenzie b P.R.Adams		13...... 30.0/	6/108/2
449	N.D.McKenzie	c M.L.Hayden		
450	A.G.Prince	c M.E.Waugh		

102   Australia v Pakistan, 1st Test, P.Saravanamuttu Stadium, Colombo, October 3, 4, 5, 6, 7, 2002

1st innings	c Faisal Iqbal b Shoaib Akhtar		0...... 24.3/	7/ 94/7
451	Abdur Razzaq	cw A.C.Gilchrist		
452	Misbah-ul Haq	c M.E.Waugh		
453	Faisal Iqbal	c M.E.Waugh		
454	Saqlain Mushtaq	lbw		
455	Waqar Younis	lbw		
456	Rashid Latif	c D.R.Martyn		
457	Shoaib Akhtar	c G.D.McGrath		
2nd innings	lbw b Shoaib Akhtar		0...... 30.3/	3/ 94/4
458	Imran Nazir	c G.D.McGrath		
459	Abdur Razzaq	lbw		
460	Misbah-ul Haq	c S.R.Waugh		
461	Younis Khan	lbw		

103   Australia v Pakistan, 2nd Test, Sharjah Cricket Association Stadium, October 11, 12, 2002

1st innings	c Younis Khan b Saqlain Mushtaq		19...... 11.0/	4/ 11/4 ..c1
462	Faisal Iqbal	lbw		
463	Abdur Razzaq	c D.R.Martyn		
464	Saqlain Mushtaq	lbw		
465	Waqar Younis	lbw		
2nd innings	dnb		6.5/	2/ 13/4 ..c1
466	Imran Nazir	cw A.C.Gilchrist		
467	Faisal Iqbal	c M.E.Waugh		
468	Shoaib Akhtar	c S.R.Waugh		
469	Waqar Younis	lbw		

104 *Australia v Pakistan, 3rd Test, Sharjah Cricket Association Stadium, October 19, 20, 21, 22, 2002*

1st innings	lbw b Danish Kaneria		11 ..... 30.1/10/ 74/5
470	Imran Farhat	lbw	
471	Faisal Iqbal	c w A.C.Gilchrist	
472	Rashid Latif	c M.E.Waugh	
473	Mohammad Sami	lbw	
474	Danish Kaneria	st A.C.Gilchrist	
2nd innings	dnb		21.0/ 3/ 56/3
475	Misbah-ul Haq	lbw	
476	Rashid Latif	lbw	
477	Saqlain Mushtaq	lbw	

105 *Australia v England, 1st Test, Brisbane Cricket Ground, Woolloongabba, November 7, 8, 9, 10, 2002*

1st innings	c M.A.Butcher b A.R.Caddick		57 ..... 26.5/ 4/ 87/1
478	M.J.Hoggard	c M.L.Hayden	
2nd innings	dnb		10.2/ 3/ 29/3
479	A.J.Stewart	c M.L.Hayden	
480	M.A.Butcher	c R.T.Ponting	
481	A.R.Caddick	c D.S.Lehmann	

106 *Australia v England, 2nd Test, Adelaide Oval, November 21, 22, 23, 24, 2002*

1st innings	c and b R.K.J.Dawson		25 ..... 34.0/10/ 93/4 ..c1
482	R.W.T.Key	c R.T.Ponting	
483	N.Hussain	c w A.C.Gilchrist	
484	R.K.J.Dawson	lbw	
485	A.R.Caddick	b	
2nd innings	dnb		25.0/ 7/ 36/3
486	M.P.Vaughan	c G.D.McGrath	
487	A.J.Stewart	lbw	
488	S.J.Harmison	lbw	

107   *Australia v England, 3rd Test, Western Australia Cricket Association Ground, Perth, November 29, 30, December 1, 2002*

1st innings	run out		35......9.0/ 0/ 32/1
489	A.J.Tudor	c D.R.Martyn	
2nd innings	dnb......		26.0/ 5/ 70/2
490	N.Hussain	c w A.C.Gilchrist	
491	C.White	st A.C.Gilchrist	

108   *Australia v Sri Lanka, 1st Test, Galle International Stadium, March 8, 9, 10, 11, 12, 2004*

1st innings	c w K.C.Sangakkara b W.PU.J.C.Vaas......		23......42.4/ 9/116/5 ..c1
492	S.T.Jayasuriya	lbw	
493	H.P.Tillakaratne	lbw	
494	U.D.U.Chandana	c w A.C.Gilchrist	
495	H.D.P.K.Dharmasena	c M.L.Hayden	
496	M.Muralidaran	c & b	
2nd innings	st K.C.Sangakkara b M.Muralidaran		0......15.0/ 5/ 43/5
497	M.S.Atapattu	c M.L.Hayden	
498	T.M.Dilshan	lbw	
499	D.P.M.D.Jayawardene	c M.L.Hayden	
500	H.P.Tillakaratne	c A.Symonds	
501	H.D.P.K.Dharmasena	c M.L.Hayden	

109   *Australia v Sri Lanka, 2nd Test, Asgiriya Stadium, Kandy, March 16, 17, 18, 19, 20, 2004*

1st innings	c M.Muralidaran b W.PU.J.C.Vaas		18......20.1/ 3/ 65/5
502	D.P.M.D.Jayawardene	c A.Symonds	
503	T.M.Dilshan	lbw	
504	H.P.Tillakaratne	c w A.C.Gilchrist	
505	K.S.Lokuarachchi	c M.S.Kasprowicz	
506	M.Muralidaran	c A.Symonds	
2nd innings	c D.N.T.Zoysa b M.Muralidaran		6......21.2/ 2/ 90/5 ..c1
507	K.C.Sangakkara	c & b	
508	H.P.Tillakaratne	c R.T.Ponting	
509	T.M.Dilshan	b	

510   W.P.U.J.C.Vaas   c J.L.Langer
511   K.S.Lokuarachchi   lbw

110   Australia v Sri Lanka, 3rd Test, Sinhalese Sports Club Ground, Colombo, March 24, 25, 26, 27, 28, 2004

1st innings   lbw b M.Muralidaran .... 32 ...... 36.0/ 7/115/2 ..c1
512   W.P.U.J.C.Vaas   b
513   H.M.R.K.B.Herath   c D.R.Martyn
2nd innings   c T.T.Samaraweera b H.M.R.K.B.Herath ...... 0 ..... 33.0/11/ 92/4
514   K.C.Sangakkara   b
515   T.M.Dilshan   c D.R.Martyn
516   D.N.T.Zoysa   b
517   W.P.U.J.C.Vaas   lbw

111   Australia v Sri Lanka, 1st Test, Marrara Cricket Ground, Darwin, July 1, 2, 3, 2004

1st innings   run out .... 2 ...... 6.5/ 1/ 20/3
518   U.D.U.Chandana   cw A.C.Gilchrist
519   W.P.U.J.C.Vaas   c M.L.Hayden
520   S.L.Malinga   c J.N.Gillespie
2nd innings   lbw b S.L.Malinga .... 1 ..... 19.0/ 2/ 61/0 ..c1

112   Australia v Sri Lanka, 2nd Test, Cazaly's Stadium, Cairns, July 9, 10, 11, 12, 13, 2004

1st innings   c T.T.Samaraweera b U.D.U.Chandana .... 2 ..... 38.0/ 7/129/3 ..c1
521   K.C.Sangakkara   c J.N.Gillespie
522   T.M.Dilshan   c M.S.Kasprowicz
523   U.D.U.Chandana   st A.C.Gilchrist
2nd innings   c T.T.Samaraweera b U.D.U.Chandana .... 4 ..... 37.0/14/ 70/4 ..c2
524   S.T.Jayasuriya   cw A.C.Gilchrist
525   R.S.Kaluwitharana   c D.S.Lehmann
526   K.C.Sangakkara   b
527   U.D.U.Chandana   st A.C.Gilchrist

113   Australia v India, 1st Test, M.Chinnaswamy Stadium, Bangalore, October 6, 7, 8, 9, 10, 2004

1st innings   c R.S.Dravid b Harbhajan Singh .... 1 ..... 28.0/ 4/ 78/2

528	V.V.S.Laxman	b			
529	I.K.Pathan	cw A.C.Gilchrist			
2nd innings	c Yuvraj Singh b Harbhajan Singh		31	32.0/	8/115/2
530	V.V.S.Laxman	lbw			
531	P.A.Patel	lbw			

114 Australia v India, 2nd Test, M.A.Chidambaram Stadium, Chepauk, Chennai, October 14, 15, 16, 17, 18, 2004

1st innings	c and b A.Kumble		4	42.3/	5/125/6 ..c1
532	Yuvraj Singh	cw A.C.Gilchrist			
533	I.K.Pathan	c M.L.Hayden			
534	V.K.Sehwag	c M.J.Clarke			
535	P.A.Patel	cw A.C.Gilchrist			
536	A.Kumble	b			
537	Harbhajan Singh	c & b			
2nd innings	c V.V.S.Laxman b A.Kumble		0		

115 Australia v India, 3rd Test, Vidarbha Cricket Association Ground, Nagpur, October 26, 27, 28, 29, 2004

1st innings	st P.A.Patel b M.Kartik		2	23.0/	8/ 47/2 ..c3
538	V.V.S.Laxman	c M.J.Clarke			
539	P.A.Patel	c M.L.Hayden			
2nd innings	dnb			14.3/	2/ 56/2
540	V.K.Sehwag	c M.J.Clarke			
541	Zaheer Khan	c D.R.Martyn			

116 Australia v New Zealand, 1st Test, Brisbane Cricket Ground, Woolloongabba, November 18, 19, 20, 21, 2004

1st innings	lbw b D.L.Vettori		10	29.3/	3/ 97/4 ..c2
542	C.D.McMillan	cw A.C.Gilchrist			
543	B.B.McCullum	st A.C.Gilchrist			
544	K.D.Mills	c M.L.Hayden			
545	C.S.Martin	c R.T.Ponting			
2nd innings	dnb			10.2/	3/ 15/4 ..c1

546	S.B.Styris	lbw
547	J.D.P.Oram	c M.L.Hayden
548	D.L.Vettori	c M.L.Hayden
549	C.S.Martin	lbw

117 Australia v New Zealand, 2nd Test, Adelaide Oval, November 26, 27, 28, 29, 30, 2004

1st innings not out......53 ...... 28.0/ 5/ 65/1 ..c1
550 J.E.C.Franklin lbw

2nd innings dnb...... 27.3/ 6/ 79/2
551 S.B.Styris c M.J.Clarke
552 C.S.Martin c R.T.Ponting

118 Australia v Pakistan, 1st Test, Western Australia Cricket Association Ground, Perth, December 16, 17, 18, 19, 2004

1st innings c Yousuf Youhana b Abdur Razzaq......12 ...... 21.0/ 9/ 38/3 ..c1
553 Younis Khan c J.N.Gillespie
554 Abdur Razzaq b
555 Mohammad Khalil b

2nd innings dnb......c1

119 Australia v Pakistan, 2nd Test, Melbourne Cricket Ground, December 26, 27, 28, 29, 2004

1st innings c and b Shoaib Akhtar......10 ...... 28.3/ 2/103/3
556 Yousuf Youhana st A.C.Gilchrist
557 Mohammad Sami lbw
558 Shoaib Akhtar st A.C.Gilchrist

2nd innings dnb...... 25.0/ 7/ 66/3
559 Yousuf Youhana c R.T.Ponting
560 Kamran Akmal lbw
561 Shoaib Malik c J.N.Gillespie

120 Australia v Pakistan, 3rd Test, Sydney Cricket Ground, January 2, 3, 4, 5, 2005

1st innings c Younis Khan b Danish Kaneria......16 ...... 24.0/ 4/ 84/1 ..c2
562 Yasir Hameed c M.J.Clarke

2nd innings dnb...... 26.0/ 2/111/4 ..c1

563 Yasir Hameed — lbw
564 Kamran Akmal — c M.L.Hayden
565 Naved-ul-Hasan — lbw
566 Shoaib Akhtar — c D.R.Martyn

121 Australia v New Zealand, 1st Test, Jade Stadium, Christchurch, March 10, 11, 12, 13, 2005

1st innings — c N.J.Astle b D.L.Vettori .... 2 ..... 40.0/ 6/112/2
567 S.P.Fleming — lbw
568 H.J.H.Marshall — b
2nd innings — dnb 14.0/ 3/ 39/5
569 C.D.McMillan — c S.M.Katich
570 H.J.H.Marshall — b
571 D.L.Vettori — lbw
572 I.E.O'Brien — lbw
573 C.S.Martin — lbw

122 Australia v New Zealand, 2nd Test, Basin Reserve, Wellington, March 18, 19, 20, 21, 22, 2005

1st innings — not out .... 50 ..... 28.1/ 7/ 69/3 ..c1
574 B.B.McCullum — c M.J.Clarke
575 C.D.McMillan — b
576 D.L.Vettori — c D.R.Martyn
2nd innings — dnb 3.2/ 0/ 14/0

123 Australia v New Zealand, 3rd Test, Eden Park, Auckland, March 26, 27, 28, 29, 2005

1st innings — c S.P.Fleming b J.E.C.Franklin .... 1 .... 23.0/ 4/ 63/3
577 H.J.H.Marshall — c R.T.Ponting
578 J.E.C.Franklin — c S.M.Katich
579 P.J.Wiseman — c J.N.Gillespie
2nd innings — dnb 23.0/ 5/ 77/4
580 B.B.McCullum — lbw
581 N.J.Astle — c S.M.Katich
582 J.E.C.Franklin — c R.T.Ponting
583 D.L.Vettori — c G.D.McGrath

124 *Australia v England, 1st Test, Lord's Cricket Ground, St John's Wood, London, July 21, 22, 23, 24, 2005*

1st innings	b S.J.Harmison		28 .... 7.0/ 2/ 19/2 ..c1
584	M.J.Hoggard	c M.L.Hayden	
585	K.P.Pietersen	c D.R.Martyn	
2nd innings	c A.F.Giles b S.J.Harmison		2 ...... 20.0/ 2/ 64/4 ..c1
586	M.E.Trescothick	c M.L.Hayden	
587	I.R.Bell	lbw	
588	A.Flintoff	cw A.C.Gilchrist	
589	S.J.Harmison	lbw	

125 *Australia v England, 2nd Test, Edgbaston, Birmingham, August 4, 5, 6, 7, 2005*

1st innings	b A.F.Giles		8 .... 25.2/ 4/116/4
590	A.J.Strauss	b	
591	A.F.Giles	lbw	
592	S.J.Harmison	b	
593	M.J.Hoggard	lbw	
2nd innings	hw b A.Flintoff		42 ...... 23.1/ 7/ 46/6
594	A.J.Strauss	b	
595	K.P.Pietersen	cw A.C.Gilchrist	
596	I.R.Bell	cw A.C.Gilchrist	
597	A.Flintoff	b	
598	A.F.Giles	c M.L.Hayden	
599	S.J.Harmison	c R.T.Ponting	

126 *Australia v England, 3rd Test, Old Trafford, Manchester, August 11, 12, 13, 14, 15, 2005*

1st innings	c A.F.Giles b S.P.Jones		90 ...... 33.2/ 5/ 99/4
600	M.E.Trescothick	cw A.C.Gilchrist	
601	A.Flintoff	c J.L.Langer	
602	A.F.Giles	c M.L.Hayden	
603	S.P.Jones	b	
2nd innings	cw G.O.Jones b A.Flintoff		34 ...... 25.0/ 3/ 74/0

127 Australia v England, 4th Test, Trent Bridge, Nottingham, August 25, 26, 27, 28, 2005

1st innings   c I.R.Bell b S.P.Jones ...... 0 ...... 29.1/ 4/102/4

604	A.J.Strauss	c M.L.Hayden
605	A.F.Giles	lbw
606	S.J.Harmison	st A.C.Gilchrist
607	M.J.Hoggard	cw A.C.Gilchrist

2nd innings   st G.O.Jones b A.F.Giles... 45 ...... 13.5/ 2/ 31/4

608	M.E.Trescothick	c R.T.Ponting
609	M.P.Vaughan	c M.L.Hayden
610	A.J.Strauss	c M.J.Clarke
611	G.O.Jones	c M.S.Kasprowicz

128 Australia v England, 5th Test, The Oval, Kennington, London, September 8, 9, 10, 11, 12, 2005

1st innings   c M.P.Vaughan b A.Flintoff... 0 ...... 37.3/ 5/122/6 ..c1

612	M.E.Trescothick	c M.L.Hayden
613	M.P.Vaughan	c M.J.Clarke
614	I.R.Bell	lbw
615	K.P.Pietersen	b
616	A.J.Strauss	c S.M.Katich
617	A.F.Giles	lbw

2nd innings   dnb... 38.3/ 3/124/6 ..c2

618	A.J.Strauss	c S.M.Katich
619	M.E.Trescothick	lbw
620	A.Flintoff	c & b
621	P.D.Collingwood	c R.T.Ponting
622	A.F.Giles	b
623	S.J.Harmison	c M.L.Hayden

129 Australia v West Indies, 1st Test, Brisbane Cricket Ground, Woolloongabba, November 3, 4, 5, 6, 2005

1st innings   cw D.C.Ramdin b D.B.Powell ...... 47 ...... 28.0/ 9/ 48/5

| 624 | S.Chanderpaul | c N.W.Bracken |
| 625 | D.B.Powell | cw A.C.Gilchrist |

626   F.H.Edwards   b
627   C.D.Collymore   c M.J.Clarke
628   J.J.C.Lawson   lbw

2nd innings   dnb .... 2.0/ 1/ 1/0 ..c2

130   *Australia v West Indies, 2nd Test, Bellerive Oval, Hobart, November 17, 18, 19, 20, 21, 2005*

1st innings   c R.R.Sarwan b D.B.Powell   1...... 11.0/ 2/ 48/0 ..c1
2nd innings   dnb ...... 39.0/ 4/112/4 ..c1

629   B.C.Lara   cw A.C.Gilchrist
630   M.N.Samuels   c B.J.Hodge
631   D.J.J.Bravo   b
632   C.D.Collymore   cw A.C.Gilchrist

131   *Australia v West Indies, 3rd Test, Adelaide Oval, November 25, 26, 27, 28, 29, 2005*

1st innings   c & b D.J.J.Bravo ...... 0...... 19.2/ 2/ 77/1
633   F.H.Edwards   c M.L.Hayden

2nd innings   dnb ...... 33.0/ 9/ 80/6 ..c1

634   W.W.Hinds   st A.C.Gilchrist
635   D.B.Powell   b
636   B.C.Lara   c M.L.Hayden
637   S.Chanderpaul   c B.J.Hodge
638   D.R.Smith   lbw
639   D.C.Ramdin   cw A.C.Gilchrist

132   *Australia v South Africa, 1st Test, Western Australia Cricket Association Ground, Perth, December 16, 17, 18, 19, 20, 2005*

1st innings   lbw b C.K.Langeveldt ...... 24 ......29.0/ 4/ 92/3
640   A.B.de Villiers   b
641   A.G.Prince   lbw
642   M.V.Boucher   c M.L.Hayden

2nd innings   lbw b J.M.Kemp ...... 5 ......47.0/21/ 83/3 ..c1
643   A.B.de Villiers   c B.J.Hodge
644   A.G.Prince   lbw
645   J.M.Kemp   c R.T.Ponting

133   Australia v South Africa, 2nd Test, Melbourne Cricket Ground, December 26, 27, 28, 29, 30, 2005

1st innings   c N.Boje b A.Nel .... 9 ...... 21.0/ 7/ 62/2
646   A.G.Prince   c R.T.Ponting
647   N.Boje   b

2nd innings   not out .... 0 ...... 28.0/ 7/ 74/4
648   A.B.de Villiers   st A.C.Gilchrist
649   H.H.Gibbs   b
650   M.V.Boucher   c R.T.Ponting
651   A.G.Prince   c M.L.Hayden

134   Australia v South Africa, 3rd Test, Sydney Cricket Ground, January 2, 3, 4, 5, 6, 2006

1st innings   c w M.V.Boucher b A.Nel .... 0 ...... 36.0/ 5/106/2
652   A.G.Prince   lbw
653   A.Nel   c B.J.Hodge

2nd innings   dnb 11.0/ 1/ 45/0

135   Australia v South Africa, 1st Test, Newlands, Cape Town, March 16, 17, 18, 2006

1st innings   c A.B.de Villiers b N.Boje .... 7 ...... 9.0/ 0/ 41/0

2nd innings   dnb 18.5/ 1/ 77/3
654   G.C.Smith   lbw
655   J.A.Rudolph   b
656   M.Ntini   c M.S.Kasprowicz

136   Australia v South Africa, 2nd Test, Kingsmead, Durban, March 24, 25, 26, 27, 28, 2006

1st innings   c A.B.de Villiers b S.M.Pollock .... 36 ...... 25.0/ 2/ 80/2
657   A.G.Prince   c A.Symonds
658   J.A.Rudolph   c M.E.K.Hussey

2nd innings   dnb .... 35.5/ 9/ 86/6 ..c1
659   A.B.de Villiers   st A.C.Gilchrist
660   G.C.Smith   c J.L.Langer
661   J.H.Kallis   lbw
662   J.A.Rudolph   c J.L.Langer
663   A.Nel   c M.L.Hayden
664   M.Ntini   lbw

**137   Australia v South Africa, 3rd Test, New Wanderers Stadium, Johannesburg,
March 31, April 1, 2, 3, 4, 2006**

1st innings	c S.M.Pollock b M.Ntini	36	13.0/ 2/ 49/1
665	J.A.Rudolph	c M.L.Hayden	
2nd innings	cw M.V.Boucher b M.Ntini	3	26.0/ 5/ 90/3
666	H.H.Gibbs	c D.R.Martyn	
667	A.G.Prince	c A.Symonds	
668	N.Boje	c A.Symonds	

**138   Australia v Bangladesh, 1st Test, Narayanganj Osmani Stadium, Fatullah,
April 9, 10, 11, 12, 13, 2006**

1st innings	cw Khaled Mashud b Enamul Haque	6	20.0/ 1/112/0
2nd innings	lbw b Mohammad Rafique	5	13.0/ 4/ 28/3
669	Mohammad Rafique	lbw	
670	Mashrafe Bin Mortaza	b	
671	Enamul Haque	lbw	

**139   Australia v Bangladesh, 2nd Test, Bir Shrestha Shahid Ruhul Amin Stadium, Chittagong,
April 16, 17, 18, 19, 20, 2006**

1st innings	dnb		18.2/ 3/ 47/3
672	Mohammad Ashraful	c M.L.Hayden	
673	Aftab Ahmed	cw A.C.Gilchrist	
674	Shahadat Hossain	c J.N.Gillespie	
2nd innings	dnb		36.0/ 4/113/5 ..c1
675	Habibul Bashar	c M.L.Hayden	
676	Rajin Saleh	c R.T.Ponting	
677	Mohammad Ashraful	b	
678	Shahriar Nafees	cw A.C.Gilchrist	
679	Mashrafe Bin Mortaza	c J.N.Gillespie	

**140   Australia v England, 1st Test, Brisbane Cricket Ground, Woolloongabba,
November 23, 24, 25, 26, 27, 2006**

1st innings	cw G.O.Jones b S.J.Harmison	17	9.0/ 0/ 25/0 ..c1

2nd innings — dnb .... 34.0/ 7/124/4 ..c2

No.	Batsman	Dismissal
680	I.R.Bell	lbw
681	A.N.Cook	c M.E.K.Hussey
682	P.D.Collingwood	st A.C.Gilchrist
683	A.Flintoff	c J.L.Langer

141 Australia v England, 2nd Test, Adelaide Oval, December 1, 2, 3, 4, 5, 2006

1st innings — lbw b M.J.Hoggard .... 43 ..... 53.0/ 9/167/1

No.	Batsman	Dismissal
684	G.O.Jones	c D.R.Martyn

2nd innings — dnb 32.0/12/ 49/4

No.	Batsman	Dismissal
685	A.J.Strauss	c M.E.K.Hussey
686	K.P.Pietersen	b
687	A.F.Giles	c M.L.Hayden
688	M.J.Hoggard	b

142 Australia v England, 3rd Test, Western Australia Cricket Association Ground, Perth, December 14, 15, 16, 17, 18, 2006

1st innings — cw G.O.Jones b M.S.Panesar .... 25 ...... 9.0/ 0/ 41/1 ..c1

No.	Batsman	Dismissal
689	M.J.Hoggard	c M.L.Hayden

2nd innings — dnb 39.2/ 6/115/4

No.	Batsman	Dismissal
690	I.R.Bell	c J.L.Langer
691	A.Flintoff	b
692	S.J.Harmison	lbw
693	M.S.Panesar	b

143 Australia v England, 4th Test, Melbourne Cricket Ground, December 26, 27, 28, 2006

1st innings — not out .... 40 ..... 17.2/ 4/ 39/5 ..c1

No.	Batsman	Dismissal
694	A.J.Strauss	b
695	C.M.W.Read	c R.T.Ponting
696	S.J.Harmison	c M.J.Clarke
697	K.P.Pietersen	c A.Symonds
698	M.S.Panesar	c A.Symonds

2nd innings — dnb 19.0/ 3/ 46/2

No.	Batsman	Dismissal
699	S.I.Mahmood	lbw

700   S.J.Harmison   lbw

144   Australia v England, 5th Test, Sydney Cricket Ground, January 2, 3, 4, 5, 2007

1st innings

701   st C.M.W.Read b M.S.Panesar .... 71 ...... 22.4/ 1/ 69/1

     M.S.Panesar   lbw

2nd innings

702   dnb.. 6.0/ 1/ 23/1

     A.Flintoff   st A.C.Gilchrist

SHANE WARNE'S RECORD IN LIMITED OVER INTERNATIONALS

The following abbreviations are used throughout this section:

MISCELLANEOUS
Comp   Competition V Venue   *not out

COMPETITION

AAC	Australasian Cup	Aiwa	AIWA Cup
B&H	Benson & Hedges (SAf) Cup	BNZ	Bank of New Zealand Cup
C&U	Carlton & United/Carlton Series	C&W	Cable & Wireless
CoCo	Coca Cola Cup	ICC	ICC Champion Trophy
NWT	NatWest Trophy	PTC	Pepsi Triangular Cup
SBI	Standard Bank International	SS	Super Series
SWS	Singer World Series	Tri	Triangular/Tri-nation Tournament
TT	Texaco Trophy	VB	VB Series
WC	World Cup	WSC	World Series/World Series Cup

COUNTRY

B	Bangladesh	E	England
I	India	K	Kenya
N	New Zealand	P	Pakistan
SA	South Africa	Sc	Scotland
SL	Sri Lanka	U	United Arab Emirates
W	West Indies	Z	Zimbabwe

BATTING AND FIELDING RECORD IN EACH SERIES

Series	Comp	V	M	I	NO	Runs	HS	Avge	100s	50s	0s	C
1992-93	BNZ	N	1	1	0	3	3	3.00	0	0	0	0
1993-94	WSC	A	10	6	1	15	9	3.00	0	0	1	4
1993-94	B&H	SA	8	3	0	87	55	29.00	0	1	0	3
1993-94	AAC	U	3	1	0	4	4	4.00	0	0	0	1
1994-95	SWS	SL	3	2	0	31	30	15.50	0	0	0	1
1994-95	Tri	P	6	3	2	39	15*	39.00	0	0	0	0
1994-95	WSC	A	4	2	0	26	21	13.00	0	0	0	2
1994-95	BNZ	N	4	2	2	7	5*	-	0	0	0	2
1994-95	C&W	W	4	3	2	22	12	22.00	0	0	0	1
1995-96	WSC	A	9	2	1	6	3*	6.00	0	0	0	3
1995-96	WC	I/P	7	5	2	32	24	10.66	0	0	1	1
1996-97	C&U	A	8	5	1	38	11	9.50	0	0	0	3
1996-97	SBI	SA	6	5	1	45	23	11.25	0	0	1	3
1997	TT	E	3	3	1	20	11*	10.00	0	0	0	1
1997-98	C&U	A	10	6	1	35	17	7.00	0	0	1	7
1997-98	PTC	I	5	4	1	27	14	9.00	0	0	1	2
1997-98	CoCo	U	5	3	2	32	19	32.00	0	0	0	0
1998-99	C&U	A	12	8	2	43	11	7.16	0	0	1	6
1998-99	C&W	W	7	5	2	84	29	28.00	0	0	0	0

Series	Comp	V	M	I	NO	Runs	HS	Avge	100s	50s	0s	C
1999	WC	E	10	4	1	34	18	11.33	0	0	0	1
1999-2000	Aiwa	SL	5	4	0	43	21	10.75	0	0	0	1
1999-2000		Z	3						0	0	0	2
1999-2000	C&U	A	4	3	2	29	9	29.00	0	0	0	4
1999-2000	BNZ	N	6	2	0	19	12	9.50	0	0	0	2
1999-2000	SS	SA	3	2	0	32	32	16.00	0	0	1	2
2000-01	SS	SA	3	2	1	16	9*	16.00	0	0	0	2
2000-01	C&U	A	9	1	0	7	7	7.00	0	0	0	8
2000-01	PC	I	4	2	0	31	18	15.50	0	0	0	3
2001	NWT	E	5	2	1	28	14*	28.00	0	0	0	5
2001-02	C&U	A	8	6	0	72	29	12.00	0	0	1	2
2001-02	SBI	SA	3	2	1	7	4*	7.00	0	0	0	0
2002-03	SS	A	3	2	0	32	31	16.00	0	0	0	2
2002-03	Tri	K	5	1	0	15	15	15.00	0	0	0	3
2002-03	ICC	SL	3	2	0	36	36	18.00	0	0	1	1
2002-03	VB	A	4	2	1	19	19*	19.00	0	0	1	2
TOTAL			193	106	28	1016	55	13.02	0	1	10	80

BATTING AND FIELDING RECORD AGAINST EACH COUNTRY

Opponent	M	I	NO	Runs	HS	Avge	100s	50s	0s	C
Bangladesh	2						0	0	0	0
England	18	11	4	108	21	15.42	0	0	1	8
India	18	15	5	109	19	10.90	0	0	2	5
Kenya	3	2	1	15	15	15.00	0	0	0	1
New Zealand	27	13	1	143	29	11.91	0	0	1	12
Pakistan	22	12	2	129	31	12.90	0	0	0	14
Scotland	1						0	0	0	0
South Africa	45	29	6	275	55	11.95	0	1	5	18
Sri Lanka	18	10	2	89	36	11.12	0	0	1	4
West Indies	27	12	6	132	29	22.00	0	0	0	11
Zimbabwe	12	2	1	16	11*	16.00	0	0	0	7
TOTAL	193	106	28	1016	55	13.02	0	1	10	80

Bangladesh	Comp	V	M	I	NO	Runs	HS	Avge	100s	50s	0s	C
1999B	WC	E	1						0	0	0	0
2002-03B	ICC	SL	1						0	0	0	0
TOTAL			2						0	0	0	0

England	Comp	V	M	I	NO	Runs	HS	Avge	100s	50s	0s	C
1994-95E	WSC	A	2	1	0	21	21	21.00	0	0	0	1
1997E	TT	E	3	3	1	20	11*	10.00	0	0	0	1
1998-99E	C&U	A	7	4	1	34	11	11.33	0	0	0	3
2001E	NWT	E	2	1	1	14	14*	-	0	0	0	1
2002-03E	VB	A	4	2	1	19	19*	19.00	0	0	1	2
TOTAL			18	15	4	108	21	15.42	0	0	1	2

India	Comp	V	M	I	NO	Runs	HS	Avge	100s	50s	0s	C
1993-94I	AAC	U	1	1	0	4	4	4.00	0	0	0	0
1994-95I	SWS	SL	1	1	0	1	1	1.00	0	0	0	0
1994-95I	BNZ	N	1	1	1	5	5*	-	0	0	0	0
1995-96I	WC	I	1	1	0	0	0	0.00	0	0	1	0
1997-98I	PTC	I	3	3	0	16	14	5.33	0	0	1	0
1997-98I	CoCo	U	3	3	2	32	19	32.00	0	0	0	0
1999I	WC	E	1	1	1	0	0*	-	0	0	0	0
1999-2000I	Aiwa	SL	2	1	0	4	4	4.00	0	0	0	1
1999-2000I	C&U	A	1	1	1	16	16*	-	0	0	0	1
2000-01I	PC	I	4	2	0	31	18	15.50	0	0	0	3
TOTAL			18	15	5	109	19	10.90	0	0	2	5

Kenya	Comp	V	M	I	NO	Runs	HS	Avge	100s	50s	0s	C
1995-96K	WC	I	1	1	1	0	0*	-	0	0	0	0
2002-03K	Tri	K	2	1	0	15	15	15.00	0	0	0	1
TOTAL			3	2	1	15	15	15.00	0	0	0	1

New Zealand	Comp	V	M	I	NO	Runs	HS	Avge	100s	50s	0s	C
1992-93N	BNZ	N	1	1	0	3	3	3.00	0	0	0	0
1993-94N	WSC	A	4	1	0	9	9	9.00	0	0	0	2
1993-94N	AAC	U	1						0	0	0	1
1994-95N	BNZ	N	2					-	0	0	0	2
1995-96N	WC	I	1	1	0	24	24	24.00	0	0	0	0
1997-98N	CoCo	U	2						0	0	0	0
1997-98N	C&U	A	4	2	1	5	5	5.00	0	0	0	3
1999N	WC	E	1	1	0	15	15	15.00	0	0	0	0
1999-2000N	BNZ	N	6	2	0	19	12	9.50	0	0	0	2
2001-02N	C&U	A	4	4	0	68	29	17.00	0	0	0	1
2002-03N	ICC	SL	1	1	0	0	0	0.00	0	0	1	1
TOTAL			27	13	1	143	29	11.91	0	0	1	12

Pakistan	Comp	V	M	I	NO	Runs	HS	Avge	100s	50s	0s	C
1994-95P	SWS	SL	1	1	0	30	30	30.00	0	0	0	1
1994-95P	Tri	P	3	1	1	11	11*	-	0	0	0	0
1996-97P	C&U	A	4	4	0	28	11	7.00	0	0	0	2
1999P	WC	E	2	1	0	1	1	1.00	0	0	0	0
1999-2000P	C&U	A	3	2	1	13	9	13.00	0	0	0	3
2001P	NWT	E	3	1	0	14	14	14.00	0	0	0	4
2002-03P	SS	A	3	2	0	32	31	16.00	0	0	0	2
2002-03P	Tri	K	3						0	0	0	2
TOTAL			22	12	2	129	31	12.90	0	0	0	14

Scotland	Comp	V	M	I	NO	Runs	HS	Avge	100s	50s	0s	C
1999Sc	WC	E	1						0	0	0	0

South Africa	Comp	V	M	I	NO	Runs	HS	Avge	100s	50s	0s	C
1993-94SA	WSC	A	6	5	1	6	3	1.50	0	0	1	2
1993-94SA	B&H	SA	8	3	0	87	55	29.00	0	1	0	3
1994-95SA	Tri	P	3	2	1	28	15*	28.00	0	0	0	0
1994-95SA	BNZ	N	1	1	1	2	2*	-	0	0	0	0
1996-97SA	SBI	SA	6	5	1	45	23	11.25	0	0	1	3
1997-98SA	C&U	A	6	4	0	30	17	7.50	0	0	1	4
1999SA	WC	E	2	1	0	18	18	18.00	0	0	0	1
1999-2000SA	SS	SA	3	2	0	32	32	16.00	0	0	1	2
2000-01SA	SS	SA	3	2	1	16	9*	16.00	0	0	0	2
2001-02SA	C&U	A	4	2	0	4	4	2.00	0	0	1	1
2001-02SA	SBI	SA	3	2	1	7	4*	7.00	0	0	0	0
TOTAL			45	29	6	275	55	11.95	0	1	5	18

Sri Lanka	Comp	V	M	I	NO	Runs	HS	Avge	100s	50s	0s	C
1993-94SL	AAC	U	1						0	0	0	0
1994-95SL	SWS	SL	1						0	0	0	0
1995-96SL	WSC	A	6	1	1	3	3*	-	0	0	0	1
1995-96SL	WC	P	1	1	0	2	2	2.00	0	0	0	0
1998-99SL	C&U	A	5	4	1	9	5	3.00	0	0	1	3
1999-2000SL	Aiwa	SL	3	3	0	39	21	13.00	0	0	0	0
2002-03SL	ICC	SL	1	1	0	36	36	36.00	0	0	0	0
TOTAL			18	10	2	89	36	11.12	0	0	1	4

West Indies	Comp	V	M	I	NO	Runs	HS	Avge	100s	50s	0s	C
1994-95W	C&W	W	4	3	2	22	12	22.00	0	0	0	1
1995-96W	WSC	A	3	1	0	3	3	3.00	0	0	0	2
1995-96W	WC	I	2	1	1	6	6*	-	0	0	0	1
1996-97W	C&U	A	4	1	1	10	10*	-	0	0	0	1
1998-99W	C&W	W	7	5	2	84	29	28.00	0	0	0	0
1999W	WC	E	1						0	0	0	0
2000-01W	C&U	A	6	1	0	7	7	7.00	0	0	0	6
TOTAL			27	12	6	132	29	22.00	0	0	0	11

Zimbabwe	Comp	V	M	I	NO	Runs	HS	Avge	100s	50s	0s	C
1994-95Z	WSC	A	2	1	0	5	5	5.00	0	0	0	1
1995-96Z	WC	I	1						0	0	0	0
1997-98Z	PTC	I	2	1	1	11	11*	-	0	0	0	2
1999Z	WC	E	1						0	0	0	0
1999-2000Z		Z	3						0	0	0	2
2000-01Z	C&U	A	3						0	0	0	2
TOTAL			12	2	1	16	11*	16.00	0	0	0	7

The following bowlers dismissed Warne in LOI's:

4 S.M.Pollock(SA)

3 C.L.Cairns(N), A.Kumble(I), Shahid Afridi(P), W.P.U.J.C.Vaas(SL), B.K.Venkatesh Prasad(I)

2 N.Boje(SA), P.S.de Villiers(SA), C.Z.Harris(N), L.Klusener(SA), M.Muralidaran(SL), Saqlain Mushtaq(P)

1 A.R.Adams(N), G.I.Allott(N), R.P.Arnold(SL), K.L.T.Arthurton(W), N.J.Astle(N), Azhar Mahmood(P), R.E.Bryson(SA), W.J.Cronje(SA), C.E.Cuffy(W), D.J.Cullinan(SA), A.A.Donald(SA), M.A.Ealham(E), G.W.Flower(Z), A.R.C.Fraser(E), D.Gough(E), A.J.Hollioake(E), R.C.Irani(E), S.T.Jayasuriya(SL), G.R.Larsen(N), C.R.Matthews(SA), Mohammad Zahid(P), M.Ntini(SA), J,P.D.Oram(N), P.V.Simmons(W), J.Srinath(I), P.L.Symcox(SA), S.L.Venkatapathy, Raju(I), D.L.Vettori(N), Waqar Younis(P), Wasim Akram(P), J.W.Wilson(N).

Details of Warne's dismissals:

Caught .... 27 .... 34.61%
Bowled .... 19 .... 24.36%
Run out .... 16 .... 20.51%
Caught by wicket-keeper .... 7 .... 8.97%
Leg before wicket .... 5 .... 6.41%
Caught & bowled .... 2 .... 2.57%
Stumped .... 2 .... 2.57%

TOTAL .... 78 .... 100.00%

BOWLING RECORD IN EACH SERIES

Series	Comp	V	M	Balls	Mdns	Runs	Wkts	Avge	5wi	Best
1992-93	BNZ	N	1	60	0	40	2	20.00	0	2/40
1993-94	WSC	A	10	540	5	301	22	13.68	0	4/19
1993-94	B&H	SA	8	414	3	285	11	25.90	0	4/36
1993-94	AAC	U	3	174	1	103	9	11.44	0	4/34
1994-95	SWS	SL	3	168	1	109	7	15.57	0	3/29
1994-95	Tri	P	6	350	5	238	6	39.33	0	4/40
1994-95	WSC	A	4	234	1	133	6	22.16	0	2/27
1994-95	BNZ	N	4	240	6	140	5	28.00	0	2/18
1994-95	C&W	W	4	235	4	204	4	51.00	0	2/33
1995-96	WSC	A	9	481	7	317	15	21.13	0	3/20
1995-96	WC	I/P	7	411	3	263	12	21.91	0	4/34
1996-97	C&U	A	8	454	6	325	19	17.10	1	5/33
1996-97	SBI	SA	6	325	2	272	10	27.20	0	2/36
1997	TT	E	3	174	0	129	1	129.00	0	1/39
1997-98	C&U	A	10	561	3	405	12	33.75	0	3/48
1997-98	PTC	I	5	294	0	219	5	43.80	0	2/45
1997-98	CoCo	U	5	282	2	221	4	55.25	0	2/28
1998-99	C&U	A	12	677	2	532	19	28.00	0	3/16
1998-99	C&W	W	7	378	10	254	13	19.53	0	3/28
1999	WC	E	10	566	13	361	20	18.05	0	4/29
1999-2000	Aiwa	SL	5	240	1	214	6	35.66	0	2/36
1999-2000		Z	3	114	1	82	4	20.50	0	2/40
1999-2000	C&U	A	4	216	4	170	4	42.50	0	2/52
1999-2000	BNZ	N	6	294	4	194	9	21.55	0	3/50
1999-2000	SS	SA	3	168	3	98	3	32.66	0	2/30
2000-01	SS	SA	3	180	2	101	2	50.50	0	2/38
2000-01	C&U	A	9	509	5	377	18	20.94	0	4/48
2000-01	PC	I	4	228	0	222	4	55.00	0	3/38
2001	NWT	E	5	270	3	232	10	23.20	0	3/52

Series	Comp	V	M	Balls	Mdns	Runs	Wkts	Avge	5wi	Best
2001-02	C&U	A	8	450	4	324	6	54.00	0	2/65
2001-02	SBI	SA	3	150	0	154	5	30.80	0	2/44
2002-03	SS	A	3	180	2	118	5	23.60	0	2/42
2002-03	Tri	K	5	234	3	150	4	37.50	0	1/4
2002-03	ICC	SL	3	122	4	60	3	20.00	0	1/2
2002-03	VB	A	4	227	0	167	6	27.83	0	2/39
TOTAL			193	10600	110	7514	291	25.82	1	5/33

BOWLING RECORD AGAINST EACH COUNTRY

Opponent	M	Balls	Mdns	Runs	Wkts	Avge	5wi	Best
Bangladesh	2	120	4	51	2	25.50	0	1/18
England	18	1012	2	732	22	33.27	0	3/16
India	18	974	2	844	15	56.26	0	3/38
Kenya	3	132	0	76	3	25.33	0	1/4
New Zealand	27	1456	16	943	49	19.24	0	4/19
Pakistan	22	1249	20	879	37	23.75	0	4/33
Scotland	1	60	0	39	3	13.00	0	3/39
South Africa	45	2364	23	1718	60	28.63	0	4/29
Sri Lanka	18	996	9	743	29	25.62	0	3/20
West Indies	27	1504	29	1045	50	20.90	1	5/33
Zimbabwe	12	633	5	444	21	21.14	0	4/34
TOTAL	193	10600	110	7514	291	25.82	1	5/33

Bangladesh	Comp	V	M	Balls	Mdns	Runs	Wkts	Avge	5wi	Best
1999B	WC	E	1	60	2	18	1	18.00	0	1/18
2002-03B	ICC	SL	1	60	2	33	1	33.00	0	1/33
TOTAL			2	120	4	51	2	25.50	0	1/18

England	Comp	V	M	Balls	Mdns	Runs	Wkts	Avge	5wi	Best
1994-95E	WSC	A	2	120	0	83	3	27.66	0	2/37
1997E	TT	E	3	174	0	129	1	129.00	0	1/39
1998-99E	C&U	A	7	395	0	289	10	28.90	0	3/16
2001E	NWT	E	2	96	2	64	2	32.00	0	2/16
2002-03E	VB	A	4	227	0	167	6	27.83	0	2/39
TOTAL			18	1012	2	732	22	33.27	0	3/16

India	Comp	V	M	Balls	Mdns	Runs	Wkts	Avge	5wi	Best
1993-94I	AAC	U	1	54	0	40	2	20.00	0	2/40
1994-95I	SWS	SL	1	60	0	53	2	26.50	0	2/53
1994-95I	BNZ	N	1	60	0	61	0	-	0	0/61
1995-96I	WC	I	1	60	1	28	1	28.00	0	1/28
1997-98I	PTC	I	3	174	0	120	2	60.00	0	1/35
1997-98I	CoCo	U	3	162	1	137	1	137.00	0	1/37
1999I	WC	E	1	38	0	49	0	-	0	0/49
1999-2000I	Aiwa	SL	2	84	0	77	2	38.50	0	2/36
1999-2000I	C&U	A	1	54	0	57	1	57.00	0	1/57
2000-01I	PC	I	4	228	0	222	4	55.00	0	3/38
TOTAL			18	974	2	844	15	56.26	0	3/38

Kenya	Comp	V	M	Balls	Mdns	Runs	Wkts	Avge	5wi	Best
1995-96K	WC	I	1	60	0	25	1	25.00	0	1/25
2002-03K	Tri	K	2	72	0	51	2	25.50	0	1/4
TOTAL			3132	0	76	3	25.33	0	1/4	

New Zealand	Comp	V	M	Balls	Mdns	Runs	Wkts	Avge	5wi	Best
1992-93N	BNZ	N	1	60	0	40	2	20.00	0	2/40
1993-94N	WSC	A	4	240	4	99	13	7.61	0	4/19
1993-94N	AAC	U	1	60	0	34	4	8.50	0	4/34
1994-95N	BNZ	N	2	120	3	61	3	20.33	0	2/21
1995-96N	WC	I	1	60	0	52	2	26.00	0	2/52
1997-98N	C&U	A	4	206	2	142	7	20.28	0	3/48
1997-98N	CoCo	U	2	120	1	84	3	28.00	0	2/28
1999N	WC	E	1	60	1	44	1	44.00	0	1/44
1999-2000N	BNZ	N	6	294	4	194	9	21.55	0	3/50
2001-02N	C&U	A	4	234	1	191	4	47.75	0	2/65
2002-03N	ICC	SL	1	2	0	2	1	2.00	0	1/2
TOTAL			27	1456	16	943	49	19.24	0	4/19

Pakistan	Comp	V	M	Balls	Mdns	Runs	Wkts	Avge	5wi	Best
1994-95P	SWS	SL	1	60	1	29	3	9.66	0	3/29
1994-95P	Tri	P	3	174	4	108	1	108.00	0	1/29
1996-97P	C&U	A	4	223	4	161	10	16.10	0	4/37
1999P	WC	E	2	114	1	83	5	16.60	0	4/33
1999-2000P	C&U	A	3	162	4	113	3	37.66	0	2/52
2001P	NWT	E	3	174	1	168	8	21.00	0	3/52
2002-03P	SS	A	3	180	2	118	5	23.60	0	2/42
2002-03P	Tri	K	3	162	3	99	2	49.50	0	1/20
TOTAL			22	1249	20	879	37	23.75	0	4/33

Scotland	Comp	V	M	Balls	Mdns	Runs	Wkts	Avge	5wi	Best
1999Sc	WC	E	1	60	0	39	3	13.00	0	3/39

South Africa	Comp	V	M	Balls	Mdns	Runs	Wkts	Avge	5wi	Best
1993-94SA	WSC	A	6	300	1	202	9	22.44	0	3/42
1993-94SA	B&H	SA	8	414	3	285	11	25.90	0	4/36
1994-95SA	Tri	P	3	176	0	130	5	26.00	0	4/40
1994-95SA	BNZ	N	1	60	3	18	2	9.00	0	2/18
1996-97SA	SBI	SA	6	325	2	272	10	27.20	0	2/36
1997-98SA	C&U	A	6	355	1	263	5	52.60	0	3/52
1999SA	WC	E	2	120	5	62	6	10.33	0	4/29
1999-2000SA	SS	SA	3	168	3	98	3	32.66	0	2/30
2000-01SA	SS	SA	3	180	2	101	2	50.50	0	2/38
2001-02SA	C&U	A	4	216	3	133	2	66.50	0	1/13
2001-02SA	SBI	SA	3	150	0	154	5	30.80	0	2/44
TOTAL			45	2364	23	1718	60	28.63	0	4/29

Sri Lanka	Comp	V	M	Balls	Mdns	Runs	Wkts	Avge	5wi	Best
1993-94SL	AAC	U	1	60	1	29	3	9.66	0	3/29
1994-95SL	SWS	SL	1	48	0	27	2	13.50	0	2/27
1995-96SL	WSC	A	6	330	3	224	10	22.40	0	3/20
1995-96SL	WC	P	1	60	0	58	0	-	0	0/58
1998-99SL	C&U	A	5	282	2	243	9	27.00	0	3/45
1999-2000SL	Aiwa	SL	3	156	1	137	4	34.25	0	2/39
2002-03SL	ICC	SL	1	60	2	25	1	25.00	0	1/25
TOTAL			18	996	9	743	29	25.62	0	3/20

West Indies	Comp	V	M	Balls	Mdns	Runs	Wkts	Avge	5wi	Best
1994-95W	C&W	W	4	235	5	204	4	51.00	0	2/33
1995-96W	WSC	A	3	151	4	93	5	18.60	0	3/30
1995-96W	WC	I	2	114	1	66	4	16.50	0	4/36
1996-97W	C&U	A	4	231	2	164	9	18.22	1	5/33
1998-99W	C&W	W	7	378	10	254	13	19.53	0	3/28
1999W	WC	E	1	60	4	11	3	3.66	0	3/11
2000-01W	C&U	A	6	335	3	253	12	21.08	0	4/48
TOTAL			27	1504	29	1045	50	20.90	1	5/33

Zimbabwe	Comp	V	M	Balls	Mdns	Runs	Wkts	Avge	5wi	Best
1994-95Z	WSC	A	2	114	1	50	3	16.66	0	2/27
1995-96Z	WC	I	1	57	1	34	4	8.50	0	4/34
1997-98Z	PTC	I	2	120	0	99	3	33.00	0	2/45
1999Z	WC	E	1	54	0	55	1	55.00	0	1/55
1999-2000Z		Z	3	114	1	82	4	20.50	0	2/40
2000-01Z	C&U	A	3	174	2	124	6	20.66	0	2/21
TOTAL			12	633	5	444	21	21.14	0	4/34

Warne dismissed the following batsmen:

8   D.J.Cullinan(SA)

7   W.J.Cronje(SA)

6   Inzamamul Haq(P), C.D.McMillan(N), J.N.Rhodes(SA)

5   J.C.Adams(W), J.H.Kallis(SA)

4   C.L.Cairns(N), S.L.Campbell(W), M.J.Greatbatch(N), Moin Khan(P),
    A.C.Parore(N), S.M.Pollock(SA), H.P.Tillakaratne(SL)

3   Abdur Razzaq(P), C.E.L.Ambrose(W), D.J.Callaghan(SA), M.A.Ealham(E),
    A.Flower(Z), G.W.Flower(Z), C.Z.Harris(N), A.D.Jadeja(I),
    R.S.Kaluwitharana(SL), G.Kirsten(SA), B.C.Lara(W), N.D.McKenzie(SA),
    R.S.Mahanama(SL), R.L.Powell(W), Wasim Akram(P), S.C.Williams(W),
    Yousuf Youhana(P)

2   N.J.Astle(N), Azhar Mahmood(P), K.C.G.Benjamin(W), T.E.Blain(N),
    A.D.R.Campbell(Z), S.V.Carlisle(Z), P.A.de Silva(SL), P.S.de Villiers(SA),
    S.P.Fleming(N), M.W.Goodwin(Z), D.Gough(E), C.L.Hooper(W),
    M.J.Horne(N), N.Hussain(E), S.T.Jayasuriya(SL), S.C.Joseph(W),
    R.S.Kalpage(SL), P.N.Kirsten(SA), N.V.Knight(E), B.M.McMillan(SA),
    C.R.Matthews(SA), N.R.Mongia(I), J.R.Murray(W), A.S.A.Perera(SL),
    Rashid Latif(P), M.N.Samuels(W), Shahid Afridi(P), P.V.Simmons(W),
    G.C.Smith(SA), A.J.Stewart(E), S.A.Thomson(N), R.G.Twose(N),
    W.P.U.J.C.Vaas(SL), D.L.Vettori(N), D.P.Viljoen(Z), C.A.Walsh(W), Waqar
    Younis(P)

1   Aamer Sohail(P), A.B.Agarkar(I), Akram Khan(B), M.J.D.Allingham(Sc),
    K.L.T.Arthurton(W), M.S.Atapattu(SL), A.M.Bacher(SA), H.K.Badani(I),
    Basit Ali(P), I.R.Bishop(W), A.M.Blignaut(Z), S.E.Bond(N), J.E.Brinkley(Sc),
    C.O.Browne(W), U.D.U.Chandana(SL), S.Chanderpaul(W)
    P.D.Collingwood(E), C.E.Cuffy(W), V.A.Dahiya(I), P.B.Dasanayake(SL),
    H.D.P.K.Dharmasena(SL), M.W.Douglas(N), R.S.Dravid(I), C.E.Eksteen(SA),
    C.N.Evans(Z), N.H.Fairbrother(E), D.J.Gandhi(I), H.H.Gibbs(SA),
    O.D.Gibson(W), G.A.Gooch(E), A.J.Hall(SA), G.M.Hamilton(Sc),
    R.A.Harper(W), B.R.Hartland(N), G.A.Hick(E), W.W.Hinds(W), R.I.C.Holder(W),
    A.J.Hollioake(E), B.C.Hollioake(E), A.C.Hudson(SA), Ijaz Ahmed(P),
    R.D.Jacobs(W), W.R.James(Z), D.P.M.D.Jayawardene(SL), A.H.Jones(N),
    Khaled Mashud(B), R.D.King(W), L.Klusener(SA), A.P.Kuiper(SA),
    G.R.Larsen(N), R.T.Latham(N), V.V.S.Laxman(I), A.C.I.Lock(Z),
    N.A.M.McLean(W), Mohammad Wasim(P), A.D.Mullally(E), D.J.Nash(N),
    C.J.Nevin(N), T.M.Odoyo(K), B.J.Patel(K), S.G.Peall(Z), M.Prabhakar(I),
    M.S.K.Prasad(I), M.W.Pringle(SA), C.P.H.Ramanayake(SL), A.Ranatunga(SL),
    M.H.Richardson(N), K.R.Rutherford(N), Saeed Anwar(P), Saleem Elahi(P),
    Saleem Malik(P), Saqlain Mushtaq(P), O.A.Shah(E), N.S.Sidhu(I),
    L.P.C.Silva(SL), E.O.Simons(SA), M.S.Sinclair(N), E.R.L.Stewart(SA),
    H.H.Streak(Z), S.B.Styris(N), P.L.Symcox(SA), S.R.Tendulkar(I), S.O.Tikolo(K),
    M.P.Vaughan(E), V.J.Wells(E), A.R.Whittall(Z), L.R.Williams(W), J.W.Wilson(N),
    B.A.Young(N), Younis Khan(P), Zahoor Elahi(P), D.N.T.Zoysa(SL).

Details of Warne's wickets in LOI's:

Caught	109	37.46%
Bowled	49	16.84%
Stumped	50	17.18%
Leg before wicket	48	16.49%
Caught by wicket-keeper	21	7.22%
Caught & bowled	13	4.47%
Hit wicket	1	0.34%
TOTAL	291	100.00%

SHANE WARNE'S MATCH BY MATCH RECORD IN LIMITED OVER INTERNATIONALS

1 v New Zealand (Wellington)   24.03.1993   b J.W.Wilson 3   10.0/0/40/2
  1   A.H.Jones   st I.A.Healy
  2   J.W.Wilson   c S.R.Waugh

2 v South Africa (Melbourne)   9.12.1993   run out............3   10.0/0/43/1
  3   D.J.Cullinan   b

3 v New Zealand (Adelaide)   12.12.1993   dnb............   10.0/1/25/4 .c1
  4   C.L.Cairns   c A.R.Border
  5   M.J.Greatbatch   lbw
  6   C.Z.Harris   c & b
  7   G.R.Larsen   c P.R.Reiffel

4 v South Africa (Sydney)   14.12.1993   c D.J.Cullinan b P.S.de Villiers 0
5 v New Zealand (Melbourne)   16.12.1993   dnb............   10.0/1/19/4
  8   R.T.Latham   st I.A.Healy
  9   C.L.Cairns   cw I.A.Healy
  10   M.J.Greatbatch   lbw
  11   T.E.Blain   c A.R.Border

6 v New Zealand (Sydney)   11.01.1994   b C.L.Cairns 9   10.0/1/27/2
  12   M.J.Greatbatch   lbw
  13   S.A.Thomson   st I.A.Healy

7 v South Africa (Perth)   16.01.1994   run out............1   10.0/0/36/2 .c2
  14   D.J.Callaghan   lbw
  15   C.R.Matthews   st T.J.Zoehrer

8 v New Zealand (Melbourne)   19.01.1994   dnb............   10.0/1/28/3 .c1
  16   M.J.Greatbatch   c P.R.Reiffel
  17   B.A.Young   b
  18   T.E.Blain   c M.L. Hayden

#	Match	Date	Dismissal	Runs	Bowling
9	v South Africa (Melbourne)	21.01.1994	c B.M.McMillan b P.S.de Villiers	1	10.0/1/45/1
19	W.J.Cronje		c D.M.Jones		
10	v South Africa (Sydney)	23.01.1994	dnb		10.0/0/42/3
20	W.J.Cronje		st I.A.Healy		
21	D.J.Cullinan		c S.R.Waugh		
22	B.M.McMillan		lbw		
11	v South Africa (Sydney)	25.01.1994	not out	1	10.0/0/36/2
23	E.L.R.Stewart		b		
24	J.N.Rhodes		c w I.A.Healy		
12	v South Africa (Johannesburg)	19.02.1994	dnb		10.0/0/56/0
13	v South Africa (Verwoerdburg)	20.02.1994	c K.C.Wessels b W.J.Cronje	9	8.0/1/41/1
25	J.N.Rhodes		lbw		
14	v South Africa (Port Elizabeth)	22.02.1994	dnb		10.0/0/36/4
26	P.N.Kirsten		c G.D.McGrath		
27	P.L.Symcox		c D.C.Boon		
28	C.R.Matthews		b		
29	P.S.de Villiers		b		
15	v South Africa (Durban)	24.02.1994	b C.R.Matthews	23	8.0/2/32/1
30	J.N.Rhodes		c M.E.Waugh		
16	v South Africa (East London)	2.04.1994	dnb		10.0/0/34/1 . c2
31	P.N.Kirsten		c M.E.Waugh		
17	v South Africa (Port Elizabeth)	4.04.1994	run out	55	3.0/0/18/0 . c1
18	v South Africa (Cape Town)	6.04.1994	dnb		10.0/0/31/3
32	A.C.Hudson		lbw		
33	W.J.Cronje		c M.A.Taylor		
34	J.N.Rhodes		st I.A.Healy		
19	v South Africa (Bloemfontein)	8.04.1994	dnb		10.0/0/37/1
35	A.P.Kuiper		c M.E.Waugh		
20	v Sri Lanka (Sharjah)	14.04.1994	dnb		10.0/1/29/3
36	R.S.Kalpage		c M.G.Bevan		
37	P.B.Dassanayake		lbw		
38	C.P.H.Ramanayake		lbw		

No	Match	Date	Batting	Score	Bowling
21	v New Zealand (Sharjah)	16.04.1994	dnb		10.0/0/34/4 .c1
39	B.R.Hartland		lbw		
40	M.W.Douglas		lbw		
41	A.C.Parore		c & b		
42	C.Z.Harris		lbw		
22	v India (Sharjah)	19.04.1994	run out	4	9.0/0/40/2
43	A.D.Jadeja		c D.C.Boon		
44	N.S.Sidhu		st J.L.Langer		
23	v Pakistan (Colombo,PIS)	7.09.1994	b Wasim Akram	30	10.0/1/29/3 .c1
45	Inzamamul Haq		st I.A.Healy		
46	Basit Ali		c & b		
47	Waqar Younis		c M.J.Slater		
24	v India (Colombo,SSC)	9.09.1994	b S.L.Venkatapathy Raju	1	10.0/0/53/2
48	M.Prabhakar		c M.J.Slater		
49	N.R.Mongia		cw I.A.Healy		
25	v Sri Lanka (Colombo,PSS)	13.09.1994	dnb		8.0/0/27/2
50	R.S.Mahanama		b		
51	P.A.de Silva		st I.A.Healy		
26	v South Africa (Lahore)	12.10.1994	dnb		10.0/0/39/0
27	v Pakistan (Multan)	14.10.1994	dnb		10.0/1/29/1
28	v South Africa (Faisalabad)	18.10.1994	not out	15	9.2/0/40/4
52	Saleem Malik		cw I.A.Healy		
53	E.O.Simons		st I.A.Healy		
54	D.N.Crookes		st I.A.Healy		
55	M.W.Pringle		lbw		
56	P.S.de Villiers		st I.A.Healy		
29	v Pakistan (Rawalpindi)	22.10.1994	not out	11	9.0/1/47/0
30	v South Africa (Peshawar)	24.10.1994	run out	13	10.0/0/51/1
57	D.J.Cullinan		b		
31	v Pakistan (Lahore)	30.10.1994	dnb		10.0/2/32/0
32	v Zimbabwe (Perth)	2.12.1994	c & b G.W.Flower	5	10.0/1/27/2 .c1

No.	Victim	Dismissal	Match	Date	Warne batting	Bowling figures
58	A.D.R.Campbell	hit wicket				10.0/0/46/1 .c1
59	H.H.Streak	c D.W.Fleming				
			33 v England (Sydney)	6.12.1994	dnb	
60	G.A.Gooch	c C.J.McDermott				9.0/0/23/1
			34 v Zimbabwe (Hobart)	8.12.1994	dnb	
61	W.R.James	cw I.A.Healy				10.0/0/37/2
62	G.A.Hick	c D.W.Fleming			b A.R.C.Fraser 21	
63	N.H.Fairbrother	cw I.A.Healy				
			35 v England (Melbourne)	10.01.1995	b A.R.C.Fraser 21	
64	D.J.Cullinan	st I.A.Healy				10.0/3/18/2
65	D.J.Callaghan	c S.R.Waugh				
			36 v South Africa (Wellington)	15.02.1995	not out 2	
66	K.R.Rutherford	st I.A.Healy				10.0/1/40/1 .c1
			37 v New Zealand (Auckland)	19.02.1995		
			38 v India (Dunedin)	22.02.1995	not out 5	10.0/0/61/0
67	S.A.Thomson	c & b				10.0/2/21/2 .c1
68	A.C.Parore	c M.A.Taylor				
			39 v New Zealand (Auckland)	26.02.1995		
69	P.V.Simmons	c M.A.Taylor				10.0/1/56/1 .c1
			40 v West Indies (Bridgetown)	8.03.1995	dnb	
70	C.L.Hooper	c G.S.Blewett				10.0/0/63/1
			41 v West Indies (Port-of-Spain)	11.03.1995	not out 4	
			42 v West Indies (Port-of-Spain)	12.03.1995	b P.V.Simmons 12	10.0/1/52/0
71	P.V.Simmons	cw I.A.Healy				9.1/3/33/2
72	S.L.Campbell	st I.A.Healy				
			43 v West Indies (Arnos Vale)	15.03.1995	not out 6	
			44 v West Indies (Adelaide)	17.12.1995	dnb	7.0/1/22/0
73	R.A.Harper	st I.A.Healy				9.1/1/41/2
74	C.A.Walsh	cw I.A.Healy				
			45 v West Indies (Melbourne)	19.12.1995	dnb	
			46 v Sri Lanka (Sydney)	21.12.1995	dnb	10.0/1/53/0
			47 v West Indies (Sydney)	1.01.1996	run out 3	9.0/2/30/3 .c2

No.	Match / Wicket	Dismissal	Score	Bowling
75	S.L.Campbell	lbw		
76	J.C.Adams	c M.E.Waugh		
77	C.E.L.Ambrose	b		
48	v Sri Lanka (Melbourne) 9.01.1996	dnb		10.0/1/37/1
78	R.S.Kalpage	b		
49	v Sri Lanka (Perth) 12.01.1996	dnb		10.0/0/45/1
79	W.P.U.J.C.Vaas	st I.A.Healy		
50	v Sri Lanka (Melbourne) 16.01.1996	dnb		10.0/0/40/3
80	R.S.Kaluwitharana	c M.E.Waugh		
81	H.P.Tillakaratne	cw I.A.Healy		
82	R.S.Mahanama	b		
51	v Sri Lanka (Melbourne) 18.01.1996	not out	3	10.0/1/29/2
83	P.A.de Silva	c M.A.Taylor		
84	H.P.Tillakaratne	cw I.A.Healy		
52	v Sri Lanka (Sydney) 20.01.1996	dnb		5.0/0/20/3 .c1
85	S.T.Jayasuriya	c G.D.McGrath		
86	A.Ranatunga	c S.G.Law		
87	H.D.P.K.Dharmasena	c S.R.Waugh		
53	v Kenya (Vishakhapatnam) 23.02.1996	not out	0	10.0/0/25/1
88	T.M.Odoyo	st I.A.Healy		
54	v India (Mumbai) 27.02.1996	c M.Azharuddin b B.K.Venkatesh Prasad	0	10.0/1/28/1
89	N.R.Mongia	c M.A.Taylor		
55	v Zimbabwe (Nagpur) 1.03.1996	dnb		9.3/1/34/4
90	A.Flower	st I.A.Healy		
91	C.N.Evans	cw I.A.Healy		
92	S.G.Peall	cw I.A.Healy		
93	A.C.I.Lock	b		
56	v West Indies (Jaipur) 4.03.1996	dnb		10.0/1/30/0
57	v New Zealand (Madras) 11.03.1996	lbw b N.J.Astle	24	10.0/0/52/2
94	C.Z.Harris	c P.R.Reiffel		
95	A.C.Parore	lbw		
58	v West Indies (Mohali) 14.03.1996	not out	6	9.0/0/36/4 .c1

No.	Batsman / Match	Dismissal	Runs	Bowling
96	C.O.Browne	c & b		
97	O.D.Gibson	cw I.A.Healy		
98	J.C.Adams	lbw		
99	I.R.Bishop	lbw		
59	v Sri Lanka (Lahore) 17.03.1996	st R.S.Kaluwitharana b M.Muralidaran	2	10.0/0/58/0
60	v West Indies (Melbourne) 6.12.1996	dnb		10.0/0/34/2.c1
100	J.R.Murray	c G.S.Blewett		
101	K.C.G.Benjamin	b		
61	v West Indies (Sydney) 8.12.1996	dnb		9.3/1/33/5
102	R.I.C.Holder	b		
103	J.R.Murray	c M.G.Bevan		
104	N.A.M.McLean	c P.R.Reiffel		
105	K.C.G.Benjamin	lbw		
106	C.A.Walsh	b		
62	v Pakistan (Adelaide) 15.12.1996	c Ijaz Ahmed b Saqlain Mushtaq	11	9.5/1/52/4.c1
107	Wasim Akram	st I.A.Healy		
108	Moin Khan	st I.A.Healy		
109	Saqlain Mushtaq	c M.E.Waugh		
110	Waqar Younis	b		
63	v Pakistan (Sydney) 1.01.1997	c Ijaz Ahmed b Saqlain Mushtaq	11	10.0/1/37/4.c1
111	Aamer Sohail	lbw		
112	Shahid Afridi	c G.S.Blewett		
113	Zahoor Elahi	c & b		
114	Inzamamul Haq	b		
64	v West Indies (Brisbane) 5.01.1997	dnb		9.0/0/51/0
65	v Pakistan (Hobart) 7.01.1997	c Zahoor Elahi b Mohammad Zahid	4	7.2/0/35/2
115	Mohammad Wasim	c M.A.Taylor		
116	Wasim Akram	st I.A.Healy		
66	v West Indies (Perth) 12.01.1997	not out	10	10.0/1/46/2
117	S.L.Campbell	c M.A.Taylor		
118	B.C.Lara	c S.G.Law		
67	v Pakistan (Melbourne) 16.01.1997	lbw b Shahid Afridi	2	10.0/2/37/0

#	Opponent (Venue)	Date	Dismissal	Runs	Bowling
68	v South Africa (East London)	29.03.1997	c D.J.Cullinan b A.A.Donald	4	10.0/0/36/2 . c1
119			J.H.Kallis st A.C.Gilchrist		
120			L Klusener b		
69	v South Africa (Port Elizabeth)	31.03.1997	lbw b P.L.Symcox	0	6.0/0/39/1
121			S.M.Pollock c A.C.Dale		
70	v South Africa (Cape Town)	2.04.1997	run out	23	10.0/0/64/2
122			J.H.Kallis b		
123			S.M.Pollock lbw		
71	v South Africa (Durban)	5.04.1997	b R.E.Bryson	12	8.1/1/36/2 . c2
124			A.M.Bacher lbw		
125			D.J.Cullinan c & b		
72	v South Africa (Johannesburg)	8.04.1997	not out	6	10.0/0/45/1
126			S.M.Pollock c S.G.Law		
73	v South Africa (Centurion)	10.04.1997	dnb		10.0/1/52/2
127			D.J.Cullinan c M.E.Waugh		
128			J.H.Kallis st I.A.Healy		
74	v England (Leeds)	22.05.1997	c G.P.Thorpe b A.J.Hollioake	4	10.0/0/46/0
75	v England (The Oval)	24.05.1997	not out	11	10.0/0/39/1 . c1
129			A.J.Stewart b		
76	v England (Lord's)	25.05.1997	cw A.J.Stewart b M.A.Ealham	5	9.0/0/44/0
77	v South Africa (Sydney)	4.12.1997	lbw b D.J.Cullinan	17	10.0/0/33/0 . c1
78	v New Zealand (Adelaide)	7.12.1997	b G.R.Larsen	5	10.0/0/48/3 . c1
130			M.J.Horne lbw		
131			C.D.McMillan c I.J.Harvey		
132			R.G.Twose c M.G.Bevan		
79	v South Africa (Melbourne)	9.12.1997	c H.H.Gibbs b L.Klusener	5	10.0/0/36/0 . c1
80	v New Zealand (Melbourne)	17.12.1997	dnb		10.0/2/25/1 . c1
133			C.D.McMillan c I.J.Harvey		
81	v South Africa (Brisbane)	11.01.1998	run out	8	10.0/0/47/0 . c1
82	v New Zealand (Sydney)	14.01.1998	not out	0	6.1/0/19/2 . c1
134			D.J.Nash b		
135			D.L.Vettori c M.G.Bevan		

No.	Opponent (Venue)	ID	Date	Batting / Wickets	R	Bowling
83	v New Zealand (Melbourne)	136	21.01.1998	dnb		8.1/0/50/1
				C.D.McMillan lbw		
84	v South Africa (Melbourne)	137	23.01.1998	b S.M.Pollock	0	10.0/1/52/3
				D.J.Cullinan st A.C.Gilchrist		
		138		S.M.Pollock c M.G.Bevan		
		139		B.M.McMillan lbw		
85	v South Africa (Sydney)	140	26.01.1998	dnb		10.0/0/52/1 .c1
				W.J.Cronje c M.G.Bevan		
86	v South Africa (Sydney)	141	27.01.1998	dnb		9.1/0/43/1
				W.J.Cronje st A.C.Gilchrist		
87	v India (Kochi)		1.04.1998	c H.H.Kanitkar b A.Kumble	0	10.0/0/42/0
88	v Zimbabwe (Motera)	142	3.04.1998	not out	11	10.0/0/45/2 .c1
		143		G.W.Flower c M.G.Bevan		
				M.W.Goodwin b		
89	v India (Kanpur)	144	7.04.1998	cw N.R.Mongia b A.Kumble	2	9.0/0/43/1
				S.R.Tendulkar c sub		
90	v Zimbabwe (Delhi)	145	11.04.1998	dnb		10.0/0/54/1 .c1
				G.W.Flower b		
91	v India (Delhi)	146	14.04.1998	b B.K.Venkatesh Prasad	14	10.0/0/35/1
				A.B.Agarkar c S.R.Waugh		
92	v New Zealand (Sharjah)	147	18.04.1998	dnb		10.0/1/28/2
				M.J.Horne c T.M.Moody		
		148		C.D.McMillan c D.S.Lehmann		
93	v India (Sharjah)	149	19.04.1998	c Harbhajan Singh b B.K.Venkatesh Prasad	19	8.0/1/37/1
				A.D.Jadeja st A.C.Gilchrist		
94	v New Zealand (Sharjah)	150	21.04.1998	dnb		10.0/0/56/1
				C.L.Cairns st A.C.Gilchrist		
95	v India (Sharjah)		22.04.1998	not out	7	9.0/0/39/0
96	v India (Sharjah)		24.04.1998	not out	6	10.0/0/61/0
97	v England (Brisbane)		10.01.1999	run out	8	10.0/0/42/0
98	v Sri Lanka (Sydney)	151	13.01.1999	dnb		10.0/1/44/2
				R.S.Kaluwitharana b		

No.	Match (Venue)	Batsman / Date	Dismissal	Bowling
152		M.S.Atapattu 15.01.1999 dnb	c M.E.Waugh	10.0/0/44/1 .c1
99	v England (Melbourne)	N.V.Knight	c M.E.Waugh	
153		17.01.1999 not out ...6		10.0/0/57/0
100	v England (Sydney)	21.01.1999 c U.D.U.Chandana b W.PU.J.C.Vaas ...5		10.0/0/45/3
101	v Sri Lanka (Hobart)	U.D.U.Chandana	c A.C.Dale	
154		H.P.Tillakaratne	c sub	
155		R.S.Mahanama	b	
156		24.01.1999 c H.P.Tillakaratne b W.PU.J.C.Vaas ...0		9.0/0/53/0 .c2
102	v Sri Lanka (Adelaide)	26.01.1999 run out ...11		10.0/0/39/3 .c2
103	v England (Adelaide)	N.V.Knight	c & b	
157		M.A.Ealham	c & b	
158		D.Gough	c A.C.Dale	
159		31.01.1999 not out ...1		10.0/0/53/3 .c1
104	v Sri Lanka (Perth)	H.P.Tillakaratne	c R.T.Ponting	
160		W.PU.J.C.Vaas	c B.P.Julian	
161		D.PM.D.Jayawardene	c A.C.Dale	
162		5.02.1999 dnb		10.0/0/48/1
105	v England (Sydney)	M.A.Ealham	c M.G.Bevan	
163		7.02.1999 c H.P.Tillakaratne b W.PU.J.C.Vaas ...3		8.0/1/51/1
106	v Sri Lanka (Melbourne)	R.S.Kaluwitharana	c D.R.Martyn	
164		10.02.1999 b D.Gough ...9		10.0/0/40/2
107	v England (Sydney)	N.Hussain	st A.C.Gilchrist	
165		A.J.Hollioake	lbw	
166		13.02.1999 dnb		5.5/0/16/3
108	v England (Melbourne)	V.J.Wells	b	
167		M.A.Ealham	b	
168		A.D.Mullally	lbw	
169		11.04.1999 b K.L.T.Arthurton ...11		10.0/3/30/2
109	v West Indies (Kingstown)	K.L.T.Arthurton	st A.C.Gilchrist	
170		H.R.Bryan	lbw	
171		14.04.1999 dnb		10.0/2/39/3
110	v West Indies (St George's)			

No.	Opponent (Venue) / Batsman — how out	Date	Bat	Runs	O/M/R/W
111	v West Indies (Port-of-Spain)	17.04.1999	not out	5	9.0/0/59/0
172	J.C.Adams — b				
173	S.C.Williams — c sub				
174	H.R.Bryan — lbw				
112	v West Indies (Port-of-Spain)	18.04.1999	run out	29	10.0/1/35/3
175	B.C.Lara — b				
176	S.C.Williams — b				
177	C.E.L.Ambrose — lbw				
113	v West Indies (Georgetown)	21.04.1999	not out	19	6.0/0/35/2
178	J.C.Adams — b				
179	C.L.Hooper — st A.C.Gilchrist				
114	v West Indies (Bridgetown)	24.04.1999	dnb		10.0/1/28/3
180	S.L.Campbell — cw A.C.Gilchrist				
181	R.D.Jacobs — c B.P.Julian				
182	S.C.Williams — st A.C.Gilchrist				
115	v West Indies (Bridgetown)	25.04.1999	run out	20	8.0/3/28/0
116	v Scotland (Worcester)	16.05.1999	dnb		10.0/0/39/3
183	M.J.D.Allingham — st A.C.Gilchrist				
184	G.M.Hamilton — b				
185	J.E.Brinkley — c A.C.Dale				
117	v New Zealand (Cardiff)	20.05.1999	b G.I.Allott	15	10.0/1/44/1
186	C.D.McMillan — c D.W.Fleming				
118	v Pakistan (Leeds)	23.05.1999	run out	1	10.0/0/50/1
187	Abdur Razzaq — c D.W.Fleming				
119	v Bangladesh (Chester-le-Street)	27.05.1999	dnb		10.0/2/18/1
188	Akram Khan — lbw				
120	v West Indies (Manchester)	30.05.1999	dnb		10.0/4/11/3
189	S.Chanderpaul — b				
190	C.E.L.Ambrose — lbw				
191	R.D.King — lbw				
121	v India (The Oval)	4.06.1999	not out	0	6.2/0/49/0

No	Match	Date	Batting	Runs	Bowling
122	v Zimbabwe (Lord's)	9.06.1999	dnb		9.0/0/55/1
	192		D.P.Viljoen st A.C.Gilchrist		
123	v South Africa (Leeds)	13.06.1999	dnb		10.0/1/33/2 . c1
	193		D.J.Cullinan b		
	194		W.J.Cronje lbw		
124	v South Africa (Birmingham)	17.06.1999	c W.J.Cronje b S.M.Pollock	18	10.0/4/29/4
	195		G.Kirsten b		
	196		H.H.Gibbs b		
	197		W.J.Cronje c M.E.Waugh		
	198		J.H.Kallis c S.R.Waugh		
125	v Pakistan (Lord's)	20.06.1999	dnb		9.0/1/33/4
	199		Ijaz Ahmed b		
	200		Moin Khan cw A.C.Gilchrist		
	201		Shahid Afridi lbw		
	202		Wasim Akram c S.R.Waugh		
126	v Sri Lanka (Galle)	22.08.1999	c U.D.U.Chandana b S.T.Jayasuriya	3	9.0/1/39/2
	203		A.S.A.Perera c M.G.Bevan		
	204		D.N.T.Zoysa c D.S.Lehmann		
127	v India (Galle)	23.08.1999	dnb		7.0/0/36/2
	205		A.D.Jadeja c D.W.Fleming		
	206		M.S.K.Prasad b		
128	v Sri Lanka (Colombo,PIS)	26.08.1999	run out	15	9.0/0/52/2
	207		L.P.C.Silva st A.C.Gilchrist		
	208		A.S.A.Perera st A.C.Gilchrist		
129	v India (Colombo,SSC)	28.08.1999	c sub b A.Kumble	4	7.0/0/41/0 . c1
130	v Sri Lanka (Colombo,PIS)	31.08.1999	c U.D.U.Chandana b R.P.Arnold	21	8.0/0/46/0
131	v Zimbabwe (Bulawayo)	21.10.1999	dnb		9.0/1/40/2
	209		A.Flower st A.C.Gilchrist		
	210		A.R.Whittall c M.E.Waugh		
132	v Zimbabwe (Harare)	23.10.1999	dnb		..........c1

No	Opponent (Venue)	Inn	Date	Batting	Score	Bowling	Wickets
133	v Zimbabwe (Harare)	211	24.10.1999	dnb		10.0/0/42/2 . c1	M.W.Goodwin c A.Symonds
		212					A.M.Blignaut c M.G.Bevan
134	v Pakistan (Brisbane)	213	9.01.2000	c Ijaz Ahmed b Waqar Younis	9	10.0/0/52/2	Inzamamul Haq lbw
		214					Moin Khan c M.E.Waugh
135	v India (Perth)	215	30.01.2000	not out	16	9.0/0/57/1 . c1	D.J.Gandhi c D.R.Martyn
136	v Pakistan (Melbourne)	216	2.02.2000	dnb		10.0/2/33/1 . c2	Moin Khan c D.R.Martyn
137	v Pakistan (Sydney)		4.02.2000	not out	4	7.0/2/28/0 . c1	
138	v New Zealand (Wellington)	217	17.02.2000	dnb			R.G.Twose b
139	v New Zealand (Auckland)	218	19.02.2000	dnb		10.0/0/35/2	S.B.Styris c M.E.Waugh
140	v New Zealand (Dunedin)	219	23.02.2000	dnb		10.0/1/50/2	N.J.Astle b
		220					C.D.McMillan c sub
141	v New Zealand (Christchurch)	221	26.02.2000	dnb		9.0/0/50/3 . c1	N.J.Astle lbw
		222					SP Fleming c S.R.Waugh
		223					D.L.Vettori b
142	v New Zealand (Napier)	224	1.03.2000	cw C.J.Nevin b D.L.Vettori	12	10.0/2/34/1 . c1	C.J.Nevin c D.R.Martyn
143	v New Zealand (Auckland)	225	3.03.2000	cw C.J.Nevin b C.L.Cairns	7	10.0/1/25/1	M.S.Sinclair c S.Lee
144	v South Africa (Durban)	226	12.04.2000	cw M.V.Boucher b M.Ntini	0	8.0/0/47/0	
145	v South Africa (Cape Town)		14.04.2000	dnb		10.0/1/21/1 . c2	D.J.Callaghan cw A.C.Gilchrist
146	v South Africa (Johannesburg)	227	16.04.2000	c N.Boje b S.M.Pollock	32	10.0/2/30/2	A.J.Hall c A.Symonds
		228					J.N.Rhodes c sub

No.	Match	Date	Batting	Score	Wicket	Dismissal	Bowling
147	v South Africa (Melbourne,CS)	16.08.2000	dnb			st A.C.Gilchrist	10.0/0/38/2
229			G.Kirsten			c D.R.Martyn	
230			J.N.Rhodes	9			
148	v South Africa (Melbourne,CS)	18.08.2000	not out	9			10.0/0/33/0 .c2
149	v South Africa (Melbourne,CS)	20.08.2000	c G.Kirsten b N.Boje	7			10.0/2/30/0
150	v West Indies (Melbourne)	11.01.2001	dnb				10.0/1/38/0
151	v West Indies (Brisbane)	14.01.2001	dnb				10.0/0/41/3 .c1
231			W.W.Hinds			c & b	
232			M.N.Samuels			c M.E.Waugh	
233			R.L.Powell			c M.E.Waugh	
152	v West Indies (Sydney)	17.01.2001	dnb				10.0/0/62/3 .c2
234			J.C.Adams			b	
235			R.L.Powell			c N.W.Bracken	
236			L.R.Williams			st A.C.Gilchrist	
153	v Zimbabwe (Melbourne)	21.01.2001	dnb				10.0/2/21/2 .c1
237			S.V.Carlisle			c I.J.Harvey	
238			G.W.Flower			c & b	
154	v West Indies (Adelaide)	26.01.2001	dnb			lbw	8.0/1/36/1 .c1
239			S.C.Joseph				
155	v Zimbabwe (Sydney)	28.01.2001	dnb			lbw	10.0/0/52/2 .c1
240			S.V.Carlisle				
241			D.P.Viljoen			b	
156	v Zimbabwe (Hobart)	30.01.2001	dnb			st B.J.Haddin	9.0/0/51/2
242			A.D.R.Campbell				
243			A.Flower			c D.R.Martyn	
157	v West Indies (Sydney)	7.02.2001	cw R.D.Jacobs b C.E.Cuffy	7			9.2/1/28/1 .c2
244			S.C.Joseph			c & b	
158	v West Indies (Melbourne)	9.02.2001	dnb			lbw	8.3/0/48/4
245			R.L.Powell			lbw	
246			B.C.Lara			c D.R.Martyn	
247			M.N.Samuels			c D.R.Martyn	
248			C.E.Cuffy			c D.R.Martyn	

No.	Match	Date	Batsman / Dismissal		Figures
159	v India (Bangalore)	25.03.2001	b J.Srinath	13	10.0/0/58/1
	249		H.K.Badani	c M.E.Waugh	
160	v India (Indore)	31.03.2001	run out	18	10.0/0/64/0
161	v India (Visakhapatnam)	3.04.2001	dnb		10.0/0/38/3 .c3
	250		V.V.S.Laxman	st A.C.Gilchrist	
	251		R.S.Dravid	c & b	
	252		V.A.Dahiya	c M.L. Hayden	
162	v India (Margao)	6.04.2001	dnb		8.0/0/62/0
163	v Pakistan (Cardiff)	9.06.2001	dnb		10.0/0/52/3 .c2
	253		Abdur Razzaq	st A.C.Gilchrist	
	254		Inzamamul Haq	st A.C.Gilchrist	
	255		Azhar Mahmood	cw A.C.Gilchrist	
164	v England (Bristol)	10.06.2001	dnb		9.0/0/48/0 .c1
165	v England (Manchester)	14.06.2001	not out	14	7.0/2/16/2
	256		B.C.Hollioake	st A.C.Gilchrist	
	257		D.Gough	lbw	
166	v Pakistan (Nottingham)	19.06.2001	c Wasim Akram b Azhar Mahmood	14	9.0/1/60/2
	258		Saleem Elahi	lbw	
	259		Yousuf Youhana	st A.C.Gilchrist	
167	v Pakistan (Lord's)	23.06.2001	dnb		10.0/0/56/3 .c2
	260		Inzamamul Haq	lbw	
	261		Rashid Latif	b	
	262		Azhar Mahmood	b	
168	v New Zealand (Melbourne)	11.01.2002	b C.Z.Harris	3	10.0/0/37/0
169	v South Africa (Melbourne)	13.01.2002	c S.M.Pollock b L.Klusener	4	10.0/1/19/1
	263		N.D.McKenzie	c A.Symonds	
170	v New Zealand (Sydney)	17.01.2002	c M.H.Richardson b C.Z.Harris	14	9.0/0/65/2
	264		M.H.Richardson	st R.J.Campbell	
	265		A.C.Parore	c M.E.Waugh	
171	v South Africa (Brisbane)	20.01.2002	dnb		10.0/1/48/0
172	v South Africa (Sydney)	21.01.2002	dnb		6.0/1/13/1 .c1
	266		G.Kirsten	lbw	

#	Match	No.	Date	Batting	Runs	Bowling
173	v New Zealand (Adelaide)	267	26.01.2002	cw A.C.Parore b C.L.Cairns	22	10.0/1/33/1
174	v New Zealand (Melbourne)	268	29.01.2002	c S.E.Bond b A.R.Adams	29	10.0/0/56/1 .c1
	S.P.Fleming			st A.C.Gilchrist		
	C.L.Cairns			c M.G.Bevan		
175	v South Africa (Perth)	269	3.02.2002	b S.M.Pollock	0	10.0/0/53/0
176	v South Africa (Durban)	270	3.04.2002	dnb		10.0/0/44/2
	G.C.Smith			cw A.C.Gilchrist		
	N.D.McKenzie			cw A.C.Gilchrist		
177	v South Africa (Port Elizabeth)	271	6.04.2002	not out	4	7.0/0/58/1
	G.C.Smith			c D.S.Lehmann		
178	v South Africa (Cape Town)	272	9.04.2002	b N.Boje	3	8.0/0/52/2
	J.H.Kallis	273		c J.P.Maher		
	N.D.McKenzie			lbw		
179	v Pakistan (Melbourne,CS)	274	12.06.2002	dnb		10.0/1/27/1 .c1
	Yousuf Youhana			cw A.C.Gilchrist		
180	v Pakistan (Melbourne,CS)	275	15.06.2002	lbw b Shahid Afridi	1	10.0/0/49/2
	Yousuf Youhana	276		c D.R.Martyn		
	Rashid Latif			b		
181	v Pakistan (Brisbane)	277	19.06.2002	b Shahid Afridi	31	10.0/1/42/2 .c1
	Saeed Anwar	278		lbw		
	Inzamamul Haq			lbw		
182	v Pakistan (Nairobi)	279	30.08.2002	dnb		8.0/1/20/1
	Younis Khan			cw A.C.Gilchrist		
183	v Kenya (Nairobi)	280	2.09.2002	dnb		3.0/0/ 4/1 .c1
	B.J.Patel			st A.C.Gilchrist		
184	v Pakistan (Nairobi)	281	4.09.2002	dnb		9.0/2/35/1 .c1
	Abdur Razzaq			b		
185	v Kenya (Nairobi)	282	5.09.2002	run out	15	9.0/0/47/1
	S.O.Tikolo			lbw		
186	v Pakistan (Nairobi)		7.09.2002	dnb		10.0/0/44/0 .c1

187 v New Zealand (Colombo,SSC) 15.09.2002 c S.E.Bond b J.P.D.Oram............0   0.2/0/ 2/1 .c1
283   S.E.Bond   st A.C.Gilchrist

188 v Bangladesh (Colombo,SSC) 19.09.2002 dnb.............................   10.0/2/33/1
284   Khaled Mashud   b

189 v Sri Lanka (Colombo,PIS) 27.09.2002 st K.C.Sangakkara b M.Muralidaran 36   10.0/2/25/1
285   S.T.Jayasuriya   b

190 v England (Sydney) 13.12.2002 dnb............................   10.0/0/42/1 .c1
286   R.C.Irani   lbw

191 v England (Melbourne) 15.12.2002 not out................19   7.5/0/39/2 .c1
287   N.Hussain   b
288   O.A.Shah   c G.D.McGrath

192 v England (Sydney) 23.01.2003 dnb............................   10.0/0/28/1
289   P.D.Collingwood   st A.C.Gilchrist

193 v England (Melbourne) 25.01.2003 c & b R.C.Irani.............0   10.0/0/58/2
290   M.P.Vaughan   c R.T.Ponting
291   A.J.Stewart   c B.Lee

SHANE WARNE'S RECORD IN MAJOR LIMITED OVER MATCHES

Batting & fielding in each season in limited over matches

Season	M	I	NO	Runs	HS	Avge	100s	50s	C
1991-92 (Zimbabwe)	3	3	2	17	11*	17.00	0	0	1
1992-93 (Australia)	1	1	0	26	26	26.00	0	0	0
1992-93 (New Zealand)	2	2	1	6	3*	6.00	0	0	0
1993-94 (Australia)	12	6	1	15	9	3.00	0	0	4
1993-94 (South Africa)	9	3	0	87	55	29.00	0	1	3
1993-94 (United Arab Emirates)	3	1	0	4	4	4.00	0	0	1
1993-94 (Sri Lanka)	3	2	0	31	30	15.50	0	0	1
1994-95 (Pakistan)	6	3	2	39	15*	39.00	0	0	0
1994-95 (Australia)	8	4	0	66	32	16.50	0	0	2
1994-95 (New Zealand)	4	2	2	7	5*	-	0	0	2
1994-95 (West Indies)	4	3	2	22	12	22.00	0	0	1
1995-96 (Australia)	12	4	1	26	15	8.66	0	0	4
1995-96 (India)	6	4	2	30	24	15.00	0	0	1
1995-96 (Pakistan)	1	1	0	2	2	2.00	0	0	0
1996-97 (Australia)	11	7	2	50	12*	10.00	0	0	9
1996-97 (South Africa)	7	5	1	45	23	11.25	0	0	4
1997 (England)	5	5	1	24	11*	6.00	0	0	4
1997-98 (Australia)	12	8	1	67	18	9.57	0	0	7
1997-98 (India)	5	4	1	27	14	9.00	0	0	2
1997-98 (United Arab Emirates)	5	3	2	32	19	32.00	0	0	0
1998-99 (Australia)	13	9	2	67	24	9.57	0	0	6
1998-99 (West Indies)	7	5	2	84	29	28.00	0	0	0
1999 (England)	10	4	1	34	18	11.33	0	0	1
1999-2000 (Sri Lanka)	5	4	0	43	21	10.75	0	0	1
1999-2000 (Zimbabwe)	3					-	0	0	2
1999-2000 (Australia)	6	5	2	60	22	20.00	0	0	4
1999-2000 (New Zealand)	6	2	0	19	12	9.50	0	0	2
1999-2000 (South Africa)	3	2	0	32	32	16.00	0	0	2
2000 (England)	21	19	2	197	34	11.58	0	0	6
2000-01 (Australia)	14	5	1	24	9*	6.00	0	0	10
2000-01 (India)	4	2	0	31	18	15.50	0	0	3
2001 (England)	6	3	1	35	14*	17.50	0	0	5
2001-02 (Australia)	12	10	0	102	29	10.20	0	0	4
2001-02 (South Africa)	3	2	1	7	4*	7.00	0	0	0
2002-03 (Australia)	10	6	1	60	31	12.00	0	0	5
2002-03 (Kenya)	5	1	0	15	15	15.00	0	0	3
2002-03 (Sri Lanka)	3	2	0	36	36	18.00	0	0	1
2003-04 (Australia)	2	2	0	9	7	4.50	0	0	0
2004 (England)	14	12	0	117	48	9.75	0	0	4

Season	M	I	NO	Runs	HS	Avge	100s	50s	C
2004-05 (Australia)	4	3	1	4	2*	2.00	0	0	2
2004-05 (New Zealand)	3	2	0	26	26	13.00	0	0	1
2005 (England)	10	8	0	97	27	12.12	0	0	6
2005-06 (Australia)	2					-	0	0	0
2006 (England)	12	10	0	97	30	9.70	0	0	5
Total	297	189	35	1819	55	11.81	0	1	119

Bowling in each season in limited over matches

Season	M	Balls	Mdns	Runs	Wkts	Ave	5wi	Best
1991-92 (Zimbabwe)	3	156	3	102	2	51.00	0	1/32
1992-93 (Australia)	1	35	0	31	3	10.33	0	3/31
1992-93 (New Zealand)	2	108	2	75	2	37.50	0	2/40
1993-94 (Australia)	12	660	6	385	22	17.50	0	4/19
1993-94 (South Africa)	9	414	3	285	11	25.90	0	4/36
1993-94 (United Arab Emirates)	3	174	1	103	9	11.44	0	4/34
1993-94 (Sri Lanka)	3	168	1	109	7	15.57	0	3/29
1994-95 (Pakistan)	6	350	4	238	6	39.66	0	4/40
1994-95 (Australia)	8	474	6	299	13	23.00	0	3/40
1994-95 (New Zealand)	4	240	6	140	5	28.00	0	2/18
1994-95 (West Indies)	4	235	5	204	4	51.00	0	2/33
1995-96 (Australia)	12	613	8	421	16	26.31	0	3/20
1995-96 (India)	6	351	3	205	12	17.08	0	4/34
1995-96 (Pakistan)	1	60	0	58	0	-	0	0/58
1996-97 (Australia)	11	634	9	432	28	15.42	2	5/33
1996-97 (South Africa)	7	385	2	334	12	27.83	0	2/36
1997 (England)	5	270	1	186	5	37.20	0	2/21
1997-98 (Australia)	12	669	6	484	17	28.47	0	3/43
1997-98 (India)	5	294	0	219	5	43.80	0	2/45
1997-98 (United Arab Emirates)	5	282	2	221	4	55.25	0	2/28
1998-99 (Australia)	13	725	3	555	20	27.75	0	3/16
1998-99 (West Indies)	7	378	10	254	13	19.53	0	3/28
1999 (England)	10	566	13	361	20	18.05	0	4/29
1999-2000 (Sri Lanka)	5	240	1	214	6	35.66	0	2/36
1999-2000 (Zimbabwe)	3	114	1	82	4	20.50	0	2/40
1999-2000 (Australia)	6	312	4	244	7	34.85	0	2/31
1999-2000 (New Zealand)	6	294	4	194	9	21.55	0	3/50
1999-2000 (South Africa)	3	168	3	98	3	32.66	0	2/30
2000 (England)	21	1092	18	661	39	16.94	0	4/23
2000-01 (Australia)	14	785	9	573	23	24.91	0	4/48
2000-01 (India)	4	228	0	222	4	55.50	0	3/38
2001 (England)	6	330	4	271	11	24.63	0	3/52

2001-02 (Australia)	12	672	8	483	10	48.30	0	2/40
2001-02 (South Africa)	3	150	0	154	5	30.80	0	2/44
2002-03 (Australia)	10	575	3	424	18	23.55	0	4/45
2002-03 (Kenya)	5	234	3	150	4	37.50	0	1/4
2002-03 (Sri Lanka)	3	122	4	60	3	20.00	0	1/2
2003-04 (Australia)	2	120	1	91	2	45.50	0	1/43
2004 (England)	14	713	7	497	22	22.59	0	4/23
2004-05 (Australia)	4	206	0	152	6	25.33	0	2/20
2004-05 (New Zealand)	3	78	0	70	1	70.00	0	1/26
2005 (England)	10	450	2	328	15	21.86	0	3/20
2005-06 (Australia)	2	120	1	92	1	92.00	0	1/39
2006 (England)	12	455	4	327	23	14.21	1	6/42
Total	297	5699	171	11088	452	24.53	3	6/42

Batting & fielding for each team in limited over matches

Team	M	I	NO	Runs	HS	Avge	100s	50s	C
Australia	197	108	28	1042	55	13.02	0	1	80
Australia B	3	3	2	17	11*	17.00	0	0	1
Australians	6	4	1	14	7	4.66	0	0	4
FICA World XI	3	2	0	26	26	13.00	0	0	1
Hampshire	57	49	2	508	48	10.80	0	0	21
ICC World XI	1	1	1	2	2*	-	0	0	0
Victoria	30	22	1	210	32	10.00	0	0	12
Total	297	189	35	1819	55	11.81	0	1	119

Bowling for each team in limited over matches

Team	M	Balls	Mdns	Runs	Wkts	Ave	5wi	Best
Australia	197	10840	115	7682	298	25.77	1	5/33
Australia B	3	156	3	102	2	51.00	0	1/32
Australians	6	264	4	193	7	27.57	0	2/21
FICA World XI	3	78	0	70	1	70.00	0	1/26
Hampshire	57	2710	31	1813	99	18.31	1	6/42
ICC World XI	1	42	0	27	2	13.50	0	2/27
Victoria	30	1609	18	1201	43	27.93	1	5/35
Total	297	5699	171	11088	452	24.53	3	6/42

Batting & fielding against each opponent in limited over matches

Opponent	M	I	NO	Runs	HS	Avge	100s	50s	C
Asian Cricket Council XI	1	1	1	2	2*	-	0	0	0
Australia A	4	2	0	26	18	13.00	0	0	0
Australian Capital Territory	1	1	0	9	9	9.00	0	0	0
Bangladesh	2					-	0	0	0
Boland	1					-	0	0	1
Cheshire	1	1	0	1	1	1.00	0	0	0
Derbyshire	1	1	0	0	0	0.00	0	0	0
Durham	3	3	2	47	29	47.00	0	0	1
England	18	11	4	108	21	15.42	0	0	8
Essex	6	5	0	53	30	10.60	0	0	2
Glamorgan	7	6	0	44	22	7.33	0	0	5
Gloucestershire	6	5	0	67	48	13.40	0	0	2
India	18	15	5	109	19	10.90	0	0	5
Kent	4	3	0	7	4	2.33	0	0	3
Kent Cricket Board	1					-	0	0	0
Kenya	3	2	1	15	15	15.00	0	0	1
Lancashire	1	1	0	15	15	15.00	0	0	1
Middlesex	6	6	0	77	21	12.83	0	0	2
New South Wales	6	6	0	69	25	11.50	0	0	1
New Zealand	30	15	1	169	29	12.07	0	0	13
NZ Cricket Council Pres. XI	1	1	1	3	3*	-	0	0	0
Northamptonshire	5	5	0	35	27	7.00	0	0	1
Nottinghamshire	3	3	0	59	29	19.66	0	0	1
Pakistan	22	12	2	129	31	12.90	0	0	14
Queensland	6	2	0	22	22	11.00	0	0	3
Scotland	1					-	0	0	0
Shropshire	1					-	0	0	0
Somerset	2	1	0	19	19	19.00	0	0	0
South Africa	45	29	6	275	55	11.95	0	1	18
South African Board Pres. XI	1					-	0	0	0
South Australia	6	4	1	49	32	16.33	0	0	3
Sri Lanka	18	10	2	89	36	11.12	0	0	4
Surrey	4	3	0	42	34	14.00	0	0	1
Sussex	2	2	0	1	1	0.50	0	0	0
Tasmania	4	3	0	42	26	14.00	0	0	3
Warwickshire	4	4	0	22	10	5.50	0	0	1
West Indians	1	1	0	13	13	13.00	0	0	1
West Indies	27	12	6	132	29	22.00	0	0	11
Western Australia	7	6	0	19	15	3.16	0	0	2
Worcestershire	2	2	0	17	14	8.50	0	0	3

Opponent	M	I	NO	Runs	HS	Avge	100s	50s	C
Zimbabwe	12	2	1	16	11*	16.00	0	0	7
Zimbabwe B	3	3	2	17	11*	17.00	0	0	1
Total	297	189	35	1819	55	11.81	0	1	119

Bowling against each opponent in limited over matches

Opponent	M	Balls	Mdns	Runs	Wkts	Ave	5wi	Best
Asian Cricket Council XI	1	1142	0	27	2	13.50	0	2/27
Australia A	4	240	5	168	7	24.00	0	3/40
Australian Capital Territory	1	60	0	31	2	15.50	0	2/31
Bangladesh	2	120	4	51	2	25.50	0	1/18
Boland	1	60	0	62	2	31.00	0	2/62
Cheshire	1	42	0	24	0	-	0	0/42
Derbyshire	1	54	2	23	4	5.75	0	4/23
Durham	3	150	4	71	6	11.83	0	2/12
England	18	1012	2	729	22	33.13	0	3/16
Essex	6	282	1	211	9	23.44	0	4/32
Glamorgan	7	338	2	258	9	28.66	0	2/16
Gloucestershire	6	263	2	177	13	13.61	0	4/23
India	18	974	2	844	15	56.26	0	3/38
Kent	4	201	6	122	11	11.09	0	4/14
Kent Cricket Board	1	60	0	34	4	8.50	0	4/34
Kenya	3	132	0	76	3	25.33	0	1/4
Lancashire	1	42	0	22	1	22.00	0	1/22
Middlesex	6	318	4	204	12	17.00	0	4/48
New South Wales	6	270	3	233	6	38.83	0	3/43
New Zealand	30	1534	16	1013	50	20.26	0	4/19
NZ Cricket Council Pres. XI	1	48	2	35	0	-	0	0/35
Northamptonshire	5	252	1	192	5	38.40	0	2/21
Nottinghamshire	3	162	3	140	4	35.00	0	2/59
Pakistan	22	1249	20	879	37	23.75	0	4/33
Queensland	6	320	2	238	7	34.00	0	2/20
Scotland	1	60	0	39	3	13.00	0	3/39
Shropshire	1	48	0	20	3	6.66	0	3/20
Somerset	2	48	0	26	0	-	0	0/26
South Africa	45	2464	23	1718	60	28.63	0	4/29
South African Board Pres. XI	1	did not bowl						
South Australia	6	342	7	228	9	25.33	0	4/45
Sri Lanka	18	996	9	746	29	25.72	0	3/20
Surrey	4	165	3	106	11	9.63	1	6/42
Sussex	2	120	2	59	2	29.50	0	1/22
Tasmania	4	215	2	155	11	14.09	1	5/35

Opponent	M	Balls	Mdns	Runs	Wkts	Ave	5wi	Best
Warwickshire	4	201	2	157	7	22.42	0	2/31
West Indians	1	60	0	27	1	27.00	0	1/27
West Indies	27	1504	29	1045	50	20.90	1	5/33
Western Australia	7	402	4	316	8	39.50	0	3/48
Worcestershire	2	60	1	36	2	18.00	0	2/36
Zimbabwe	12	633	5	444	21	21.14	0	4/34
Zimbabwe B	3	156	3	102	2	51.00	0	1/32
Total	297	5699	171	11088	452	24.53	3	6/42

Batting & fielding on each ground in limited over matches

Ground	M	I	NO	Runs	HS	Avge	100s	50s	C
Adelaide Oval	13	9	1	106	32	13.25	0	0	11
Ahmedabad (Sardar Patel)	1	1	1	11	11*	-	0	0	1
Alderley Edge (Moss Lane)	1	1	0	1	1	1.00	0	0	0
Auckland (Eden Park)	4	1	0	7	7	7.00	0	0	2
Ballarat (Eastern Oval)	1					-	0	0	1
Bangalore (M.Chinnaswamy)	1	1	0	13	13	13.00	0	0	0
Bankstown Oval	1	1	0	25	25	25.00	0	0	1
Basingstoke (May's Bounty)	1	1	1	18	18*	-	0	0	1
Birmingham (Edgbaston)	3	3	0	28	18	9.33	0	0	0
Bloemfontein (Goodyear Park)	1					-	0	0	0
Bridgetown (Kensington Oval)	3	1	0	20	20	20.00	0	0	1
Brisbane (Woolloongabba)	9	5	0	78	31	15.60	0	0	4
Bristol (County Ground)	4	3	0	48	48	16.00	0	0	2
Bulawayo (Athletic Club)	1	1	1	3	3*	-	0	0	0
Bulawayo (Queens Sports Club)	1					-	0	0	0
Canterbury (St Lawrence Ground)	3	2	0	3	3	1.50	0	0	2
Cape Town (Newlands)	4	2	0	26	23	13.00	0	0	2
Cardiff (Sophia Gardens)	6	5	0	50	22	10.00	0	0	4
Carlton (Princes Park)	1					-	0	0	3
Centurion Park	2	1	0	9	9	9.00	0	0	0
Chelmsford (County Ground)	2	1	0	15	15	15.00	0	0	0
Chennai (M.A.Chidambaram)	1	1	0	24	24	24.00	0	0	0
Chester-le-Street (Riverside)	3	2	1	29	29	29.00	0	0	0
Christchurch (Lancaster Park)	2	1	0	26	26	26.00	0	0	1
Colombo (P.Saravanamuttu)	1					-	0	0	0
Colombo (R.Premadasa)	4	4	0	73	36	18.25	0	0	0
Colombo (Sinhalese S.C.)	4	3	0	34	30	11.33	0	0	3
Croydon (Whitgift School)	1					-	0	0	0
Delhi (Feroz Shah Kotla)	2	1	0	14	14	14.00	0	0	1
Devonport (Formby Recreation)	1	1	0	26	26	26.00	0	0	0
Dunedin (Carisbrook)	2	1	1	5	5*	-	0	0	0
Durban (Kingsmead)	4	3	0	35	23	11.66	0	0	2

Ground	M	I	NO	Runs	HS	Avge	100s	50s	C
East London (Buffalo Park)	2	1	0	4	4	4.00	0	0	3
Faisalabad (Iqbal Stadium)	1	1	1	15	15*	-	0	0	0
Galle (International Stadium)	2	1	0	3	3	3.00	0	0	0
Georgetown (Bourda)	1	1	1	19	19*	-	0	0	0
Hamilton (Seddon Park)	1	1	0	0	0	0.00	0	0	0
Harare (Sports Club)	4	2	1	14	11*	14.00	0	0	3
Hobart (Bellerive Oval)	5	3	0	18	9	6.00	0	0	0
Hove (County Ground)	2	2	0	1	1	0.50	0	0	0
Indore (Nehru Stadium)	1	1	0	18	18	18.00	0	0	0
Jaipur (Sawai Mansingh)	1					-	0	0	0
Johannesburg (New Wanderers)	3	2	1	38	32	38.00	0	0	0
Kanpur (Modi Stadium)	1	1	0	2	2	2.00	0	0	0
Kennington Oval	4	4	2	52	34	26.00	0	0	1
Kingstown (Arnos Vale)	2	2	1	17	11	17.00	0	0	0
Kochi (Nehru Stadium)	1	1	0	0	0	0.00	0	0	0
Lahore (Gaddafi Stadium)	3	1	0	2	2	2.00	0	0	0
Leeds (Headingley)	3	2	0	5	4	2.50	0	0	1
Lord's Cricket Ground	8	5	0	63	21	12.60	0	0	3
Manchester (Old Trafford)	3	2	1	29	15	29.00	0	0	1
Margao (Nehru Stadium)	1					-	0	0	0
Melbourne (Docklands)	5	3	1	17	9*	8.50	0	0	3
Melbourne Cricket Ground	37	20	3	148	29	8.70	0	0	11
Milton Keynes (Campbell Park)	1	1	0	0	0	0.00	0	0	0
Mohali (Punjab C.A. Stadium)	1	1	1	6	6*	-	0	0	1
Multan (Ibn-e-Qasim Bagh)	1					-	0	0	0
Mumbai (Wankhede Stadium)	1	1	0	0	0	0.00	0	0	0
Nagpur (Vidarbha C.A. Ground)	1					-	0	0	0
Nairobi (Gymkhana Club)	5	1	0	15	15	15.00	0	0	3
Napier (McLean Park)	1	1	0	12	12	12.00	0	0	1
Nelson (Trafalgar Park)	1	1	1	3	3*	-	0	0	0
North Sydney Oval	2	2	0	15	14	7.50	0	0	0
Northampton (County Ground)	2	2	0	28	27	14.00	0	0	0
Nottingham (Trent Bridge)	2	2	0	26	14	13.00	0	0	0
Paarl (Boland Bank Park)	1					-	0	0	1
Perth (W.A.C.A. Ground)	10	9	3	35	16*	5.83	0	0	6
Peshawar (Arbab Niaz)	1	1	0	13	13	13.00	0	0	0
Port Elizabeth (St George's Park)	4	3	1	59	55	29.50	0	1	1
Port of Spain (Queen's Park)	4	4	2	50	29	25.00	0	0	0
Portsmouth	1	1	0	7	7	7.00	0	0	1
Potchefstroom (Witrand)	1					-	0	0	0
Rawalpindi Cricket Stadium	1	1	1	11	11*	-	0	0	0
Richmond Cricket Ground	3	3	0	9	9	3.00	0	0	1
Sharjah C.A. Stadium	8	4	2	36	19	18.00	0	0	1
Southampton (County Ground)	6	6	0	50	29	8.33	0	0	3

Ground	M	I	NO	Runs	HS	Avge	100s	50s	C
Southampton (The Rose Bowl)	17	14	0	133	30	9.50	0	0	9
St George's (Queen's Park, New)	1					-	0	0	0
St Kilda (Junction Oval)	2					-	0	0	0
Sydney Cricket Ground	29	14	4	99	18	9.90	0	0	16
Taunton (County Ground)	1					-	0	0	0
Uxbridge Cricket Club Ground	1	1	0	12	12	12.00	0	0	0
Visakhapatnam (Indira Priyadarshini)	2	1	1	0	0*	-	0	0	3
Wellington (Basin Reserve)	2	2	1	5	3	5.00	0	0	0
Wellington (Westpac Stadium)	2					-	0	0	1
Whitchurch (Heath Road)	1					-	0	0	0
Worcester (New Road)	2	1	0	3	3	3.00	0	0	3
Total	297	189	35	1819	55	11.81	0	1	119

Bowling on each ground in limited over matches

Ground	M	Balls	Mdns	Runs	Wkts	Ave	5wi	Best
Adelaide Oval	13	725	11	476	23	20.69	0	4/25
Ahmedabad (Sardar Patel)	1	60	0	45	2	22.50	0	2/45
Alderley Edge (Moss Lane)	1	42	0	24	0	-	0	0/24
Auckland (Eden Park)	4	240	4	121	6	20.16	0	2/21
Ballarat (Eastern Oval)	1	50	0	20	2	10.00	0	2/20
Bangalore (M.Chinnaswamy)	1	60	0	58	1	58.00	0	1/58
Bankstown Oval	1	60	1	49	1	49.00	0	1/49
Basingstoke (May's Bounty)	1	54	1	40	2	20.00	0	2/40
Birmingham (Edgbaston)	3	153	5	115	7	16.42	0	4/29
Bloemfontein (Goodyear Park)	1	60	0	37	1	37.00	0	1/37
Bridgetown (Kensington Oval)	3	168	5	112	4	28.00	0	3/28
Brisbane (Woolloongabba)	9	504	3	402	9	44.66	0	3/41
Bristol (County Ground)	4	179	2	113	10	11.30	0	4/23
Bulawayo (Athletic Club)	1	60	1	37	1	37.00	0	1/37
Bulawayo (Queens Sports Club)	1	54	1	40	2	20.00	0	2/40
Canterbury (St Lawrence Ground)	3	147	5	72	11	6.54	0	4/14
Cape Town (Newlands)	4	4228	1	168	8	21.00	0	3/31
Cardiff (Sophia Gardens)	6	330	2	267	9	29.66	0	3/52
Carlton (Princes Park)	1	60	1	35	5	7.00	1	5/35
Centurion Park	2	108	2	93	3	31.00	0	2/52
Chelmsford (County Ground)	2	114	0	106	0	-	0	0/44
Chennai (M.A.Chidambaram)	1	60	0	52	2	26.00	0	2/52
Chester-le-Street (Riverside)	3	156	5	49	5	9.80	0	2/12
Christchurch (Lancaster Park)	2	72	0	76	4	19.00	0	3/50

Ground	M	I	NO	Runs	HS		Avge	100s	50s	C
Colombo (P.Saravanamuttu)	1	148	0	27	2		13.50	0		2/27
Colombo (R.Premadasa)	4	222	2	176	5		35.20	0		2/52
Colombo (Sinhalese S.C.)	4	164	3	105	5		21.00	0		3/29
Croydon (Whitgift School)	1	56	0	42	6		7.00	1		6/42
Delhi (Feroz Shah Kotla)	2	120	0	89	2		44.50	0		1/35
Devonport (Formby Recreation)	1	35	0	31	3		10.33	0		3/31
Dunedin (Carisbrook)	2	120	1	111	2		55.50	0		2/50
Durban (Kingsmead)	4	205	3	159	5		31.80	0		2/36
East London (Buffalo Park)	2	120	0	70	3		23.33	0		2/36
Faisalabad (Iqbal Stadium)	1	56	0	40	4		10.00	0		4/40
Galle (International Stadium)	2	96	1	75	4		18.75	0		2/36
Georgetown (Bourda)	1	36	0	35	2		17.50	0		2/35
Hamilton (Seddon Park)	1			did not bowl						
Harare (Sports Club)	4	156	2	107	3		35.66	0		2/42
Hobart (Bellerive Oval)	5	272	0	195	10		19.50	0		3/45
Hove (County Ground)	2	120	2	59	2		29.50	0		1/22
Indore (Nehru Stadium)	1	160	0	64	0		-	0		0/64
Jaipur (Sawai Mansingh)	1	60	1	30	0		-	0		0/30
Johannesburg (New Wanderers)										
	3	180	2	131	3		43.66	0		2/30
Kanpur (Modi Stadium)	1	54	0	43	1		43.00	0		1/43
Kennington Oval	4	153	1	120	4		30.00	0		2/6
Kingstown (Arnos Vale)	2	115	6	63	4		15.75	0		2/30
Kochi (Nehru Stadium)	1	160	0	42	0		-	0		0/42
Lahore (Gaddafi Stadium)	3	180	2	129	0		-	0		0/32
Leeds (Headingley)	3	180	1	129	3		43.00	0		2/33
Lord's Cricket Ground	8	432	5	314	15		20.93	0		4/33
Manchester (Old Trafford)	3	3144	6	49	6		8.16	0		3/11
Margao (Nehru Stadium)	1	48	0	62	0		-	0		0/62
Melbourne (Docklands)	5	300	3	177	5		35.40	0		2/38
Melbourne Cricket Ground	37	22061	21	1435	55		26.09	0		4/19
Milton Keynes (Campbell Park)	1	54	1	33	0		-	0		0/33
Mohali (Punjab C.A. Stadium)	1	54	0	36	4		9.00	0		4/36
Multan (Ibn-e-Qasim Bagh)	1	60	1	29	1		29.00	0		1/29
Mumbai (Wankhede Stadium)	1	60	1	28	1		28.00	0		1/28
Nagpur (Vidarbha C.A. Ground)	1	57	1	34	4		8.50	0		4/34
Nairobi (Gymkhana Club)	5	234	3	150	4		37.50	0		1/4
Napier (McLean Park)	1	60	2	34	1		34.00	0		1/34
Nelson (Trafalgar Park)	1	48	2	35	0		-	0		0/35
North Sydney Oval	2	284	1	90	3		30.00	0		3/43
Northampton (County Ground)	2	90	0	74	4		18.50	0		2/21
Nottingham (Trent Bridge)	2	108	3	92	3		30.66	0		2/60
Paarl (Boland Bank Park)	1	60	0	62	2		31.00	0		2/62

Ground	M	I	NO	Runs	HS	Avge	100s	50s	C
Perth (W.A.C.A. Ground)	10	588	6	433	17	25.47	0		3/48
Peshawar (Arbab Niaz)	1	60	0	51	1	51.00	0		1/51
Port Elizabeth (St George's Park)	4	156	0	151	6	25.16	0		4/36
Port of Spain (Queen's Park)	4	234	2	209	4	52.25	0		3/35
Portsmouth	1	150	0	30	1	30.00	0		1/30
Potchefstroom (Witrand)	1	did not bowl							
Rawalpindi Cricket Stadium	1	54	1	47	0	-	0		0/47
Richmond Cricket Ground	3	180	1	126	5	25.20	0		2/31
Sharjah C.A. Stadium	8	456	3	324	13	24.92	0		4/34
Southampton (County Ground)	6	330	6	194	14	13.85	0		4/23
Southampton (The Rose Bowl)	17	758	3	566	21	26.95	0		3/21
St George's (Queen's Park, New)	1	60	2	39	3	13.00	0		3/39
St Kilda (Junction Oval)	2	1120	1	92	1	92.00	0		1/39
Sydney Cricket Ground	29	1561	15	1105	47	23.51	1		5/33
Taunton (County Ground)	1	did not bowl							
Uxbridge Cricket Club Ground	1	58	0	48	4	12.00	0		4/48
Visakhapatnam (Indira Priyadarshini)	2	120	0	63	4	15.75	0		3/38
Wellington (Basin Reserve)	2	120	3	58	4	14.50	0		2/18
Wellington (Westpac Stadium)	2	60	0	44	0	-	0		0/44
Whitchurch (Heath Road)	1	48	0	20	3	6.66	0		3/20
Worcester (New Road)	2	120	1	75	5	15.00	0		3/39
Total		297	5699	171	11088	452	24.53	3	6/42

OTHER MISCELLANEOUS MATCHES

Youth Tests in West Indies 1990

Batting & fielding record	M	I	No	Runs	HS	Avge	100	50	C
Australian Youth	3	4	1	27	18*	9.00	0	0	2

Bowling record	M	Balls	Mdns	Runs	Wkts	Avge	5w	10w	Best
Australian Youth	3	329	14	175	6	29.16	0	0	3/28

Lancashire League 1991

Batting & fielding record	M	I	No	Runs	HS	Avge	100	50	C
Accrington	24	24	0	390	51	16.25	0	2	13

Bowling record	M	Balls	Mdns	Runs	Wkts	Avge	5w		Best
Accrington	24	2310	75	1226	78	15.71	8		6/33

SHANE WARNE'S FIRST XI RECORD FOR ST KILDA IN VICTORIAN DISTRICT PREMIER CRICKET

This information was provided by Ken Williams

First XI batting and fielding in each season

Season	M	I	NO	Runs	HS	Avge	100s	50s	C
1989-90	11	7	5	56	18*	28.00	0	0	6
1990-91	6	2	1	6	6*	6.00	0	0	2
1991-92	12	8	2	141	62	23.50	0	1	3
1992-93	4	3	0	50	33	16.66	0	0	3
1993-94	3	3	0	78	73	26.00	0	1	1
1995-96	1	1	0	22	22	22.00	0	0	1
1996-97	2	1	0	10	10	10.00	0	0	1
1997-98	2	2	0	18	15	9.00	0	0	0
1998-99	5	4	0	159	109	39.75	1	0	6
2000-01	3	3	0	121	95	40.33	0	1	0
2001-02	1	1	0	0	0	0.00	0	0	0
2005-06	5	3	1	156	105*	78.00	1	0	0
2006-07	3	3	0	47	27	15.66	0	0	0
Total	58	41	9	864	109	27.00	2	3	23

First XI bowling in each season

Season	M	Balls	Mdns	Runs	Wkts	Avge	5wi	10wm	Best
1989-90	11	718	33	274	9	30.44	0	0	3/29
1990-91	6	576	24	275	11	25.00	0	0	3/25
1991-92	12	1008	62	358	17	21.05	0	0	4/31
1992-93	4	168	7	66	5	13.20	0	0	4/36
1993-94	3	264	10	124	6	20.66	0	0	3/80
1995-96	1	60	1	22	2	11.00	0	0	2/22
1996-97	2	162	9	91	1	91.00	0	0	1/58
1997-98	2	72	1	60	1	60.00	0	0	1/8
1998-99	5	186	1	92	2	46.00	0	0	1/13
2000-01	3	216	11	70	0	-	0	0	
2001-02	1	60	2	25	1	25.00	0	0	1/25
2005-06	5	597	8	212	11	19.27	0	0	3/38
2006-07	3	138	0	88	7	12.57	0	0	4/34
Total	58	3985	169	1757	73	24.06	0	0	4/31

SHANE WARNE'S HUNDREDS

109	St Kilda	v	Melbourne	Albert Grounf	24 October 1998
105*	St Kilda	v	Richmond	Richmond	11 February 2006

His best bowling for St Kilda was 4/31 (18.0/9/31/4) v North Melbourne at St Kilda on 8 February 1992

His first XI debut for St Kilda

St Kilda v Northcote
1989-90
Played at Northcote Park, December 2, 9, 1989
St Kilda won on first innings

North Melbourne

1	G.P.Dowling	c Graf b Whiteside	67
2	†M.J.O'Sullivan	run out	13
3	*G.K.Hobbs	c Graf b Walker	13
4	E.R.Eddings	c Warne b Osborne	2
5	S.D.Williams	c Harper b Osborne	0
6	G.B.Gardiner	b Walker	4
7	A.C.Dale	not out	55
8	S.Jain	b Whiteside	5
9	A.D.McGinty	b Walker	5
10	M.B.Newell	b Whiteside	0
11	W.R.Bennett	not out	7
	Extras	b4, lb6, nb6,	16
	Total	9 wickets cc	187

FoW: 1/33, 2/70, 3/75, 4/83, 5/88, 6/140, 7/150, 8/163, 9/170

St Kilda	O	M	R	W
D.K.Walker	32	5	62	3
S.F.Graf	6	0	15	0
L.D.Harper	15	4	20	0
W.G.Whiteside	20	6	30	3
M.Osborne	26	9	47	2
S.K.Warne	1	0	3	0

St Kilda

1	A.W.Lynch	cw O'Sullivan b McGinty	9
2	†J.R.Jacoby	b Bennett	115
3	W.G.Whiteside	b Dale	15
4	R.B.Gartrell	c Dowling b Newell	111

```
 5  L.D.Harper ................. b Jain ....................................................... 14
 6  D.K.Walker ................. not out ......................................................... 4
 7  S.K.Warne ................. not out ......................................................... 7
 8  J.Murphy
 9  B.A.Robinson
10  *S.F.Graf
11  M.Osborne
    Extras ......................... lb2, nb10, ................................................ 12
    Total .......................... 5 wickets ............................................... 287
    FoW: 1/18, 2/39, 3/230, 4/268, 5/276.
```

Northcote	O	M	R	W
A.D.McGinty	18	5	49	1
M.B.Newell	22	7	59	1
W.R.Bennett	20	6	68	1
A.C.Dale	16	2	50	1
S.Jain	21	8	38	1
G.P.Dowling	2	0	15	0
S.D.Williams	1	0	6	0

Umpires: M.N.L.Day & G.M.Thies. Toss: St Kilda.